WITHDRAWN

It Happens

A Guide to Contemporary Realistic Fiction for the YA Reader

Kelly Jensen

VOYA Press

an imprint of E L Kurdyla Publishing, LLC

Bowie, Maryland

All rights reserved. Forms, worksheets, and handouts may be reproduced by librarians, teachers, and other educators for non-commercial purposes. Except for such usage, no part of this publication may be reproduced in whole or in part, or stored in a retrieval system, or transmitted in any form or by any means, electronic, mechanical, photocopying, recording, or otherwise, without written permission of the publisher. For information regarding permission, contact E L Kurdyla Publishing, PO Box 98. Bowie, MD 20718 or www.kurdylapublishing.com.

ISBN 978-1-61751-031-1

Copyright © 2014

Published by VOYA Press, an imprint of E L Kurdyla Publishing LLC

LCCN: 2014938980

The paper used in this publication meets the minimum requirements of the American National Standard for Information Sciences-Permanence of Paper for Printed Materials, ANSI Z39.48-1992.

Printed in the United States of America

Table of Contents

Acknowledgments

A huge thank you to the following people I am thrilled to have played a part in this book and in my life:

- Lenore Appelhans – for the keen eyes in reading early drafts for me, as well as the "!!!" throughout the process.

- Sophie Brookover and Elizabeth Burns – for shaping the way I think about reader's advisory. Your savvy individually, let alone together, is unmatched.

- Trish Doller – for regular word count challenges and keeping me accountable for getting writing done almost every day (or not).

- Kimberly Francisco – for being the best co-blogger I could ask for and for offering feedback along the way. Without your or our blog, this book wouldn't have happened. Whenever you're ready to check out contemporary YA, I've got a couple recommendations.

- The International Library of Awesome: Abby Johnson, Angie Manfredi, Andrea Sowers, Katie Salo, and Sarah Thompson – for the best professional network a person could ask for. Having you ladies as my go-tos for these past few years has brought me such joy.

- Jackie Parker – for showing me how to be a better reader and the ways to be a better critic. Book talking with you is always fun, even if we rarely agree.

- Tiffany Schmidt – for offering the kind of feedback I really needed to get this book into shape. Your insight and suggestions were invaluable.

- Courtney Summers – for early brainstorming about categories and for endless support and enthusiasm. Your pep talks are world class.

Thank you to everyone at VOYA Press for letting me write this book.

Thanks also go to my mom and my grandma, who encouraged reading and writing from the start. All of those trips to the library and all of the books I lost and made you pay late fees for got me to this point.

And always, thank you, Erik. Team Jensen forever – even if I'm never the next J.K. Rowling.

Introduction

I've kept a running list of every book I've read since middle school. It includes classics I read in in various classes – *The Catcher in the Rye*, *A Separate Peace*, about half of Shakespeare's works. But when I flip through and think about the books that have stuck with me, the ones that stand out are the realistic YA titles I read when I was a teen.

Speak by Laurie Halse Anderson came out when I was just entering high school. It was my first encounter reading a story about someone my own age struggling with a huge secret and the first time I realized that people I knew – the people I went to school with, the people I was friends with – could be dealing with something as horrifying as sexual violence. *The Perks of Being a Wallflower* by Stephen Chbosky came out around the same time, and the feelings of being an outsider, of never being understood – I knew those feelings, and everyone around me knew them, too, even if they never shared them. I devoured Patricia McCormick's *Cut*, which helped me be sympathetic in college when my first roommate struggled with self-harm herself.

What resonated with me then and what makes those books continue to stick with me is how real and how raw they were. How I saw myself in all of those stories, even if my own life was nothing like those portrayed on the pages. I felt and understood the emotions, since I lived them right along with the characters. There were never enough books like these in the newly-built teen area of my public library – the one where I got my first library job as a page in high school – and all I wanted was more stories like those.

My passion for realistic YA grew in college and library school. I remember where I was and how I felt when I read books like Ellen Hopkins's *Crank* for the first time, discovering how well verse could convey emotion and desperation. Or how much I loved the way E. Lockhart portrayed a smart, savvy, and strong female character in *The Disreputable History of Frankie Landau Banks*. Picking up my first Sarah Dessen book introduced me to a world full of relatable, fully-fleshed relationships between girls and significant others and girls and their families.

Blogging about books opened up a means for me to discuss titles with other readers (librarians, teachers, and those who just liked books), but it was my time serving on a committee charged with selecting a best book when I learned how wide and how deep realistic fiction goes. I will always be grateful for the opportunity to meet the "smaller," emerging, but exceptionally important voices in books by Geoff Herbach, Matthew Quick, Natalie Standiford, Courtney Summers, and more. Working with a committee taught me how to consider books critically, how to discuss them for more than their plot points, and how to make connections between and among titles.

Most importantly, I learned there is something in every book that will appeal to a reader.

It might not be a book for *me*. It might not be a book for the readers I know. But it will be a book for *someone*. That someone could walk into my library tomorrow, and I'll have exactly the right title to recommend.

I've made it a mission in my career to think about that with each and every book I read: Who does this book work for and how can I get it into their hands?

It Happens: A Guide to Contemporary Realistic Fiction for the YA Reader was born from the idea that every book has a reader, as well as from my passion for and interest in realistic fiction.

There are hundreds – maybe even thousands – more books published for young adults now than when I was a young adult. That means there are many more books to read and to share with those who want these stories.

This book is a way into sharing them.

Part 1
Real Tools

Contemporary YA fiction as we know it today arguably got its start in 1968, the year S. E. Hinton's *The Outsiders* first published. Since then, the genre has seen a number of seminal books that youth advocates, readers, and authors point to as all-time favorites and inspiration not only for their own work or reading, but in their lives more broadly.

Robert Cormier's *The Chocolate War*, Robert Lipsyte's *The Contender*, Paul Zindel's *The Pigman*, and more recently, Laurie Halse Anderson's *Speak*, Stephen Chbosky's *The Perks of Being a Wallflower*, John Green's *Looking for Alaska*, and Patricia McCormick's *Cut* are a small handful of these well-known and influential novels.

There are well-known, perennially-popular authors such as Judy Blume and Sarah Dessen who have made – and continue to make – an everlasting mark on contemporary YA. Even today, the works of both authors resonate, as Blume's *Tiger Eyes* hit the silver screen in 2013 and Dessen's novels continue to crack the *New York Times Best Seller* list. There are also authors like Blake Nelson who made an impact in the way readers find realistic fiction, as his novel *Girl* was serialized for teen readers in *Sassy* at the height of teen magazine consumption in the 1990s.

The first part of this book serves three distinct purposes:

- First, it aims to define the elements that comprise a contemporary YA novel. Because there aren't clear-cut definitions and because genres can become blurry, breaking apart and considering the elements that compose a contemporary novel offers an interesting and worthwhile discussion about the complexities of text.

- Next, it will explore why contemporary young adult fiction matters and how youth advocates and YA readers can find these books. Included are well-known and lesser-known book award lists from around the world.

Then, once the groundwork of the "what" and "how" of contemporary YA fiction have been covered, this section delves into the tools of critically reading and evaluating text. It will explore how those skills can be put to work in developing strong and creative reader's advisory programs that put these books into the hands of the right readers.

It's not always easy trying new things, but the best readers and book champions are those who reach beyond their own comfort zones. This section should help spark new, inventive means for those eager to become advocates for young adult readers and for contemporary YA fiction.

Chapter 1

Defining Contemporary YA Fiction

There is something particularly special, particularly empowering, about contemporary, realistic fiction for teens. "Here you *are," it says to them. "Your story is worth hearing.* Your *story matters. I see you." —*Angie Manfredi, youth services librarian

Though it seems like it should be straightforward, defining the contemporary young adult novel isn't easy. There are a number of phrases often associated with or substituted for "contemporary" when talking about the genre. These include the problem novel, the bildungsroman, and realistic fiction. While frequently interchangeable terms, they're not synonymous. Each has a specific meaning.

■ The Problem Novel

It is common to equate contemporary YA fiction with the phrase "problem novel." There is a central problem – drugs, teen pregnancy, delinquency, divorce, and so forth – and the real-world setting both aids and hinders this problem throughout the story. Over the course of the novel, the main character literally or metaphorically grows or dies, depending on the choices he or she makes toward solving the problem. But "problem novel" is too simplistic a definition for the whole of what contemporary YA fiction encompasses.

Michael Cart offers a readable and thorough exploration of the origins of realistic/contemporary fiction in his book *Young Adult Literature: From Romance to Realism* (ALA, 2010). He talks in depth about the history of the so-called problem novel, highlighting some of the hallmark authors and titles. "Problem novel" is a phrase weighted with specific meaning, defining a type of book published with a defined purpose. These books don't focus on characterization, don't develop their stories to the fullest potential, and don't implement techniques of strong, compelling writing. Instead, the problem novel focuses *entirely* on the problem and message of the story.

Cart uses author Jeanette Eyerly as an exemplar of the "problem novel" trend that arose in the 1960s and 1970s. Her books, with titles such as *The Drop Out* (published in 1963), *The Girl Inside* (1968), and *See Dave Run* (1978), showcased the problems associated with dropping out of high school, with teen pregnancy, and with being a runaway, respectively. The characters, the settings, and the subplots – if they even existed – didn't matter to the central problem. These elements of story could be substituted between and across books because the focus was on the issue at hand, rather than the way a specific, fully-fleshed character worked through the problem or grew as a result of working through it. In other words, the books were about alcoholism, dropping out of school, or shoplifting, and not about the character's entire journey through the experience.

Compare any of Eyerly's titles to S. E. Hinton's groundbreaking *The Outsiders* (published in 1968) and there are tremendous differences in the treatment of story, in reception, in longevity, and maybe most importantly, in appeal to readers. Hinton doesn't offer a problem with a solution; Hinton offers a story with fully-realized characters who challenge those problems, who interact with one another, and who cannot be substituted with any other character in order to make the story work. What readers remember are the characters in Hinton's novel. The same can't be said of Eyerly's books—readers most likely recall the issue at hand instead.

This isn't to say that problem novels are bad in and of themselves; they were a trend in publishing for young adults. Rather, it's to point out that the "problem novel" is a specific type of book, and it is rare to encounter a true problem novel in today's YA fiction. Using the phrase "problem novel" to define realistic/con-

> The problem novel is a specific type of story that focuses exclusively on the problem and message of the book. The characters, setting, and the subplots don't matter – they could be substituted between and across titles. The focus of the problem novel is the issue at hand, rather than the way a specific, fully-fleshed character works through the problem or grows as a result. It is entirely message-driven.

temporary fiction more broadly undercuts the richness of story, character development, and secondary plots present in books today.

At their core, contemporary novels have a problem within them, otherwise there would be no conflict. But equating the genre with the problem novel suggests both are a very specific type of book. It also suggests that other genres do not have problems at the heart of their stories. If that were the case, there would be no mystery or fantasy or science fiction genres.

The Bildungsroman

Any glossary of literary terms will define bildungsroman in virtually the same words: It is a novel about a character growing from a child into maturity. The bildungsroman follows as a character understands and recognizes his or her place in the world, then grows or changes because of it. Although the term is specific, it is in many ways the *definition* of young adult fiction more broadly. A character finds his or her place in the world through realizing he or she is no longer

> The bildungsroman is at the heart of all YA fiction: It's about the shift from childhood to maturity and the recognition that things and people can and do change.

guided by childhood beliefs and principles and must now come to terms with what it means to grow up.

Arguably, every YA book, from fantasy novels to dystopians and romances, fits the definition of bildungsroman by virtue of the age, experience, and insight garnered by the protagonists.

As with the phrase "problem novel," using bildungsroman as a synonym or definition of contemporary YA fiction undermines the complexity and range of the genre itself. The growth of a character and his or her "coming of age" is an important aspect of the book, but it is not the entire purpose. Contemporary YA encompasses the problem and the elements defining what it means to grow up and understand one's place in the world.

While bildungsroman brings us a bit closer to defining contemporary YA fiction, it is too large a term to describe what it is that separates contemporary from any other young adult genre.

■ Realistic Fiction

If neither problem novel nor bildungsroman captures what a contemporary YA novel is, then what does it mean for a novel to be considered realistic fiction? And does realistic fiction differ from contemporary?

Nilson and Donelson (2009) offer this definition of realistic YA fiction: "Young adult fiction with real-world settings in historical periods not far removed from our own. The books feature young protagonists solving problems without the help of magic." Then, quoting Marc Aronson, they further their definition by noting that the success of realistic novels for readers is in their ability to highlight intimacy: "Does a book have the potential to touch readers deeply so that, in the struggle with it, they begin to see and shape themselves?"

In teasing this apart, we see realistic fiction is one part problem novel *and* one part bildungsroman because the characters are solving problems. What sets Nilson and Donelson's definition apart from that of the problem novel and the bildungsroman, though, is their use of setting and place. The realistic novel features the real world, and the setting is in a period that isn't too far removed from our own. This explanation of the realistic novel is broad and encompassing, as it folds a number of genres within it, including mystery, romances, westerns, thrillers, and other stories about characters solving real-world problems in the real world. It is a solid and strong definition, aided only by Aronson's further suggestion that these books are ones readers relate to deeply because what happens in the story is something they can see and absorb as a method of self-exploration and understanding.

In other words, realistic fiction isn't about the runaway teen and what happens to the runaway teen. It's about the teen who chooses to run away, why she or he made the choice to do that, what the experience looks and feels like, who or what the teen encounters along the way, and what the teen chooses to do about his life situation after gathering knowledge and insight on his or her own. Because the story is about the character and what it is he or she chooses to do about the problem, the character cannot be swapped out with any other character. It is a story that belongs to that character and that character alone.

In essence, a realistic YA novel has the potential to serve as the reader's own bildungsroman experience.

What sets realistic fiction apart from genres like science fiction or fantasy, though, is the book's jumping off point. Realistic fiction never deviates from the world as we know it; it's about what happens in real life, both the good and the bad. The tone can be somber, raw, lighthearted, humorous, or anything in between. It can also be a little bit of all of these things. Because realistic fiction is rooted in emotions, actions, and the fallout from each, it can explore topics that are heavy and grim, as well as topics that are sweet and easy-going.

Nothing is off limits when it comes to topics in realistic fiction. But what separates it from the simple problem novel is that these problems are explored through diverse, thoughtfully-voiced characters; through the shifting and challenging dynamics of relationships between and among characters; and through subplots that may make what appears to be the problem of the novel not the problem at all, but instead an outcome of any number of other interactions or situations within the story.

Noteworthy in Nilson and Donelson's definition is the element of time setting. Realistic YA takes place in historical periods not far removed from our own. Perhaps this is where we can carve an understanding of what it means to be a contemporary realistic YA novel.

What is it that makes a novel historical? At what point in time does a book become historical, as opposed to contemporary? Is there a middle ground between a book that was contemporary at one point and yet doesn't portray a specific time period? Nilson and Donelson leave gray area in their decision to call the time setting in realistic YA fiction "one not far removed from our own." Likewise, it begs the question of who the "our" is: teen readers or adult readers?

◼ Contemporary vs. Realistic vs. Historical Fiction

As a descriptive term, contemporary simply means that a book is set within the current frame of time. There are contemporary mysteries, contemporary romances, contemporary fantasies, as much as there is contemporary realistic fiction. All the word means is that the story takes place in the present time period. It doesn't necessarily suggest that the books are filled with time-bound pop culture references; rather, there are enough cues within the story to make it clear it is happening in or near the present day.

Even though Rainbow Rowell's *Eleanor & Park* (St. Martin's Griffin, 2013) is a wholly realistic story, the purposeful setting in 1986 means that it is not a contemporary novel. The references to music are one element that play a role in the story; pop culture, as well as the lack of technology in the homes of both main characters, among other things, make this story historical, as opposed to contemporary. Emily Danforth's *The Miseducation of Cameron Post* (Harper Teen, 2012), while realistic, is set in the 1990s, and is not contemporary for many of the same reasons.

For today's teens, the time frames of the 1980s and 1990s are historical. Even though the books are set in the past, they are still realistic fiction. They just happen to not be *contemporary*.

Both Rowell's book and Danforth's book are explicit in their time frames when it comes to setting, but not all realistic novels are. Consider Laurie Halse Anderson's *Speak* (Putnam, 1999) or Patricia McCormick's *Cut* (Push, 2002). Each novel falls within the canon of easily-recognized realistic YA fiction, and both novels stand the test of time with readers, each having been published over a decade ago. Because neither book has a specific time period setting nor offers a specific time context, theoretically, both books could be considered contemporary YA. However, both novels date themselves in small ways: both lack daily technology interaction in and impacting the lives of the main characters and, at least in the case of McCormick's novel, the main character uses a pay phone.

The same consideration goes for Jay Asher's *13 Reasons Why* (Razorbill, 2007); even though the time frame isn't explicit in the story, the narrative plays out over a series of cassette tapes and through portable tape players, setting it in either a 90s or early 00s period.

These are tiny and arguably insignificant details to consider when trying to make a larger statement about the definition of contemporary realistic YA fiction, but they're important. Today's teens – both those who would exist within a realistic novel and those reading realistic novels – live in a world where technology is everywhere and pay phones are rare items to have access to or even see on a typical day. That's not to say technology is the line separating contemporary realistic novels, historical novels, and the broader realistic novel, but it is a distinguishing characteristic.

The pure definition of a contemporary realistic novel, then, is a novel that takes place in a world easily recognized as today's world by the characters in the book, as well as the readers taking in the book. It betrays a sense of the cultural zeitgeist, as well as the fears, the expectations, the highs, and the lows of what it means to be a teen in the present world. It doesn't need to specifically mention current events in the world, nor does it need to infuse the story with references to today's television, music, or clothing styles. Those sorts of references may date a book quickly. A contemporary realistic novel is one that is aware enough of today's world to acknowledge those benefits and challenges within the story. It understands the way teens think about their own timeframe while also offering a sense of timelessness.

> For the purposes of this book, the words contemporary and realistic are used interchangeably, though the focus within the book lists and discussion guides are solely on contemporary titles published within the last seven to ten years.

So while not all of today's teens may have cell phones at their disposal, likewise, it's not a requirement of contemporary YA to feature characters toting the latest and greatest gadget. However, contemporary fiction should acknowledge these realities in some way – would a cell phone change the entire storyline by making it an easier resolution or a harder one?

Again, it's not only the technology that situates a story. There are other elements that make a story contemporary as opposed to historical or simply realistic. These things can include the access teens have to items like fake ID cards, their access to transportation, their knowledge of the world around them (which does, in many ways, relate back to their on-the-ready access to technology), the stakes surrounding their post-high school plans, and so forth. It'd be short-sighted to suggest that today's teens or the characters in today's YA books don't share the same heartaches and desires as those in books set in 2000 or 1986 or 1924 or 1873 or 1600. It would be short-sighted, though, to suggest that their contemporary sensibilities don't give them different advantages and disadvantages to working through and toward them.

It's nearly impossible to say when a novel slides out of the artificial time frame of contemporary. While it's easy to place a finger on historical time settings, there are no immediate markers for when a novel is no longer contemporary. There are some obvious indicators – referencing televisions shows such as *Buffy the Vampire Slayer* or *Veronica Mars* as being watched on television, rather than via DVD or streaming on the web – but those pop culture cues aren't always readily apparent nor defining. It would be bold to suggest what the markers separating contemporary from realistic are, too, since the term itself is contingent on the shifts and changes within culture and the world more broadly.

Perhaps a method of thinking about what is and isn't contemporary, though, can be simplified when it's explored through the lens of what the teen years are. There are six years between the ages of thirteen and eighteen and seven or eight years, if you consider ages twelve and nineteen to be part of the teen years. So much growth and change happens on the individual level between those years that it might be an easy gauge of what it means to be contemporary. Does today's eighteen-year-old have the same interests and experiences as they did when they were thirteen? What was contemporary at age thirteen feels historical to a teen at eighteen, even if it's still a realistic memory or aspect of his or her development.

Another way to think about it is to consider whether or not the teen years of today's eighteen-year-old mirror the teen years that lay ahead of today's thirteen-year-old. While both can and will enjoy the same realistic novels, since these are ultimately stories about characters working through problems that exist in the recognizable world, the lenses through which the now-eighteen-year-old and the now-thirteen-year-old take in their teen experiences are not the same. They bring something different to the books, as much as they take something different away. Their teen years are and will be different because their worlds are different.

Because older titles are still realistic and at times foundational texts, they may be referenced as read alikes or as examples for specific appeal factors. Though these books are set within a given time frame, this book will have no problem standing the test of time. Even as these titles wane in showcasing the world as it stands right now, the core of these books are their realistic characters, challenges, hopes, and dreams. Those are the components that make a book withstand the test of time, regardless of label.

Contemporary YA features young adult protagonists set in today's world incorporating today's issues, paralleling and intertwining with the values that every teen – and every reader – thinks about: family, friendship, love, growing up, loss, faith, the future, and many, many more.

◼ References

Brannen, Jennifer. "All About Realistic Fiction for Teens," via NoveList Database, April 2012.

Brannen's genre guide offers a quick overview of realistic fiction, including foundational titles and outstanding authors in the genre. She also highlights some of the elements that define realistic fiction and what separates it from and ties it together with other genres.

Cart, Michael. *Young Adult Literature: From Romance to Realism*. American Library Association, 2010. 288p. $68.50. 978-0-8389-1045-0.

As noted earlier, Cart's exploration of the history of young adult fiction is a must-read for any fan of this category of books. It's easy to follow and offers great insight into the growth and changes in the various genres within young adult. Cart also offers insight into the genres themselves, into how to use these books with teens, and more.

Nilsen, Alleen Pace, and Kenneth L. Donelson. *Literature for Today's Young Adults*. Eighth Edition. Allyn & Bacon, 2009. 512p. $49. 978-0-205-59323-1.

Nilsen and Donelson's textbook provides definitions and examples of not only realistic books, but of the expanse of genres within young adult fiction. This is a strong primer for those new to working with or reading YA, though they do not offer a definition separating contemporary realistic fiction from realistic fiction more broadly, and they choose to include magical realism within the realm of realistic fiction, despite the fact it incorporates fantastical elements into an otherwise real world.

Chapter 2

Why Contemporary YA Fiction Matters

Life can be hard. Messy. Painful. People betray you. People ignore you. People leave you. I write contemporary YA because teens need to see they're not alone in dealing with the hard stuff life hands us. But for me, it's not about the issues so much as it is about the stumbling, falling, getting back up, and moving forward. Young adult novels that portray real issues often give teens an intimate glimpse inside another person's life. It can be helpful, I think, to see someone else go through a difficult time and come out the other side okay. It's not always easy to find hope amidst the despair, especially when it's a teen without a lot of life experience. But perhaps after closing the pages of a well-done contemporary YA novel, a teen will think: If she can make it through, I can too. – Lisa Schroeder, author of Falling for You *and* The Day Before

It's easy to lump any book genre beneath simple descriptions. Science fiction books take place in space or have aliens. Fantasy novels feature castles and unicorns. Mysteries are about figuring out who tried to hide the body. When it comes to contemporary/realistic fiction, it's probably easiest to say the books within the genre are problem novels. But as explained earlier, the truth of the matter is that, at heart, *every* book is a problem novel. Every story has a problem at its core, and it's the job of the characters to work through that problem using whatever means available to them in their world. This could be a space ship. This could be the police. This could be a katana.

In a contemporary novel, the tools available to the characters are the tools that exist in our world.

Contemporary YA fiction, despite having the ability to tackle limitless topics within its pages, still finds itself a limiting genre because it is bound to the confines of reality. There isn't a way out of a problem through magic or imagination. While there are books that certainly bend reality a bit and force the reader to question whether the story could actually happen or not, contemporary YA fiction can do this if the story's explanation lies within reality. In other words, because reality has bits of the fantastic and the magical to it, these elements can and do certainly appear in contemporary fiction and the books remain realistic.

Antonia Michaelis's *The Storyteller* (Amulet, 2012), for example, is a lengthy fairy tale about a girl, a sailboat, and the fighting off of mythical beasts and enemies. But Michaelis weaves this fairy tale into a larger narrative – the story is told through the voice and perspective of a teen boy, Abel, who constructs the fairy tale to entertain and engage his younger sister Micah. Abel has been subject to abuse and torment because of his sexuality and it's through this fairy tale that he and his sister can escape their harsh reality. So while there is a fairy tale within the story, this book is a wholly contemporary novel. The problems and challenges are not magically resolved nor do they take place in another time or in an alternate reality.

> ### Magical Realism and Bending Reality
>
> "Magical realism" is a genre that falls between contemporary/realistic fiction and fantasy. These books take elements of reality and infuse them with bits of magic and fantasy. But what makes this genre interesting is that many readers may take these stories as straight contemporary/realistic or as straight fantasy. The lines are so blurry between the two at times that readers question whether what happened in the story actually occurred or it was all inside the character's head. Interpretation becomes an act of teasing apart these pieces and making determinations about whether the story happened or whether there is something else at play. Below are a few books falling into the category of "magical realism."
>
> - *Tighter* by Adele Griffin (Alfred A. Knopf, 2011)
> - *Ask the Passengers* by A. S. King (Little, Brown, 2012)
> - *Everybody Sees the Ants* by A. S. King (Little, Brown, 2011)
> - *Please Ignore Vera Dietz* by A. S. King (Alfred A. Knopf, 2010)
> - *Before I Fall* by Lauren Oliver (HarperTeen, 2010)
> - *Lark* by Tracey Porter (Harper Collins, 2011)
> - *The Turning* by Francine Prose (HarperTeen, 2012)
> - *17 & Gone* by Nova Ren Suma (Dutton 2013)

While contemporary YA sometimes gets flack for not being an "escapist genre" because it can take on real-world problems without shying away from the gritty and painful, it's through reading these stories that readers *do* escape. Even when the story mimics something going on in their own lives, readers are able to escape their personal situations, if only to work through similar ones via another character. There is something escapist about developing sympathy and empathy for characters in difficult life moments – both in the positive and less-than-positive senses. Realistic stories ask the reader to set aside their own egos and their own biases and feel something for another.

Readers may sympathize with a bullied/bully character like Regina in Courtney Summers's *Some Girls Are* (St. Martin's Press, 2010) and understand the choices she makes because they themselves have been victims. They may understand the tension and anxiety that comes with being the person of ridicule and torment every day in school. They may see that the fallout from Regina's choice to protect herself, in fact, makes her sympathetic.

Others may find themselves understanding how challenging it is to be either the prettiest girl in the school or the ugliest one, with the responsibilities or pitfalls that come with either – and both – labels, as each of the eight characters experience in Siobhan Vivian's *The List* (Pulse, 2012). Or readers may see themselves in Tyrell's shoes, learning how to deal with the reappearance of family members in one's life after a long and painful absence, as in Coe Booth's *Bronxwood* (Pulse, 2011). Further impacting them may be the urban setting and the difficulties of making peace with the person who may or may not be the right one for them.

Visually-driven Contemporary YA

A range of storytelling styles means that both avid and more reluctant readers have options for finding the right contemporary YA. Below is a list of contemporary novels which include either illustrative elements or story-related ephemera to enhance the stories, incorporating a visual and sometimes tactile aspect to the book. Some of these are graphic novels while others use visuals as only part of the story.

- *Chasing Shadows* by Swati Avasthi (Knopf, 2013)
- *Happyface* by Stephen Emond (Little, Brown, 2010)
- *Why We Broke Up* by Daniel Handler and Maira Kalman (Little, Brown, 2011)
- *Wanderlove* by Kirstin Hubbard (Delacorte, 2012)
- *Amy and Roger's Epic Detour* by Morgan Matson (Simon & Schuster, 2010)
- *Nothing Can Possibly Go Wrong* by Prudence Shen and Faith Erin Hicks (First Second, 2013)
- *Winger* by Andrew Smith (Simon and Schuster, 2013)
- *Drama* by Raina Telgemeier (Graphix, 2012)

On the opposite end, readers may see themselves stuck in the smallest town in the world, on the plains of Nebraska, desperately hoping someone out there understands the implications of being gay in that situation, as Morgan does in Kirstin Cronn-Mills's *The Sky Always Hears Me: And the Hills Don't Mind* (Flux, 2009).

But it's not only these big stories that make a reader connect, understand, or empathize. It can be the smaller ones, too. It could be the shame and embarrassment one may feel if they accidentally lose control of their bodily functions at a high stress event, like Alex does in Adele Griffin's *All You Never Wanted* (Alfred A. Knopf Books, 2012). It could be the struggle of finding your voice again – the kind that just came to you when you were writing poetry – after losing a brother, much like Jonathan in Conrad Wesselhoeft's *Adios, Nirvana* (Houghton Mifflin, 2011).

Contemporary YA can and does reach readers on any level, and not just because of the wide span of stories being told. There is a breadth of storytelling techniques and styles that enhance the experience and make it accessible for readers across the board. There are books in alternative formats – through letters or emails, through scrapbooks or graphics, through texts or multiple points of view – which change a story's accessibility. The appeal is built in the story and in the structure simply because it's an element of being realistic. Contemporary fiction contains such a range of books that struggling or reluctant readers can find a story that fits their needs and interests in the same way that the most literary readers can find a one that engages and challenges them.

The everyday real-world lives of humans shape their personal stories. The same happens in contemporary fiction. It's through this wealth of human experience, emotion, and vulnerability that these stories grow and become important.

Contemporary YA fiction matters because it's the teen experience. It sheds light into their lives, and readers relate, even if they don't know the exact story being told. It's here readers see themselves, and it's here readers find themselves, too. These books can and do change a reader's life in profound ways.

Chapter 3

Seeking Contemporary YA Fiction

The right book at the right time can change a teen's life forever. When a teen reads a contemporary novel, they have a mirror to their own existence, a safe place for them to think about and question their place in the world. I can't ever know the full extent of what I've given them by connecting them to the right book, I can only report on what I've seen happen.

In my years of working with teens, I've seen teen girls gain the strength to seek help after reading Patricia McCormick's Cut *in Teen Book Club. A teen boy who finally saw a gay character – like him – in* Boyfriends with Girlfriends *by Alex Sanchez. And a young tween who stopped chatting with someone she didn't know via Facebook after reading Sarah Darer Littman's* Want to Go Private? *These are just a few stories that will always stay with me, as I know those contemporary novels will stay with them.* – Katie Salo, youth services librarian

It's no secret that contemporary fiction doesn't get quite the same push as other genres. Certainly, there are titles and big name authors such as Sarah Dessen, John Green, Ellen Hopkins, and a handful of others who do receive strong publicity and marketing support, but the vast majority of contemporary books fall mid-list. They have smaller print runs than other genres. While they often still see traditional trade reviews through sources like *Booklist*, *The Horn Book*, *Kirkus*, *School Library Journal*, and *VOYA*, these are not usually the titles showing up in full-colored advertising in the same trade journals. Most contemporary titles aren't being shown on the big screen as previews, nor are they the titles getting entire product lines devoted to them. These aren't the books that are on end caps at grocery stores or in the small airport book shops. They don't have high-budget trailers.

Part of why these books don't get the publisher push is that the topics are often specific, grounded in individual experiences, and they don't tend to slip into areas of popular or mass interest. In other words, the story of a pregnant teen or the snapshot of a teen struggling through losing a parent doesn't have the same kind of wide appeal that a read alike to whatever the next big trend title may be. That's not to say the next dystopia doesn't have a deeply personal meaning to readers in the same way as a contemporary novel – it certainly can and does – but these stories are packaged and sold differently.

Readers and advocates of reading aren't stuck with what's being sold and marketed heavily, though. There are outlets available for discovering titles that fall a little below the radar and outside the buzz. It requires a little extra work, but there are plenty of tools and tricks available to make saying on top of these books easier.

◼ Locating and Using Non-traditional Review Sources

Not all titles will be reviewed traditionally, but it's possible to supplement professional reviews (or lack thereof) with reviews throughout the blogosphere.

As mentioned earlier, there are books that receive a lot of promotional backing, and while there are many bloggers who review and highlight some of those big titles, those bloggers, as well as a host of others, make an effort to review and discuss other books as well. Having a title of a book or the name of the author can be enough to hunt down blog reviews. Of course, different blogs review with different criteria in mind – some are reader responses and some are more analytical reviews. Reading through a handful of blog's reviews and posts will give a sense of whether they line up more along the lines of traditional trade reviews, explaining the strengths or weaknesses of a title critically, or if they're more likely to react by their own tastes.

Most bloggers have a review policy somewhere on their website. This policy tells what kind of books they tend to like, and many bloggers will include their favorite types of reads. Knowing this can give insight into the kind of books the reviewer will see more favorably, and it can give insight into whether they're more critical or more casual reviewers. Reading a review policy can also indicate whether the reviewer writes as a professional – a librarian, a teacher, an author, an editor – or as a reader. Even those who are professionals in day jobs may blog simply as readers. Those who aren't in the book business may choose to blog with a professional eye.

The bulk of blogs are independent, meaning that they're not hosted nor supported by a publication or other media entity. Book blogs, such as *Book Riot,* are developed and written by readers for readers, but they're not connected to a professional journal or corporation. Contributors to those sites may or may not be compensated. There are some blogs, too, which are connected to trade review journals. *School Library Journal, Library Journal,* and *Kirkus,* for example, either host (and compensate) bloggers through their websites or they host blogs on their website that are contributed to by a number of bloggers who may also have their own independent blogs elsewhere. All of these perspectives make the blog world one that is rich with opinion and one that offers a wealth of information.

No style of blogger reviews is better than another. It all depends on reader preference – the critically-minded review blogs are great for their depth and insight into the literary aspects of a book, but the reader response blogs are great because they give insight into the average reader. In many cases, the average reader is one who not only reads a significant amount of YA, but many of these readers are teens. That teen voice in a review can sometimes say as much, if not more, than an adult voice when it comes to YA books. A teen voice can be powerful in crafting a strong book talk, too. What an adult picks up on in a book either via reading or via review isn't necessarily what a teen will gravitate toward.

There are blog-specific search engines like Google's BlogSearch, but any search engine can pick up blog results. While there are certainly "big name" YA bloggers out there, what matters is finding a style and voice that works for the reader. Sometimes the smallest bloggers write the most thoughtful reviews and sometimes the big bloggers aren't necessarily helpful for their reviews but instead, for things like being aware of new book release dates. Keeping an eye on a variety of blogs allows for more depth and breadth in terms of discovering new voices, new titles, and the myriad of opinions on them.

In another corner of the blogging world are author and publisher blogs. There are collaborative blogging efforts by different types of authors – for example, there have been blogs run entirely by contemporary YA authors, and there are any number of group blogs written by debut novelists. There are individual authors who blog, too, and don't simply talk about their writing; instead, they blog about different books they're reading or they offer up book lists on different topics. Different publisher imprints have taken to blogging, too. Often these blogs highlight their own titles, and many times, these blogs will use their authors to develop the blog posts. HarperCollins's Greenwillow imprint, for example, runs a strong blog at *http://greenwillowblog.com/*.

Outside of the wide world of blogs are other non-traditional sources worth checking on periodically. These include mainstream magazines both for adults and for teens, such as *Entertainment Weekly* and *Seventeen Magazine*. While the bulk of the books receiving reviews or commentary there tend to be bigger budget titles (in other words, fewer contemporary realistic titles than titles fitting the trend at the time or titles receiving significant buzz), it's very possible to discover new authors or books through these sources.

Newspapers such as *The New York Times* are worth monitoring, as well; in many cases, these papers write about YA novels and do so using YA authors. In other words, it's not necessarily writers employed by the paper doing the stories or reviews – it might be someone from within the book world. That can expose lesser-known titles, including the books that don't get the same kind of publisher push as those that may appear in print advertising or in big-name publications.

It can be challenging to balance all of this information – how much should you read if there is so much available? One solution is to pick a couple of sources and read them regularly. Another solution is to set up some sort of information management system that can be searched when necessary. For example, subscribe to many blogs of interest through an RSS tool and either periodically skim the feed or use the "search" feature within the reader to look up information when desired.

▌ Book Awards, Honors, and Selection Lists to Know

Another way to seek out contemporary realistic YA, as well as to stay aware of the range of YA fiction beyond this genre, is through familiarity with significant book awards and selection lists produced each year. This overview, which focuses on lists that include contemporary titles among their selections (as opposed to be exclusively limited to a single genre that doesn't include contemporary), offers insight into the array of awards offered not only in the United States, but also Australia, Canada, and the United Kingdom. This list is not exhaustive, but instead, compiled to showcase variety in honored titles and selection processes: some which allow teens a voice in the decisions, some which focus entirely on literary merit, and some which aim to marry teen appeal with literary merit.

Highlighted within the lists are contemporary titles honored within the last few years.

■ American Library Association Awards

Every year, the American Library Association honors a variety of books through its different divisions and roundtables. These selections are made by volunteers within the organization and its divisions. These volunteers are primarily librarians, but may also include teachers and others with an interest in the association's values.

Association for Library Services to Children Awards

Mildred A. Batchelder Award

The Batchelder honors a children's book that was originally published in a language other than English and has been translated to English. These books skew young; eligible books are published for the 14 and under age group. Recent contemporary/realistic titles honored include:

- *Nothing* by Janne Teller (Antheneum, 2010)

- More information about the Batchelder Award can be found at *http://www.ala.org/alsc/awardsgrants/bookmedia/batchelderaward*.

Notable Children's Books

The yearly Notables list highlights the books published within a given year that are not only of strong literary merit but also reflect the interests of young readers. The Notables list includes titles that span the range of youth reading levels, including an Older Readers list with older middle grade and young adult titles. Recent contemporary/realistic titles honored include:

- *Under the Mesquite* by Guadalupe Garcia McCall (Lee & Low, 2011)

- *Drama* by Raina Telgemeier (Graphix, 2012)

- *Nothing* by Janne Teller (Antheneum, 2010)

- *Bluefish* by Pat Schmatz (Candlewick, 2011)

More information about the Notable Children's Books can be found at *http://www.ala.org/alsc/awardsgrants/notalists/ncb*.

Pura Belpre Award

The annual Pura Belpre Award is given to a children's book that not only has literary merit, but which also showcases the Latino/a experience. There are winning titles, as well as honorees. Recent contemporary titles include:

- *Under the Mesquite* by Guadalupe Garcia McCall (Lee & Low, 2011)

More information about the Pura Belpre can be found at *http://www.ala.org/alsc/awardsgrants/bookmedia/belpremedal*.

Ethnic and Multicultural Information Exchange Round Table (EMIERT)

Coretta Scott King Book Awards

Every year, EMIERT presents an award to African American authors and illustrators who produce outstanding work with a focus on or appreciation for African American culture for young readers, including young adults. This award is given to authors, as opposed to individual titles, for a book they've published in the prior year. Recent contemporary titles include:

- *Mare's War* by Tanita S. Davis (Knopf, 2009)
- *Lockdown* by Walter Dean Myers (Amistad, 2010)

More information about the Coretta Scott King Awards can be found at *http://www.ala.org/emiert/cskbookawards*.

Feminist Task Force of the Social Responsibilities Round Table (FTF)

Amelia Bloomer Project List

Every year, the FTF – an arm of the Social Responsibilities Round Table – produces a list of the best feminist books for young readers of all ages, including young adults. Recent contemporary titles include:

- *Sister Mischief* by Laura Goode (Candlewick, 2011)
- *Keep Sweet* by Michele Dominguez Greene (Simon Pulse, 2010)
- *This Girl is Different* by J.J. Johnson (Peachtree, 2011)
- *Illegal* by Bettina Restrepo (Katherine Tegen, 2011)
- *The Mockingbirds* by Daisy Whitney (Little, Brown, 2010)
- *Pink* by Lili Wilkinson (Harper Teen, 2011)

More information about the Amelia Bloomer Project can be found at *http://ameliabloomer.wordpress.com/*.

Gay, Lesbian, Bisexual, and Transgender Round Table (GLBTRT)

The GLBTRT offers two honors and awards each year. In conjunction with the Social Responsibilities Round Table, they develop the Rainbow Book List and independently, the GLBTRT honors books with the Stonewall Award.

Rainbow Book List

This annual list highlights books that have realistic content in relation to GLBT characters or stories, and the list spans the entire range of youth literature, including YA titles. Recent contemporary honorees include:

- *I Am J* by Cris Beam (Little, Brown, 2011)
- *Starting From Here* by Lisa Jenn Bigelow (Skyscape, 2012)
- *Brooklyn, Burning* by Steve Brezenoff (Carolrhoda, 2011)
- *Between You and Me* by Marisa Calin (Atria, 2012)
- *Beautiful Music for Ugly Children* by Kirstin Cronn-Mills (Flux, 2012)
- *Happy Families* by Tanita S. Davis (Knopf, 2012)
- *Tessa Masterson Will Go to Prom* by Emily Franklin and Brendan Halpin (Walker, 2012)
- *Tilt* by Ellen Hopkins (Margaret K. McElderry, 2012)
- *Ask the Passengers* by A.S. King (Little, Brown, 2012)

- *Personal Effects* by E.M. Kokie (Candlewick, 2012)
- *Pink* by Lili Wilkinson (Harper Teen, 2011)

More information about the Rainbow Book List can be found at *http://glbtrt.ala.org/rainbowbooks/.*

Stonewall Book Awards

This annual award is given to the outstanding books that exemplify the GLBT experience. These titles can span any age category, but there is a specific award dedicated to youth and young adult titles. Recent contemporary selections include:

- *Sparks* by S.J. Adams (Flux, 2011)
- *Almost Perfect* by Brian Katcher (Delacorte, 2009)
- *Drama* by Raina Telgemier (Graphix, 2012)
- *Pink* by Lili Wilkinson (Harper Teen, 2011)
- *Putting Makeup on the Fat Boy* by Bil Wright (Simon & Schuster Books for Young Readers, 2011)

More information about the Stonewall can be found at *http://www.ala.org/glbtrt/award.*

Young Adult Library Services Association (YALSA)

YALSA produces a number of award and selection lists annually that highlight books of outstanding literary merit and books that appeal to teen readers. The following are a sample of what YALSA members develop, as well as a sample of some of the contemporary YA titles included on the awards and selection lists.

Best Fiction for Young Adults (BFYA)

As the name suggests, this annual annotated list highlights the best fiction published for young adults in a given year. It includes a top-ten list, as well, for those titles which are the best of the best picks. These titles marry strong writing with teen appeal. Recent contemporary titles include:

- *Me and Earl and the Dying Girl* by Jesse Andrews (Abrams, 2012)
- *Leverage* by Joshua Cohen (Dutton, 2011)
- *Graffiti Moon* by Cath Crowley (Knopf, 2012)
- *The Fault in Our Stars* by John Green (Dutton, 2012)
- *Everybody Sees the Ants* by A.S. King (Little, Brown, 2012)
- *Boy21* by Matthew Quick (Little, Brown, 2012)
- *How to Save a Life* by Sara Zarr (Little, Brown, 2011)

More information about the BFYA annual list can be found at *http://www.ala.org/yalsa/best-fiction-young-adults.*

Great Graphic Novels for Teens

The annual Great Graphic Novels list highlights well-written and illustrated titles that also appeal to teen readers. This list also includes a top ten, for the best of the best graphic novels published in the prior year. Because graphic novels are a format, as opposed to a genre, there are often strong contemporary titles included in these lists. Recent contemporary picks include:

- *Page by Paige* by Laura Lee Gulledge (Amulet, 2011)
- *Tina's Mouth: An Existential Comic Diary* by Keshni Kashyap and Mari Araki (Houghton Miffling Harcourt, 2012)
- *Drama* by Raina Telgemeier (Graphix, 2012)

More information about the Great Graphic Novels list can be found at *http://www.ala.org/yalsa/great-graphic-novels*.

William C. Morris YA Debut Award

This annual award, which began in 2009, is given to a first-time author for the strongest book that combines literary merit and teen appeal. The Morris also creates a short list of honor titles. Recent contemporary books include:

- *Love and Other Perishable Items* by Laura Buzo (Knopf, 2012)
- *Charm and Strange* by Stephanie Kuehn (St. Martins Griffin, 2013)
- *Flash Burnout* by L.K. Madigan (Houghton Mifflin Books for Children, 2009)
- *Under the Mesquite* by Guadalupe Garcia McCall (Lee & Low, 2011)
- *Sex & Violence* by Carrie Mesrobian (Carolrhoda, 2013)
- *Dr. Bird's Advice for Sad Poets* by Evan James Roskos (Houghton Mifflin, 2013)
- *Where Things Come Back* by John Corey Whaley (Atheneum, 2011)
- *The Freak Observer* by Blythe Woolston (Carolrhoda, 2011)

More information about the Morris award can be found at *http://www.ala.org/yalsa/morris-award*.

Quick Picks for Reluctant Young Adult Readers

The annual Quick Picks list aims to reach teens who aren't necessarily the most eager readers. While the books picked for this list are well-written, reader appeal is a primary evaluative measure. The Quick Picks list contains fiction and non-fiction titles, and it includes a top ten list. Recent contemporary titles include:

- *Me and Earl and the Dying Girl* by Jesse Andrews (Abrams, 2012)
- *Something Like Normal* by Trish Doller (Bloomsbury, 2012)
- *Tilt* by Ellen Hopkins (Margaret K. McElderry, 2012)
- *Bad Boy* by Dream Jordan (St. Martin's Griffin, 2012)
- *A Midsummer's Nightmare* by Kody Keplinger (Poppy, 2012)
- *Want to Go Private?* by Sarah Darer Littman (Scholastic, 2011)
- *Recovery Road* by Blake Nelson (Scholastic, 2011)

More information about Quick Picks for Reluctant Readers can be found at *http://www.ala.org/yalsa/quick-picks-reluctant-young-adult-readers*.

Popular Paperbacks for Young Adults

Every year, the committee building the Popular Paperbacks list picks a series of themes that appeal to a wide range of young adult readers. The books selected to fit these themes are titles available in paperback and span genres and publication dates. Recent themes include boarding schools and summer camps, performance arts, romance, adventure, and food and cooking. Popular Paperbacks also includes a top ten titles each year, pulled from across the lists. Recent contemporary titles include:

- *Prom and Prejudice* by Elizabeth Eulberg (Point, 2011)

- *Bunheads* by Sophie Flack (Poppy, 2011)

- *The Disreputable History of Frankie Landau-Banks* by E. Lockhart (Disney-Hyperion 2008)

- *Trapped* by Michael Northrop (Scholastic, 2011)

- *Struts & Frets* by Jon Skovron (Abrams, 2009)

More information about Popular Paperbacks can be found at *http://www.ala.org/yalsa/popular-paperbacks-young-adults*.

The Michael L. Printz Award

Arguably, the Printz Award is the most well-known award and highest honor given by YALSA. It is presented once a year to the book of strongest literary excellence, and there can be up to four honor titles each year. This award, as well as the honoree titles, does not consider teen appeal as a determining factor, though each book will appeal to the right reader. Recent contemporary winners and honorees include:

- *Stolen* by Lucy Christopher (Chicken House, 2010)

- *Why We Broke Up* by Daniel Handler (Little, Brown, 2011)

- *Please Ignore Vera Dietz* by A.S. King (Knopf, 2010)

- *Nothing* by Janne Teller (Atheneum, 2010)

- *Where Things Come Back* by John Corey Whaley (Atheneum, 2011)

More information about the Printz Award can be found at *http://www.ala.org/yalsa/printz-award*.

Teens' Top Ten

The Teens' Top Ten is YALSA's teen choice list, where teens nominate and pick their favorite books. It is the only list created through YALSA or ALA that is entirely based on teen input. Recent contemporary titles include:

- *Wintergirls* by Laurie Halse Anderson (Viking, 2009)

- *What Happened to Goodbye* by Sarah Dessen (Viking, 2011)

- *Where She Went* by Gayle Forman (Dutton, 2011)

- *The Fault in Our Stars* by John Green (Dutton, 2012)

More information about the Teens' Top Ten can be found at *http://www.ala.org/yalsa/teens-top-ten*.

◼ The National Book Award

The National Book Award is a literary award presented by the nonprofit National Book Foundation. The categories for the award include adult Fiction and Non-fiction, as well as Poetry, and there is a separate division for Young People's Literature. Judges for the National Book Award include writers of note within the field of judging. In 2013, those eligible for judging also include people of note within the field, including booksellers, librarians, and more.

The judging panels used to develop a short list of five finalists, and then using whatever criteria mutually decided upon by the panel, they selected one winner. The rules for 2013 changed a bit, and now judges are developing a long-list of ten titles to be announced in September, followed by a short list of five titles announced in October, and finally, a winner at the end of the year. Recent contemporary YA titles include:

- *Out of Reach* by Carrie Arcos (Simon Pulse, 2012)

- *Lockdown* by Walter Dean Myers (Harper, 2010)

More information about the National Book Awards can be found at *http://www.nationalbook.org/*.

◼ The Children's and Young Adult Bloggers' Literary Awards (CYBILS)

The CYBILS are an annual award given by children's and young adult bloggers. The awards honor the books that best highlight literary merit and kid or teen appeal. The nominations come from readers, and from eligible reader nominations, a first round of panelists develop a shortlist of five to seven titles. A second round of judges determine a winner in each category. Categories of most interest to the purposes of this book include Young Adult Fiction (which excludes science fiction and fantasy, but does include historical fiction) and Graphic Novels. Recent shortlisted contemporary titles include:

- *Me and Earl and the Dying Girl* by Jesse Andrews (Abrams, 2012)

- *Page by Paige* by Laura Lee Gulledge (Amulet, 2011)

- *Stupid Fast* by Geoff Herbach (Sourcebooks Fire, 2011)

- *Anna and the French Kiss* by Stephanie Perkins (Dutton, 2010)

- *Boy21* by Matthew Quick (Little, Brown, 2012)

- *Drama* by Raina Telgemeier (Graphix, 2012)

More information about the CYBILS can be found at *http://www.cybils.com*.

The Sydney Taylor Awards

The annual Sydney Taylor Awards honor the best books for kids and teens that highlight the Jewish experience. It's given by the Association of Jewish Libraries in three categories: younger readers, older readers, and teen readers. There are also silver medal winners and notable books within each category. Recent contemporary winners and honorees include:

- *OyMG* by Amy Fellner Dominy (Walker, 2011)

- *Intentions* by Deborah Heiligman (Knopf, 2012)

More information about the Sydney Taylor Awards can be found at *http://www.jewishlibraries.org/main/Awards/SydneyTaylorBookAward.aspx*.

The Asian Pacific American Award for Literature

Developed and presented by the Asian Pacific American Librarians Association (APALA), the APA Award for Literature honors strongly written books about Asian and Pacific Americans and their heritage. There are a number of categories, including one for young adult fiction. Each category can have both a winner and an honoree. Recent contemporary titles include:

- *Orchards* by Holly Thompson (Delacorte, 2011)

More information about the APALA Award for Literature can be found at *http://www.apalaweb.org/awards/literature-awards/*.

The Edgar Awards

Given annually by the Mystery Writers of America, the Edgar Awards honor the year's best writing in the genre. Mystery, though a genre in and of itself, also spans genres, as mysteries can happen in science fiction, fantasy, historical or in contemporary novels. The Edgar Award is presented to one winner within a category, including young adult, and each category also has a shortlist of honorees. Recent contemporary titles include:

- *Emily's Dress and Other Missing Things* by Kathryn Burak (Roaring Brook Press, 2012)
- *Amelia Anne is Dead and Gone* by Kat Rosenfield (Dutton, 2012)

More information about the Edgar Awards can be found at *http://www.theedgars.com/*.

Boston Globe-Horn Book Awards

The Boston Globe-Horn Book Awards are presented every year in June, selected by a panel of three judges who are chosen by the editor of *The Horn Book* magazine. The awards can honor up to two books in each category, which includes fiction published for children and young adults. Recent contemporary titles include:

- *Blink & Caution* by Tim Wynne-Jones (Candlewick, 2011)

More information about the Boston Globe-Horn Book Awards can be found at *http://archive.hbook.com/bghb/*.

Los Angeles Times Book Prize

The L.A. Times Book Prize is an annual award given to a book first published in English in the United States within a given year. The judges for the prize are appointed and typically are responsible for nominating the books, as well as naming the finalists and winners. The judges are those who work or publish within the categories they're judging, and there is a category for young adult fiction. Recent contemporary titles include:

- *The Big Crunch* by Pete Hautman (Scholastic, 2011)
- *Ask the Passengers* by A.S. King (Little, Brown, 2012)
- *Boy21* by Matthew Quick (Little, Brown, 2012)

More information about the LA Times Book Prize can be found at *http://events.latimes.com/bookprizes/*.

◼ The Bram Stoker Awards

Given annually by the Horror Writers Association, the Stoker Awards honor books for superior achievement in the arena of horror writing, and this award, unlike many others, allows for ties. Any work published in English is eligible, and there is a category for young adult fiction, which began in 2010. Because horror is a mood or feeling given by the novel, it can often include realistic fiction. Recent contemporary titles include:

- *Rotters* by Daniel Kraus (Delacorte, 2011)

More information about the Stoker Awards can be found at *http://www.horror.org/stokers.htm*.

◼ The Society of Children's Book Writers and Illustrators (SCBWI) Golden Kite Awards

Given every year, the SCBWI Golden Kite Awards and Honors are given to the best children's books published that year. Each category for the award has three judges who each write within that category. These books are both the best written titles, as well as those with great appeal to readers. There is a fiction category, which includes both middle grade and young adult titles.

As of 2013, there have been no recent contemporary titles honored.

More information about the Golden Kite Awards can be found at *http://www.scbwi.org/Pages.aspx/Golden-Kite-Award*.

◼ State Award and Honor Lists

Nearly every state in the U.S. has some type of award or selection list featuring outstanding titles for young readers. These lists are compiled by professional librarians and teachers, as well as some with input from teens themselves. Often, these lists do an excellent job of offering a mix of new and older titles, as well as titles across the genres, including contemporary. Examples of state lists worth spending time with include Illinois's Abraham Lincoln List, Texas's Tayshas List, New Jersey's Garden State Teen Book Awards, and the intermediate and senior divisions of Oregon's Reader's Choice Award. Also worth exploring are the Capitol Choices awards, developed by teachers, librarians, booksellers, reviews, and others with a vested interest in young people's literature who work near Washington, D. C.

For more information, as well as links to the various award and honor lists by state, author Cynthia Leitich Smith keeps a well-updated resource on her blog at *http://www.cynthialeitichsmith.com/lit_resources/awards/stateawards.html*.

◼ The Canadian Library Association Young Adult Book Award

Given annually, the Young Adult Book Award from the Canadian Library Association honors a book published by a Canadian author in English which appeals to teen readers. Recent contemporary titles include:

- *Half Brother* by Kenneth Oppel (Scholastic, 2010)

More information about the Canadian Library Association's Young Adult Book Award can be found at *http://www.cla.ca/AM/Template.cfm?Section=Young_Adult_Canadian_Book_Award*.

■ The White Pine Award

This yearly award, presented by the Ontario Library Association, solicits the input of teen readers in selecting a winner from a shortlist of nominated titles. Categories include fiction and non-fiction titles. The White Pine is a part of Ontario Library Association's larger "Forest of Reading" program, which honors books ranging from picture books to adult books written by Canadian authors. Recent contemporary titles include:

- *Beat the Band* by Don Calame (Candlewick, 2010)

- *Swim the Fly* by Don Calame (Candlewick, 2009)

- *Sister Wife* by Shelley Hrdlitschka (Orca, 2008)

- *Getting Over Garret Delaney* by Abby McDonald (Candlewick, 2012)

- *Cracked Up to Be* by Courtney Summers (St. Martin's Griffin, 2008)

- *Some Girls Are* by Courtney Summers (St. Martin's Griffin, 2009)

More information about the Forest of Reading program and the White Pine Award can be found at *http://www.accessola.org/OLAWEB/Forest_of_Reading/*.

■ Additional Canadian Awards for Children's and Young Adult Literature

There are a host of other awards and honors for children's and young adult literature given through different organizations and sponsorships in Canada. Information about the awards, including nominated titles, can be found through the Canadian Book Centre at *http://www.bookcentre.ca/awards/canadian_awards_index*.

■ Awards Outside North America

Although sometimes distribution of titles published in Australia or the United Kingdom can prove a hurdle, readers who are interested in awards and "best of" lists should note some of the following Australian and UK-based honors. Many of these lists, like those developed and promoted in North America, feature contemporary titles and they can offer an interesting perspective and slice-of-life for readers curious about another part of the world. This is not an exhaustive compilation of award and distinctions.

Australia

- The Children's Book Council of Australia's annual awards. Information about the award, its honorees, and more can be accessed at *http://cbca.org.au/awards.htm*.

- The Inky Awards are Australia's only teen choice awards. Information about the award, its honorees, and more can be accessed at *http://www.insideadog.com.au/page/inkys*.

- The Prime Minister's Literary Awards honor titles within the young adult category each year. Information can be found at *http://arts.gov.au/pmliteraryawards*.

The United Kingdom

- The Booktrust Award honors a teen title annually with their award. Information about the award can be found at *http://www.booktrust.org.uk/prizes-and-awards/11*.

- The annual Carnegie Medal is bestowed every year to the writer of an outstanding book for children. Information about the Medal and past recipients can be found at *http://www.carnegiegreenaway.org.uk/carnegie/*.

- Every year, *The Guardian* awards a fiction prize for children's books. Information about the award and past winners and honorees can be found at *http://www.guardian.co.uk/books/guardianchildrens-fictionprize*.

◼ The Importance of Digging Deep

Being aware of the range of contemporary YA titles helps in developing read alikes, as well as in finding similarities between and among authors and titles. When a reader has finished everything that Sarah Dessen's written, being prepared with a number of next reads is important, and most of those next reads will come from authors who aren't as well-known as she is. Those read alikes open doors to new voices and potential new favorite authors for readers.

Contemporary YA is a rich genre. While there may be a wealth of titles published that explore grief and loss, knowing that the grieving experience is different for each and every individual in real life makes it clear that the variety of books exploring that topic are necessary. What may resonate with one reader may read inauthentic to another. That reader may find a different author's take on loss, though, to be exactly what they want or need to read.

There are no one-size-fits-all books in any genre, let alone in contemporary YA. Every book has its reader, and every reader has his or her book. It's crucial to exploit the tools available in order to advocate for the reader and his or her book. Armed with the tools for finding contemporary YA books beyond the ones presented here, it's time to work through how to evaluate those books and implement them into strong, savvy, and tailored reader's advisory.

Chapter 4

Methods for Evaluating Fiction

One of the books that has influenced me greatly is Joyce Sweeney's Center Line. *It's a book I read over and over in my adolescence, and while I didn't personally relate to the story of five brothers who run away from their abusive, alcoholic father, having the opportunity to live in their world gave me such empathy for those boys. I felt sad and frustrated at some of their choices, but I very much appreciated Sweeney's willingness to look at the complex, difficult truths within each character, rather than choosing to merely evoke pity for their situation. Her approach, and its impact on me, has shaped what I strive to do in my own writing: to put as much truth on the page as possible, even when that truth feels uncomfortable. Especially when it feels uncomfortable.—Stephanie Kuehn, author of* Charm & Strange

Readers approach a book with different goals in mind. They may want to read because it's a means of escaping from their reality or because it's a way of falling into a new world, foreign from their own. They could be reading for an assignment or because it's an activity they enjoy. Whatever the reason, there is value in having a toolkit for critically evaluating texts. This can be especially true when it comes to using young adult fiction with readers, either via a book group, classroom discussion, in book talking, in book lists, and more.

Critical evaluation highlights the elements of a text that work well and those that don't work quite so well. All books have their strengths and their weaknesses, and while critical evaluation sounds like a way to tease out and emphasize only the parts that don't work, that's not the case. Exploring what does and does not work at the same time offers a thorough means for understanding not just the book at hand, but fiction more widely. Having a toolkit for critical reading helps in judging the merits and challenges of the text at hand and provides a lens for appreciating fiction on a grander scale.

This section delves into the following evaluative tools, providing definitions, examples, and explanations for how to use these tools when reading and/or discussing a text:

- Appeal
- Authenticity
- Character Arc
- Flow/Cohesion

- Pacing
- Passage of Time
- Setting
- Voice

It's not necessary to explore a text with all of these in mind. But knowing what these tools are helps when there is something working extremely well in a book and when something feels entirely off balance. These are methods of pinpointing that are useful for reader's advisory, as well as for personal reading. Readers who can name the books they like and the books they don't like are often reading through the lens of one or more of these elements.

◼ Appeal

There are two elements of appeal: reader appeal and market appeal.

What is it that makes a book appealing? What makes a book a good read alike to another one? How do you get a book into the hands of the right reader for maximum impact? These questions are at the heart of **reader appeal**. Reader appeal is based entirely on individual readers and is the heart of this book. It can come in a myriad of forms, ranging from bigger, topical interests – such a road-trip story – to more microscopic aspects of story – such as a road trip that takes place in the Pacific Northwestern United States or a road trip that features a GLBT love story within it.

Market appeal, on the other hand, is not dependent upon a reader's interest. While the market may label a book as appropriate for young adults and thus guide it toward a type of reader, the individual reader doesn't matter much. Rather, the market looks broadly at appeal to readers. Within market appeal are two other appeal aspects: commercial appeal and literary appeal.

Titles with **commercial appeal** are those which will reach a very wide audience – there's something to the story which will sell the book to a large number of readers. Commercial appeal means there is a compelling hook to the story, and that is what gets the book moving off shelves. Examples of commercially-appealing books within YA fiction more broadly include *The Hunger Games* or *Divergent*. Both of these books feature plot hooks that appeal to a vast readership; in both cases, it's girl against a broken or crumbling world.

Books with more **literary appeal** will still reach a good-size audience, but the hook of the story isn't as immediately sellable as commercial titles. Literary defines a writing style more than it does a sales point. The attention falls more on the writing, which uses literary devices such as imagery, figurative language, or metaphor to construct a story. It is not better or worse than a book with high commercial appeal; these books don't necessarily have a larger nor a smaller audience, either.

Commercial and literary appeal aren't genre-limited. There are literary science fiction titles as much as there are commercial romance novels. These are not mutually exclusive terms, and contemporary realistic fiction spans both commercial and literary novels.

While it's not unheard of for highly commercial novels to have a literary slant to them, it's rare. John Green's books may be excellent examples of when commercial and literary appeal come together. Then there are authors like Sarah Dessen who showcase strong, consistent writing, but her books lean more

Every book published has a different appeal. Included here are examples of contemporary YA authors who generally write either more commercial or more literary novels.

More Commercial	More Literary
• Jennifer Brown	• Laurie Halse Anderson
• Meg Cabot	• Justina Chen
• Ally Carter	• A. S. King
• Chris Crutcher	• Matthew Quick
• Matt de la Pena	• John Corey Whaley
• Jordan Sonnenblick	• Sara Zarr

to commercial than literary. Ellen Hopkins is another example of an author whose books are more commercial than literary, despite what she does within the writing, particularly her use of the verse format.

Most novels fall between commercial and literary. These are the **mid-list titles** – and it's these mid-list titles that comprise the bulk of good read alikes to the most commercial and most highly literary titles. It's in those mid-list titles where, as noted already, contemporary YA fiction tends to fall most often.

Evaluating Appeal

Every reader has a book that will work for him or her, and digging into those appeal factors is important for getting the right titles into the right hands. Reader appeal is at the heart of effective reader's advisory, as the books recommended to readers are selected based on those elements of story that readers find interesting.

Delving into what does and does not work for a specific reader helps that reader become stronger at identifying reading preferences. That reader becomes more critical, more discerning, and ultimately, more satisfied in his or her book selections.

The heart of this book is appeal – what is it that makes a contemporary novel appealing to a reader? What elements are he or she looking for in their next read? Does he want a book that's got an immediately-engaging premise and hook or one that's infused with literary elements to keep him unraveling layers of story? Or, does he want a book that marries both?

■ Authenticity

Does the story feel real?

Maybe the most crucial element of a contemporary YA novel is authenticity. Since the book's success hinges on its believability, it's crucial that the story be authentic. But authenticity doesn't depend entirely upon the reader's own sensibilities – gauging authenticity happens through the story itself. In other words, is what happens to the characters authentic to *their* situation? To *their* voice? To *their* place in the world?

Authenticity can often be parsed out through elements like dialog. When the characters interact, does it feel like the characters are being themselves? Are they speaking in a way that reflects who they are in the story? Are they coming across much younger or older? Much more educated or under-educated? Does the way the character talks with his or her peers differ than when he or she interacts with a person in authority?

A character who is the same in every interaction isn't necessarily the most authentic. If a character interacts in the same manner wherever they are – in a classroom, in their bedroom, at dinner with their parents, at a black-tie event – they aren't being authentic, either.

Characters are complex and dynamic.

While it's important for readers in the targeted age group for young adult novels – those between 12 and 18 – to feel like the characters reflect their realities and "sound like they do," it's not the hallmark of authenticity. It's important, too, for the characters in these books not to sound like or act like stereotypes. For instance, a novel about characters in inner-city New York shouldn't all sound like characters in a book set in the rural Midwest. But nei-

> Authenticity emerges when it's clear that the character's voice and interactions both mirror their realities and offer windows into something deeper personally.

ther should they sound like they're all hardened city teens who have dealt with every challenge possible.

Novels that incorporate diverse character lineups should give enough attention to these characters so that they don't read like tokens. Characters who may be gay or lesbian shouldn't simply be there to be there. They should be complex and dynamic outside their labels, even if they aren't in a leading role.

Because contemporary novels are set in today's world, the authenticity to time period is less crucial than it is in historical novels, but it's not entirely absent. Teens who are able to get around much in the story because they lack access to technology isn't authentic; even if the main characters don't have a cell phone or a lap top, chances are they're still impacted by these tech tools by simply being teenagers surrounded by peers who are using them all the time. In other words, there are no islands in realistic fiction. That doesn't mean that a contemporary novel requires the use of pop culture or other easily-dated references to give it authenticity. Rather, it means that complete avoidance of certain aspects of modern daily life can discredit the reality of the story and characters.

Also important with authenticity is the story's readability and the character's behaviors and actions. Are they reflective of real teens? Again, there is no prescription for an average teenager, as some are capable of incredibly intellectual actions, behaviors, and thoughts and some operate without much maturity at all. Teenagers are not stereotypes; every teen is an individual with his or her own personalities, quirks, dreams, desires, emotions, reactions, and responses. Authentic stories reflect this range. They don't stop the reader and beg him/her to question whether or not he's reading about characters in a certain life stage.

Evaluating Authenticity

Books shouldn't talk down to their readers, nor should they pander to them, either. The best payoffs are those which are earned through the course of the entire story, where readers see a character through highs and lows, through true dialog, and through scenarios which test the limits of both the character and his story more grandly.

Authenticity is about trust in the characters, in the story, and in the reader. It's a partnership between the book and the reader. The more the story trusts itself and its characters, the more the reader can trust the storytelling.

■ Character Arc

While there are important elements of character worth looking at critically, the most important one is the character arc. How does the character change from the beginning of the novel through to the end? Is there an entire journey? Is there a payoff in reading the story or is the character flat-lined from start to finish?

Because contemporary fiction tends to depend upon the characters to drive the story, the way a character acts and changes propels the action forward. While not always the case, character development and arc follow less of an actual arc and more of a "W" shape. The story starts on a high of some sort, then it dips down to the lowest point. The character then pushes upward toward a climax, but because nothing can be cut and dry, it's not truly the climax for the character, nor his/her development. Instead, further challenges push that character down into another valley before allowing him or her to come to a conclusion.

Contemporary novels may also follow the hero's journey structure of character arc. It's not that much

Arc Styles

In terms of recent contemporary fiction illuminating these arc styles, Emily Murdoch's *If You Find Me* (St. Martin's Griffin, 2013) showcases the "W" plot well and Michael Hassan's *Crash and Burn* (Balzar + Bray, 2013) gives a strong example of the hero's journey.

At the beginning of Murdoch's book, Carey and her younger sister are rescued from their trailer in the woods. Neither girl had gone to school; their mother had taken them out and raised them deep in the wilderness. But when they're rescued, instead of things becoming better for the sisters, things worsen. They were sent to live with their father, who they knew nothing about. And it wasn't just their father. They also met a new stepmother and stepsister. The girls then enrolled in public school. Just when things are going up hill and Carey feels as though she's adjusting to this new life (wherein she reaches the middle peak of the "W"), another plot element emerges and she's tossed into a downward regression. This comes at the time when she's being asked to talk about an incident that happened in the woods, which caused her to be traumatized in the way that she is. Reliving this is a nightmare, but as she works through it, she's able to walk through to the final peak of the "W."

In Hassan's novel – which follows the more traditional hero's journey – readers get to know Crash through the entirety of his life, all of the highs and lows, and he gives us his story through the journey from point A to point B. We're exposed to Crash's ordinary life before he's given a call to action, which is to write the story of his relationship with Burn and how that relationship and the insight gained from it helped him ultimately solve the ordeal Burn initiates. This novel is epic because it is that journey, and through the journey, that readers see and experience the entire arc of both Crash and Burn.

For further explanation and examples of the "W" plot, check out Kathleen Wall's blog at *http://kathleenwall.wordpress.com/2010/05/27/wow-for-the-w-plot/*. An explanation of the hero's journey can be found on The Writer's Journey at http://www.thewritersjourney.com/hero's_journey.htm.

different from the "W" plot, though it can focus more heavily on action than on character's emotional development (which is the focus of the "W").

It's not always necessary for there to be a cut and dry arc to a character. Sometimes there's value in an ambiguous character ending. As readers, we can watch a character make choices and decisions throughout the book which beg us to consider how the outcome may emerge. Will that character ultimately be redeemed in some way? A big story doesn't always mean a character will come away "better" nor changed positively for the experience. They can, however, still have a full and complete arc.

Evaluating Character Arc

What it comes down to is that the main character or characters in a story are complex and that they contain multitudes. They don't face every challenge before them in the same manner, and as readers, we come to expect that something comes out of those challenges that either improves or weakens the character.

It's okay for readers to question the characters and their arcs, and it's okay for things to come around full-circle to where they were in the beginning. The purpose of the arc is to offer depth and insight into the emotions and accompanying actions and behaviors of the character. Stories with no character arc are stories which die before they begin or are stories where it's clear there is a message to be delivered and the character is the method of delivery.

■ Flow/Cohesion

Flow – which can also be called cohesion – is about *how* the story reads. It's not about pacing but the construction of the book itself.

Some short books are speedy reads while others are much slower paced. Below are a few examples of each:

Slow Paced

The Children and the Wolves by Adam Rapp (Candlewick, 2011)

Catch & Release by Blythe Woolston (Carolrhoda, 2012)

Fast Paced

Never Eighteen by Megan Bostick (Houghton Mifflin Harcourt, 2012)

Dirty Little Secrets by C.J. Omololu (Walker, 2010)

Unlocked by Ryan G. Van Cleave (Walker, 2011)

If there is backstory woven into the narrative, does it make sense how it's presented? Is it done throughout the story naturally or is it inserted in a more unnatural methodology, such as through different chapters? Through italicized portions? Even if the method of insertion is more artificial, it doesn't mean that the flow of the story won't work.

Jennifer Brown masters this technique in *Thousand Words* (Little, Brown, 2013) as she offers Ashleigh's present moment in community service between chapters of back story, explaining the events leading up to that punishment. The flow makes sense to the reader, as it doesn't force large periods of backstory into the present narrative. There is no "info dumping" here.

Flow isn't only about backstory, though. It's also about present and forward motion. Chapters that are too short or too long can impact flow of the story, either dragging down the narrative or speeding it up to a point where the reader feels he/she may have missed something. Flow can be impacted on a sentence-by-sentence level, too: if the sentence doesn't read well or relies too heavily on long or Latinate words, on adverbs, or on lengthy descriptive passages that don't offer insight into the story or character, it can slow down flow.

Readers can usually discover an issue with flow and cohesion by reading passages aloud. If they come out clunky or don't roll off the tongue naturally, usually there is something clogging up the movement. Novels which are cohesive and have good flow should beg for reading aloud.

There are books where flow is purposefully choppy or staccato. This choice in writing and story development should make sense and not feel like a gimmick. An example of short, clipped writing that works with the story's flow, rather than against it, is Erica Lorraine Scheidt's *Uses for Boys* (St. Martin's, 2013). The main character's thoughts are very short and scattered, and this translates into what she shares over the course of the novel.

Dialog also impacts flow. Does dialog make sense where it is? Is the story development too dependent upon it? Or is there too much sharing of backstory in the narrative when it could instead be put into dialog? Dialog can hook a reader immediately, but it can slow down a story or push it forward too quickly.

In alternatively formatted novels – those told through verse, multiple perspectives, or other methods – flow is important. If it feels like the verse isn't natural, that can make the novel challenging to get through. Verse novels in particular should beg to be read aloud if the flow is strong. Ellen Hopkins has this down pat, and she goes the extra mile in crafting much of her verse to be visual to the reader, as well. This visual translation enhances the flow, rather than detracts from it. In stories told through multiple voices, the change in voices should make sense and be clear to the reader; chapter headings or breaks that indicate change in perspective are often helpful in flow, rather than hindering.

Evaluating Flow/Cohesion

A novel that flows well is one that compels the reader to keep going. It is also likely a novel that has good pacing, solid character development, and strong writing mechanics more wholly.

While flow and cohesion aren't appeal factors, per se, they can impact the reader's experience. Clunky flow is a turn-off.

Pacing

How fast or slow the story moves defines the pacing. The length of the book doesn't define the pacing, but rather, the way in which the story is told. A book can be packed with quick-moving action or it can have a methodical unraveling of plot that purposefully makes the reader take the story in at a slower speed.

Whether the book unravels at a swift pace or a slower pace doesn't impact the strength of the book nor does it project a judgment upon the book's literary merits. There are books with speedy pacing that are as literary as those with more leisurely pacing and vice versa. The style of the book can impact pacing, but not always. Novels written in verse, for example, are not always fast paced, despite the style.

Longer books go both ways, too, in terms of pacing. There are books like Andrew Smith's *Winger* (Simon and Schuster, 2013) with nearly 500 pages that read quickly. Then there are books like Eishes Chayil/Judy Brown's *Hush* (Walker, 2010) that require the reader to slow down and focus intensely through the story.

Lengthy books in alternative storytelling formats can go both ways, as well. As mentioned earlier, some of Ellen Hopkins's verse novels have rapid pacing, despite their length, and there are books like Joshua Cohen's *Leverage* (Dutton, 2011) which features two points of view and two voices that speed right along pace-wise.

Evaluating Pacing

The bulk of contemporary fiction tends to fall somewhere in the middle pace-wise because there's less focus on building new worlds or in driving the story forward through action.

That said, pacing can make or break a book if it doesn't feel right – the character development and the story arc can suffer under pacing that's too quick or too slow in equal measure.

Passage of time can be an appeal factor for many readers. There are stories which take place in a single day, including titles like Omololu's *Dirty Little Secrets*, Cath Crowley's *Graffiti Moon* (Knopf, 2012), and Matthew Quick's *Forgive Me, Leonard Peacock* (Little, Brown 2013).

There are books like National Book Award Finalist Carrie Arcos's *Out of Reach* (Simon Pulse, 2012) wherein the actual passage of time within the story is one day, but the story itself covers a longer period of time – the flashbacks interspersed throughout the narrative lengthen it.

The Statistical Probability of Love at First Sight by Jennifer E. Smith (Little, Brown, 2012) is another example of a story that passes over the course of little more than a day in real time, but which infuses depth to the story through backstory and flashbacks.

◼ Passage of Time

Similar to pacing is the story's passage of time, the length of time that progresses in-story.

Sometimes the author makes the decision to lay passage of time out for readers in chapter headings or throughout the story, but often, it's the reader who picks up the clues on how much time passes from the beginning to the end of the book. Gayle Forman's *Just One Day* (Dutton, 2013), for example, uses the month of the year to open most chapters in order to indicate passage of time (which, despite the title, takes place over the course of more than just one day). These clues to the reader also appear in books such as Amy Reed's *Crazy* (Simon Pulse, 2012) via the email date and time stamps, and Tiffany Schmidt's *Bright Before Sunrise* (Walker, 2014) uses time stamps over the course of the single night through which the story plays out.

There are books like the previously mentioned Hassan title, *Crash and Burn*, that cover great periods of time. This particular novel spans a period between the main character's elementary school days until the present, the summer prior to beginning college. The way it's written allows for this passage of time to make sense, and the length to which Hassan allows his character to inform his present situation with his past experiences further permits the lengthy passage of time. There aren't odd gaps, wherein the character doesn't offer insight; rather, the passage is logical and doesn't over- or under- serve the story.

Passage of time is different than pacing and different than setting or time period. Passage of time is the actual period covered from the start of the book until the end. Pacing, as discussed above, is the speed at which the story unfolds. Setting is where the story takes place. Time period is when it takes place. In historical fiction, there can be a relationship between a time period and passage of time (if it unfolds over one year and therefore the passage of time is one year) but they are not the same thing.

Evaluating Passage of Time

Passage of time isn't dependent upon the book's length. It's dependent upon whether that story's time frame and the way the story unfolds throughout that frame makes sense. If there are gaping holes in the time or if there are weeks or months that pass within pages – or even sentences – that aren't logical, then chances are the passage of time is working against the story in some way. Either the character isn't offering enough insight or backstory or the story itself tries to cram in far too much unnecessary information.

From an evaluative standpoint, passage of time isn't the most crucial of critical tools. Often, stories fall apart for bigger reasons than passage of time.

That said, it *is* a critical tool in understanding and unlocking reader appeal. Does a reader want a story that takes place in a short period of time? Or do they want one that's expansive? So even if this tool isn't necessary all the time, it's an element worth keeping in mind for those stories where passage of time *does* play a big role in the narrative or character development.

◼ Setting

All books have some sort of setting to them, but the role that setting plays depends upon the story itself. Sometimes, it's at the forefront and other times, it's there simply as backdrop.

When setting plays a large role in the plot or in the development of character, it can be a big appeal factor for readers. If a story's set near them or set in a place that mirrors their own, it can make the book have a sense of immediacy and intimacy. If it's set in a place entirely unfamiliar, it can bread a sense of travel or adventure and allow for experiencing and understanding stories that may be foreign.

Noteworthy settings in novels happen everywhere. The following are a few examples of memorable settings, broken down by locale:

Foreign Settings

- *Anna and the French Kiss* by Stephanie Perkins (Dutton, 2011) set in Paris, France
- *Instructions for a Broken Heart* by Kim Culbertson (Sourcebooks, 2011) set in Italy
- *Meant to Be* by Lauren Morrill (Delacorte, 2012) set in England
- *When You Were Here* by Daisy Whitney (Little, Brown, 2013) set in Japan

Vivid Rural/Small Town Settings

- *Where Things Come Back* by John Corey Whaley (Antheneum, 2011)
- *The Freak Observer* by Blythe Woolston (Carolrhoda, 2010)
- *Beautiful Music for Ugly Children* by Kirstin Cronn-Mills (Flux, 2012)
- *Princesses of Iowa* by M. Molly Backes (Candlewick, 2012)

Strong Urban Settings

- *What Can('t) Wait* by Ashley Hope Perez (Carolrhoda, 2011)
- *Wild Awake* by Hilary T. Smith (Katherine Tegen, 2013)
- *Permanent Record* by Leslie Stella (Amazon Children's, 2013)
- *Don't Breathe A Word* by Holly Cupala (HarperTeen, 2012)

Unique Settings

- *The Girls of No Return* by Erin Saldin (Scholastic, 2012) set at a remote reform school
- *Frost* by Marianna Baer (HarperTeen, 2011) set at a boarding school
- *Clean* by Amy Reed (Simon Pulse, 2011) set at a rehabilitation center
- *Every Little Thing in the World* by Nina de Gramont (Antheneum, 2010) set at a summer reform camp
- *The Statistical Probability of Love at First Sight* by Jennifer E. Smith (Little, Brown, 2012) set in an airport and on an airplane

Traveling Abroad

- *Wanderlove* by Kirsten Hubbard (Delacorte, 2012) moves throughout Central America
- *Just One Day* by Gayle Forman (Dutton, 2013) moves throughout Europe

Road Trips in America

- *In Honor* by Jessi Kirby (Simon and Schuster, 2012)
- *Don't Stop Now* by Julie Halpern (Feiwel & Friends, 2011)
- *Kiss the Morning Star* by Elissa Janine Hoole (Marshall Cavendish/Amazon, 2012)
- *The Disenchantments* by Nina LaCour (Dutton, 2012)
- *Thou Shalt Not Road Trip* by Antony John (Dial, 2012)
- *Amy & Roger's Epic Detour* by Morgan Matson (Simon and Schuster, 2010)

Whatever the case, setting can play a significant role in a contemporary novel because the story can only take place in the real world. That's not to say that contemporary novels don't require world building, but the world building required in a realistic novel differs from that in a fantasy or science fiction novel. It has to not just feel real, but it has to *be* real, even if the actual place in the story is not.

Sarah Dessen is well-known known for her settings. Nearly all of her books take place in the same "world" of Colby. It's not a real place, but it's based on a number of ocean-side towns. This world feels fresh and real, and it's one reason that keeps readers returning to her stories. It's the reader's world as much as it is the world of her characters.

Evaluating Setting

In many ways, setting is like passage of time in that it's not necessarily a useful critical tool in and of itself. Setting can play a role in what makes a storyline succeed or fail, but the role it has as an evaluative tool comes in the way it can and is an appeal factor for many readers.

Setting can be a matter of understanding place because of experience and personal knowledge, but it can also be a matter of readers wanting to travel somewhere completely different from where they are in their own lives.

■ Voice

Voice isn't just one thing – it's two.

The first aspect of voice is that which readers may come to expect of an author whose work has been read in the past.

Authors like Sarah Dessen or Susane Colasanti have a voice to their writing that is distinctly their own. A reader picking up a book and flipping through a few pages knows they're reading a Dessen or Colasanti book by the way the authors use their language, develop their imagery, craft their sentences, and so forth. It's not to say their characters all sound the same, but rather, these authors have a voice behind their writing that is memorable. An author's voice distinguishes one person's writing from another.

The second aspect of voice – that of the character – isn't as clear-cut as authorial voice.

Not every book has a strong voice to it. That's not to say there's not voice present, but rather, it's not at the forefront of the writing. Though primarily a tool of first-person narration, it is absolutely possible for third-person narration to have strong voice. Take for example Sara Zarr's *The Lucy Variations* (Little, Brown, 2013). Despite being in third person, Lucy's voice rings through as

---

Multiple points of view novels, as well as those told in verse, need a distinct voice –or voices – to be memorable. A few examples of strong voices in these alternative format books include:

- *Freakboy* by Kristin Elizabeth Clark (Farrar, Straus and Giroux, 2013): verse novel and multiple points of view

- *Tricks* by Ellen Hopkins (Margaret K. McElderry, 2010): verse novel and multiple points of view

- *Exposed* by Kimberly Marcus (Random House Books for Young Readers, 2011): verse novel

- *Crazy* by Amy Reed (Simon Pulse, 2012): multiple points of view and epistolary format

- *Cracked* by K. M. Walton (Simon Pulse, 2012): multiple points of view

- *The List* by Siobhan Vivian (Push, 2012): multiple points of view

Voice vs. Tone

The concept of voice can be easily confused with the tone of a novel, especially as alternative format books come into the picture. But voice is much different than either of those literary concepts. A good way to illustrate the difference may be through a book like Libba Bray's *Beauty Queens* (Scholastic, 2011). The story is told through an ensemble cast, so readers don't get to know one character's voice intimately; however, there are numerous voices that can be teased out of the narrative. Bray's book isn't most known for the voice, though. It's known for its tone instead. This book is a satire, and that tone carries throughout, rather than the development of rich and distinct voices among the characters. This isn't a critique of the voice or characters; it's rather the method of storytelling. The satirical tone is what is most memorable from *Beauty Queens*.

Voice vs. Style

Voice can easily be confused with style. Style is the means of delivering the story. Verse novels are written in the style of using verse to tell the story. The epistolary novel is written in letter-style. There are books like *Morgan Matson's Amy and Roger's Epic Detour* (Simon and Schuster Books for Young Readers, 2010) which include ephemera within the narrative, making it a scrapbook styling.

But more than the execution of the story as style is the writing style more broadly. There are stories told through short, clipped sentences like Erica Lorraine Scheidt's *Uses for Boys* (St. Martin's Press, 2013) and then there are books where the story is told through a longer, more fantastical style like Antonia Michaelis's *The Storyteller* (Abrams, 2012).

While style can and often does impact voice, it's still a distinct writing technique separate from voice.

The more the tools are used during and after reading a novel, the more clear reader appeal emerges.

Through appeal, through reading the right books at the right time and for the right reasons, the messages and greater issues worth thinking about, worth discussing, and worth evaluating shine through.

someone struggling to rectify giving up a former passion with finding herself. What makes her voice stand out are the ways in which she longs for and grieves the losses in her life. Even with readers pulled a step back through third-person narration and unable to see the world straight through Lucy's eyes, the reader identifies her voice easily. It's in the way she presents her feelings and in the way her actions then express those same emotions. Zarr's own authorial voice also stands out, despite the fact *The Lucy Variations* is her first novel in third person.

A couple of noteworthy first-person contemporary titles that showcase strong and solid voice include Geoff Herbach's *Stupid Fast* (Sourcebooks, 2011) and Amy Spalding's *The Reece Malcolm List* (Entangled, 2013). Both books undercut their characters' challenges with humor in ways that make their voices unique.

Voice is crucial in books where there are multiple narrators because it is through each voice that readers discern the distinct characters. Novels written in alternative formats rely heavily on voice to drive the story. If those books don't have voice, they don't have character. They may have style but lack substance.

Not all books will have a strong voice. There are plenty of good novels that succeed without requiring the character to have a strong voice or without the author having developed his or her own authorial voice (and because there are many authors who write across genres, sometimes it's challenging for them to have a defined voice). What voice comes down to in the end is how the reader comes to know and remember the character. Is it the way the character reacted in a specific situation or in repeated situations that is especially memorable? Is it the way the character approached something with humor or grace, despite not needing to do so? Is the character hard-edged and sharp? Soft?

Evaluating Voice

Voice can highlight a character's humor or sarcasm, his or her longing or romantic sides, and much more, without ever requiring the reader to be explicitly told that is how a character is or how a character behaves. It's part and parcel of *how* characters share their story with the reader.

In contemporary YA especially, voice is what may be the driving narrative force. Since most contemporary fiction is character-focused, voice is what can make a book memorable, even more so than whatever the characters' struggles in the story may be.

Voice is what stands out when all else about a character is stripped away. It's the intimate perspective only offered by the character at hand. It can't be described in simple words but rather, it's a feeling of *knowing* the characters, even when they aren't doing anything noteworthy at all.

The above are tools for evaluating fiction on a critical level, but they have no utility in discovering meaning or message. Readers have their own unique tools for that. Instead, the tools above should be used as a way of thinking about fiction and the elements that make a novel appealing. They are means of helping craft critical exploration of *how* a novel delivers a message or idea.

Critically evaluating a book with the tools above is key to objectively exploring a novel. Because message and theme are subjective elements of story, it's impossible to say a book is only about one specific thing. The tools above allow for objective and unbiased methods of thinking about a text. Pacing is something that can be assessed without bias (it's either well-paced or it's not – it doesn't matter what that book's particular pace is). Character arc, voice, and the other elements allow for objective observation and exploration because there is no *right* or *wrong* way for it to work. Instead, it either works or it does not work. These tools allow readers to figure out the why.

Chapter 5

Reader's Advisory

As a former middle school teacher, I have seen my share of reluctant readers. When I began teaching YA literature at the university level, I thought I had put those days behind me. Instead, I was surprised to find that some students were less-than-avid readers, not an ideal situation when faced with reading tons of YA novels over the course of a semester. I knew one of the things I needed to do was make sure the early reading of YA materials reminded these students why they loved books and reading at one point in their lives. I did exactly what I had done as a middle school teacher: located a wide range of books, book talked them all, and set up a reading schedule that took students from lighter to more hearty fare. I was careful to include books with characters of color, books with settings familiar and foreign, and books with inner and outer conflicts. The books represented the range of forms, formats, and genres: graphic novels, nonfiction, picture books for older readers, series, and novels in verse to name a few. Before long, in addition to the assignments they were completing, I also received notes about how much they enjoyed this or that book, notes about them handing a title off to a friend or colleague, and (best of all, as far as I am concerned) notes about students sharing their reading with their own classrooms of students. As someone who knows and loves YA literature for its power to transform our thinking and our lives, I could ask for nothing better. – Teri Lesesne, professor of children's and young adult literature

Youth advocates know that even the most voracious readers can stumble upon reading roadblocks. There are times when a reader can't connect with a book that appears to have all the characteristics they prefer. There are times you read a book and think immediately of someone who should read the title because it's very *them* or because it is a great novel that reads similar to another favorite book or author.

Before delving too deeply into this, **it's important to establish a difference between recommending books and offering reader's advisory**. While the formal terminology of reader's advisory tends to be associated with librarianship or book selling, anyone who reads is perfectly capable of providing strong reader's advisory (RA). The difference between simply recommending books and performing RA comes through the method of delivery.

Reading recommendations primarily stem from the reader's personal interest in a book. When a book is recommended to a reader, it's because the person who recommends it sees something in it that reminds them of the reader or they want that particular book to resonate with another person.

Anyone can offer recommendations and there is nothing wrong with recommending books. A bookstore can, for example, recommend that everyone read the books on the *New York Times* bestsellers list because those books are popular and those books are being read by many people. But it's not reader's advisory for a book seller to simply suggest that someone looking for a good book try a book on the bestseller list.

Reader's advisory is a skill set that focuses on the outside reader, with recommendations given based on the in-

A Crash Course in Reader's Advisory

Reader's advisory involves talking with a reader about his or her reading preferences in order to offer book selections that meet the reader's needs or interests. Below are a few questions worth asking in an RA conversation. An RA interaction doesn't require all of these questions; pick the ones that help you, as an advisor, most understand what a reader wants:

- What was the last book (or books) you read and loved? What made you love that book – was it the characters? The setting? The genre? Something in the plot?

- What was the last book (or books) you did not like? What was it that didn't work for you in the book?

- Who are your favorite authors?

- Do you have a favorite series? What did you like about that series?

- What books have you read in school that you liked or did not like? Why?

- What are you in the mood for reading? Do you want something familiar or something different? Something challenging or something more relaxing to read?

- When you say you want a mystery (or any other broad term), do you want it to be funny? Do you want it to be serious? Do you want it to be a stand alone or part of a series?

Ask the reader leading questions to understand what it is they want in a certain type of book.

Sometimes, and with teens especially, it's not easy to get answers to these questions. If that's the case, switch gears a bit – rather than ask about books, ask about the last movie, television show, or video game they saw and enjoyed. Tease out from those answers what elements of story work for them. That may help translate into reading.

Never assume anything about your reader: the reader's gender, age, socioeconomic class, and education rarely mean anything in a reader's advisory conversation. In fact, assumptions about any of these in providing RA may make the conversation shut down entirely.

terests and the reading preferences of another reader. It's highly individual. In the example above, reader's advisory would occur if the bookseller asked the reader his or her previous favorite titles and favorite genres, as well as books that haven't worked for that person in the past. He or she would then tailor suggested titles to what the reader's history of reading had been. The reader's advisor doesn't offer up titles at random or titles on a prescribed list; instead, he/she customizes the suggested books based on what that reader's tastes and interests are.

> Reader's advisory relationships hinge on trust in that a reader trusts the person tasked with advisory to suggest next reads without advice or judgment upon taste.

Good reader's advisors can provide solid recommendations based on the reader's interest because they themselves are readers. It doesn't mean that a reader's advisor needs to know everything nor read everything. Rather, it means that she or he needs the ability to ferret out what it is a reader wants and use a combination of his/her own reading knowledge and the resources available to him/her in order to match the reader to appropriate books.

Another critical element of RA is offering title suggestions without judgment. Tough, gritty, dark books can appeal to all kinds of readers, whether or not they themselves are dealing with those things in their own lives. A good reader's advisor has the reader's needs and interests as the only elements in mind when offering recommendations.

Trust is essential in providing quality RA because as a reader's advisor, you have to trust in your own ability to tease out what it is the reader really wants. A reader saying he or she enjoys "romance" may actually want something other than another romance novel – he or she may like an element common among a number of romances recently read that has nothing to do with the romance itself. This, too, is where non-judgment of the reader matters: it could be easy to write the reader's tastes off as simplistic when really, they could be quite complex. What the reader may have enjoyed about the handful of romances he or she read was

> Appeal factors are the elements of a story that appeal to a reader. Those appeal factors within a book are teased out via critical evaluation and consideration. Discovering what appeal factors a reader desires comes through the reader's advisory interaction.

the family dynamics of the main character or it could have been a particular writing style. It could have been that the books each featured some sort of exotic locale and that setting made the book work for the reader. It could

have been the story's pacing, the arc of the characters within the story, or it could have even been the age of the characters in the book. All of these are **appeal factors**, regardless of a book's genre. And even if it was the romance within the books that worked for the reader, the way romance is written differs. It's not simplistic nor identical across all books within the genre.

Reader's advisory isn't one thing, though. There are two kinds of RA: There is **active reader's advisory** and **passive reader's advisory**.

Active RA is when the advisor interacts personally with readers in some capacity. This can come through book talking, through one-on-one conversation, through a group book discussion, or other face-on conversation.

Passive RA is just as effective as active reader's advisory, even if it's less personal. Passive advisory takes numerous forms, including writing book reviews, creating shelf talkers (reviews with appeal factors discussed and attached to book shelves), developing book displays around various topics or themes, drafting book lists, and highlighting books through means other than dialog. Even though these things may sound more like recommendations than reader's advisory, they're not. Because passive RA requires critical consideration of the material, it's more than simply offering an easy reading solution. It's an alternative method of delivering reader's advisory that allows the advisor to delve into new and creative methods of offering book selections.

Both active and passive RA are important in developing a full reader's advisory experience – they each have their strengths and their limitations, so it's important as an advisor (and as a reader) to develop skills in giving and receiving both experiences.

As mentioned earlier, RA can be performed by anyone willing to learn how to do it. The key is remembering appeal factors.

Reader's advisory is built upon the notion that all books have something within them that appeals to a reader's sensibilities. It begins broadly: Is a reader looking for a book aimed at young adults? Young adult as a category of reading is an appeal factor.

From there, it narrows down to genre. Genre is a broad appeal factor, and it's the easiest to offer suggestions through because a reader and a reader's advisor can know whether or not a book within a particular genre will or will not work. Genre is not the final determining factor of reader's advisory; it's a tool to use in pulling out more appeal factors. While readers tend to have genre preferences, a good reader's advisor can encourage readers to look beyond their comfort genre when they as an advisor are able to determine the more granular elements of a story that work for a particular reader. The most devoted science fiction readers may find a perfect-for-them story in contemporary fiction.

Beyond genre, there are the appeal factors laid out earlier in the critical assessment section of this book, including language and writing style, pacing, passage of time, voice, and others. Then there are plot elements that may matter to a reader. He or she may want a book where a pet plays a significant role in the story or she/he may want a story that's set in a community similar to his/her own. Readers may want a story that includes a non-traditional family or a family going through transition. When readers can identify the aspects of a story they like or would like to read, the reader's advisor can and should work to find books that include them. It may indeed involve going across genre.

Fortunately, and not surprisingly, readers looking for contemporary realistic fiction will find that much of what they're interested in is the real world represented in the genre. Significant pets? Plenty of them. Stories set in non-tradi-

Bibliotherapy

An aspect of RA worth noting is the more specialized practice of bibliotherapy, which can be performed via active or passive means. Bibliotherapy focuses on delivering specialized reading recommendations based on a reader's personal challenges in hopes that the reader can find some sort of solution or comfort through that reading.

The purpose isn't simply recommending; it's a method of curating reading with a specific goal in mind for the reader. It can be directed at an individual – leading someone experiencing manic depression to books and resources about manic depression – and it can also be directed more broadly – following a national tragedy, curated reading lists featuring books related to the tragedy or resources for coping with the devastation from the event.

Because contemporary fiction tackles realistic issues, plenty of books can be used for bibliotherapeutic means; however, contemporary fiction doesn't exist solely for this purpose. Bibliotherapy is only a tiny component of reader's advisory. Good reader's advisors can offer bibliotherapy through the same set of tools used to deliver RA to other readers. It's a matter of considering appeal factors, in addition to potentially triggering factors within a book (which could include anything from disordered eating to stories about cancer) before disseminating recommendations.

A further discussion of the challenges and the opportunities with bibliotherapy can be found through the American Library Association's website and related articles at *http://www.ala.org/tools/bibliotherapy*.

tional places, like boats or airplanes? They're here. Stories that feature parents in the midst of divorce? Stories that include strong male friendship? Unlikeable female characters? These are all appeal factors to readers, as well as appeal factors to think about when conducting reader's advisory, be it passive or active.

Getting to those appeal factors in books isn't always easy, especially when working with teens who are still learning about and developing their reading preferences and interests. What matters is being open to and considerate of the wide variety of appeal factors that exist with each individual book and that matter to each individual reader. By offering reader's advisory through a variety of means and by reading widely, this skill set becomes second nature.

Tools for Developing Reader's Advisory Skills

Anyone has the capacity to be a good reader's advisor. You don't have to read everything nor do you have to read extensively, though it helps if you do. If you don't do the reading yourself, if you're aware of and knowledgeable with tools out there – reviews, blogs, reader's advisory guides, proprietary databases – you can still offer good advisory.

Read Widely

As much as reader's advisory is about being objective, there is something to be said about the value of being able to personally vouch for a book or two. Those who read and enjoy doing so are enthusiastic in not only offering objective RA, but they're able to also attest to the strengths and values of the books they recommend that they have read personally. Sometimes when reader's advisors hit a snag and cannot get the person they're advising to give them enough information for recommendations, they have to go by their own personal favorites. There's also something to be said about the value of a good passive reader's advisory display of favorites – and sometimes, what a reader may want is a book that you have enjoyed yourself.

The more widely you read and force yourself to be exposed to new and different material, the better reader and reader's advisor you become. More than that, the deeper you go within a genre, the more appeal facts you can dig out of the genre and the more similarities you can pull together across books. The wider you go outside a particular genre, the same truth exists: you can find similarities and appeal factors that may not always be superficially obvious.

In the case of contemporary realistic fiction, being a deep reader allows you to understand that the vast majority of the books in the genre are not "lesson" books, nor are they driven by an agenda. They're not all stories of doom and gloom. It's a rich genre, with reader appeal to meet the needs of a variety of different types of readers.

Note Elements of Story

Go beyond the critical elements mentioned earlier and consider the other details present in a story which may be of interest to you as a reader or to other readers. What are the things that stick out as important to the plot or the things that are minor but still resonate? What's unusual? What's novel? What's the opposite of unusual or novel and instead so ordinary that it might not even seem worth noting?

Doing this doesn't mean paying attention to every single detail in a book and losing sight of the story. Instead, it's a consciousness of the careful construction of story and an awareness of what it is that could trigger interest for a reader. Even if they seem small – a setting on an airplane, a main character who spends a lot of time in a thrift store, or a character's passion for playing guitar or piccolo – these are appeal factors. The plane is an unusual setting and the hobby of thrift store shopping is both part of character development, as well as setting. Readers who want to read stories set in a different locale may be piqued by the plane or the thrift store. Readers who themselves have a thrift store interest may want to read about a character who also enjoys his or her time that way.

In noting these sorts of details, you also give yourself the pieces to build **read alikes** based on appeal factors that don't always seem obvious. Read alikes are the books suggested to a reader or curated into displays or reading lists that share similar appeal factors to one another. Are there a number of books featuring main characters who play guitar? Or who sing in competitive choir? Even if the stories are told through wildly different means and tackle entirely opposite themes, these little details build bridges among books. Those bridges then become a way for readers to try new-to-them stories, new-to-them authors, and broaden their own reading horizons. Read alikes stem from both appeal factors and critical evaluation of text – and those two things, as noted above, aren't mutually exclusive, either.

Compare Style

In addition to discovering aspects of story and thinking about the critical elements within a novel, there's the more and less obvious aspect of exploring and thinking about the styles that define the book at hand and how that style compares to other books. There is first and foremost the author's voice that distinguishes them from other authors, but more than that, style defines the overall *feel* of the work.

Thinking about style is important and it becomes much easier to define the more you read. Understanding the style of a book allows for thinking about read alikes, and this is particularly useful when a reader has exhausted the books by a single author. What is it about that author's style that is appealing? How does the book approach a subject? This can be as simple as thinking about the tense through which the story is told – is it first person, present tense? Is it third person past tense? Is it in second person, wherein the readers themselves feels they're being talked at?

Although format doesn't constitute style specifically, the format of a book can be a stylistic appeal factor. Is it in verse? Is it told scrapbook style? Through emails or letters?

Beyond format and tense are other, more subjective measures of story style. Is a book edgy or gritty? Is it a book that could be given to any reader because there's no content to be conscious of? These are subjective because the definitions of what qualifies as edgy or as "content conscious" differs among all readers and it differs among all communities. That said, these stylistic elements can be gauged via reader response and reader preference. They can also be gauged through wide reading and through consideration of the appealing elements of story noted above.

Take an author like Ellen Hopkins. Her books are usually told through the first person perspective, though the present or past tense choices vary. When told through a first person present tense, a novel has a sense of immediacy, and the reader moves right along with the main character (the "I" and "me") as the story unfolds.

In a first person past tense novel, the reader still moves with the main character, but the story unfolds with some delay. It's still immediate, but not as much as through the present tense.

Hopkins's novels tend to use first person, even when there are multiple points of view at hand. As of this writing, all of her novels have also been written in verse. Additionally, Hopkins writes about edgy and gritty topics, such as drug addiction, teen pregnancy, and teen prostitution in a way that's unflinching. The action and the challenges happen on page.

In general, Ellen Hopkins's books can be described as edgy, first-person stories in verse format. For readers looking to read books similar to hers, any or all of these elements may be of interest. These are reader appeal factors.

Thinking about those elements – the first-person perspective, the verse, and the gritty storytelling – would suggest offering read alikes in the vein of Heidi Ayarbe, who writes in first-person and who tackles

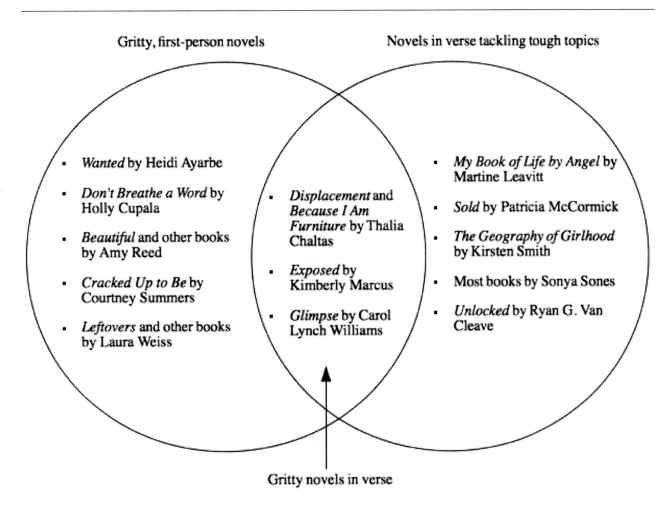

Gritty, first-person novels   Novels in verse tackling tough topics

- *Wanted* by Heidi Ayarbe

- *Don't Breathe a Word* by Holly Cupala

- *Beautiful* and other books by Amy Reed

- *Cracked Up to Be* by Courtney Summers

- *Leftovers* and other books by Laura Weiss

- *Displacement* and *Because I Am Furniture* by Thalia Chaltas

- *Exposed* by Kimberly Marcus

- *Glimpse* by Carol Lynch Williams

- *My Book of Life by Angel* by Martine Leavitt

- *Sold* by Patricia McCormick

- *The Geography of Girlhood* by Kirsten Smith

- Most books by Sonya Sones

- *Unlocked* by Ryan G. Van Cleave

Gritty novels in verse

gritty, edgy topics in her books. A bonus of Ayarbe as a read alike, particularly *Wanted* (Balzar + Bray, 2012), is that her books tend to take place in locations similar to Hopkins's – the western United States and even more specifically, Nevada. Other solid read alikes on this set of appeal factors for Hopkins fans would include Holly Cupala, Amy Reed, and Laura Weiss.

If it's the verse aspect of Hopkins's novels that is appealing to a reader, in conjunction with her head-on tackling of tough topics, then Kimberly Marcus's *Exposed* (Random House Books for Young Readers, 2011), Carol Lynch Williams's *Glimpse* (Paula Wiseman Books, 2011), and Thalia Chaltas's *Displacement* (Viking Juvenile, 2011) and *Because I Am Furniture* (Viking Juvenile, 2009) would be great read alikes.

Here's a visual way to think about developing read alikes for Ellen Hopkins, as described above. Note that "gritty" as an appeal factor can be fairly subjective and arguable.

Style is a means of quick and ready read alike creation because it's something that can be figured out by simply paging through a book or through reading the first couple of chapters. For some readers, this is in and of itself enough to compel them to try something new.

Cover Trends

Publishers put a lot of thought and money behind designing their book covers, and as simplistic and elementary as it sounds, sometimes the cover of a book can be used as RA. Many authors have a "brand," wherein their books have a similar aesthetic to them. Even though her books have been repackaged, Sarah Dessen's novels all have a similar look to them (both in their initial looks and in their repackaged looks). That look is mirrored in Deb Caletti's books, as well as books by Jessi Kirby, Susane Colasanti, Elizabeth Scott, and even some of the updated editions of Laurie Halse Anderson's books. All of these authors would make good author read alikes to Dessen.

It's worth exploring the visual element of contemporary books especially, because aside from offering read alike potential, they can offer insight into trends within the genre, as well as trends in marketing the genre. Marketing trends can aid developing read alikes, too – are there a lot of covers that have a certain look to them? Do a lot of the covers appear to be dark and feature a certain kind of model on them? These can suggest bigger trends within the books themselves. Likewise, a departure in an author's branded look on a cover can be as valuable an insight into reader appeal. If there's a book that looks dramatically different than prior titles, it could suggest a shift in the book's style, in its theme, or other elements. Elizabeth Scott's books are an excellent example of this. Her darker novels look markedly different than her more romantic ones that would have good appeal to Dessen readers.

While this isn't a hard science nor is it a perfect method to identify reader appeal qualities, it can be an effective means of RA in a pinch or a means of providing passive reader's advisory. As the YA market continues to expand, it might be smart to pay attention to cover and aesthetic design, as it can lend itself to quickly distinguishing appeal factors in story.

■ Developing a Reader's Advisory Program

Once you're able to think about reading with an eye toward reader's advisory, you can then consider the ways in which that sort of reading lends itself to implementing an RA program. As mentioned earlier, there are two aspects of reader's advisory: passive and active. Both are important, as they appeal to different types of readers in different ways. Likewise, they're valuable for the advisor who utilizes different skill sets in each.

Passive Reader's Advisory

Passive RA involves offering readily-available resources for finding and discovering books of interest without having to be personally present to guide a reader or hand sell a title. Passive reader's advisory, in addition to being a great solution for those who may not have time to interact face-to-face with readers regularly, allows for advisors to flex their creativity. It also allows for thinking about appeal factors in both specific and broad ways. Not only that, the manner in which passive reader's advisory can be delivered allows for much flexibility and innovation.

The following suggestions for passive RA programs aren't exhaustive. Instead, these are meant to be a springboard, both for those looking to begin passive reader's advisory and those looking to expand beyond their current programs.

Book Displays

There are thousands of ways to create unique displays based on any number of appeal factors. For contemporary fiction, it's easy and effective to develop displays that highlight the connections among books topically, such as books tackling grief and loss, books featuring sports, or books about bullying. There's opportunity to go well beyond thematic commonality though. Some simple and effective ideas might include:

- Books where the covers all feature beach settings or kissing scenes.

> A display today that captures the appeal factors of *Glee* might include Sara Bennett-Wealer's *Rival* (HarperTeen, 2011) for the competitive singing aspect, Amy Spalding's *The Reece Malcolm List* (Entangled, 2013) for the musical theater, and even books like Cath Crowley's *A Little Wanting Song* (Knopf Books for Young Readers, 2010), which features a main character who is a singer.

- Books that feature characters who share the same name.

- Books with characters who all play an instrument in their school band.

- Books set in your part of the world or books set in a completely foreign place.

- Books featuring animals in a prominent way.

- Books set in coffee shops.

If there's something making waves on television or in pop culture, a hot new movie or video game, create a display with books that share some of the appeal factors of whatever it is that's popular. Contemporary fiction is ripe for this sort of passive reader's advisory. For example, when the show *Glee* made waves, the perfect opportunity arose to develop a display featuring books with show choirs, with musical theater, and with performance and competition more broadly.

You can take displays up another notch and make them interactive. If you have a bunch of great books but they lack the kind of cover that catches reader attention, put them on display and ask readers to create covers that better reflect the content or that would stand out more. Use those designs to create another display.

Put displays in places where they're expected and where they might not be expected. In a library or in a classroom, using dedicated shelf space for rotating displays is the first step. While there's no rule on how often you should change the display, developing a schedule and planning for future thematic displays can make this method of passive reader's advisory become a habit. Not only does it become habit for you as advisor, but readers then come to anticipate what the next thing to be displayed may be. It builds excitement in the reader as much as it can build excitement in your role as advisor to share new books.

Don't have shelf space to dedicate to a display? Get creative. Some ideas for displays when you don't have shelf space could include:

- Using the side of a book shelf, a bulletin board, wall space, or winders to display images of book covers, rather than using the physical books themselves.

- Use a windowsill, if you have one, to display titles.

- Have a door? It's a blank canvas for book displays with printed or copied cover images.

- Take advantage of tech spaces – create digital images that can be used as computer wallpaper in the teen area or classroom. You can also create screensavers with book covers.

Shelf Talkers

Take a page from bookstores. How often do you see index-card size book reviews attached to shelves written by employees? Implement a similar shelf talking system. But rather than writing only an enthusiastic review of how great the book is, highlight the reader appeal of the book. Include read alike titles with the shelf talker so that those who may have read the book have another to turn to and vice versa.

Combine the power of the shelf talker with the power of the book display by creating page-size, attractive fliers to place on the shelves with reviews and read alikes. This can be particularly useful in shelf areas near popular authors. Displaying shelf talkers near shelves of Sarah Dessen, John Green, or Ellen Hopkins books would be a smart means of not only encouraging interest in these well-known contemporary realistic authors, but also in bringing attention to titles similar to theirs. By no means is this sort of talker limited to single authors. If there is a particularly popular book in your library or a book that's been popular for a long time, are there more recent books that tread similar ground? Create an "If you like this, you might like . . ." shelf talker.

Next to Jay Asher's *13 Reasons Why* (Razorbill, 2007), make a shelf talker suggesting titles such as Carmen Rodrigues's *34 Pieces of You* (Simon Pulse, 2012) and Lane Davis's *I Swear* (Simon & Schuster Books for Young Readers, 2012). Both read alikes follow the stories of main characters who have committed suicide and are leading those who were a part of their lives through a series of clues to help make sense of their choice. The story execution and voices give them that reader appeal.

Like with book displays, shelf talkers allow for flexibility in how frequently they're updated or shifted. Reader advisors can choose to shift through their shelf talkers on a set period of time or they can keep some of them as permanent parts of their collection space. Read alikes to Asher's title, for example, could be updated with additional titles but still kept on display.

Book and Reading Lists

Maybe the most basic tool of passive RA is the book list. While there's certainly always a concern of creating too many book lists on too many niche topics – that sort of information can become overwhelming – keeping a ready reference of different topics that could be developed into a book list is never a bad thing. This allows for variety and novelty, as book lists can always be changed out or switched up as time and space allow.

Not all book lists need to be traditional ones. Get creative:

- Develop book lists into bookmarks or into handbills that may surprise readers to find on the shelf or that capture their attention in a different way.

- With social media, book lists can be developed and shared online quite easily. Where there may be concern about too much paper vying for reader attention in the library, the online book list doesn't complicate this problem.

- Incorporate read alike lists inside of the books themselves. Include either a bookmark (with additional copies so readers may either keep the one included in the book or for when it simply doesn't come back) or adhere a small list of read alikes inside the front or back cover of a book for quick reference.

- Develop something digitally with read alikes and include the website address inside or on the back of the book cover.

Beyond the book list, though, are other interactive – but still passive – means of providing RA.

- Reader advisors can advertise what it is they're reading currently and what their thoughts are on the title. They can do this on a physical place like in their library's teen department, on the outside of a classroom door, or on a chalkboard, whiteboard, or bulletin board. They can do this same thing in a virtual space, as well. It's interactive in that you as advisor update the information regularly; but more than that, you can allow other readers to respond to what you're reading, either through providing space to ask questions, share reactions, or offer future reading suggestions.

- Allow readers to share what it is they're reading. Cover the end of a set of shelves with butcher block paper and ask the question "What are you reading?" Let anyone pitch in.

- Don't have room on a shelf? Get a piece of poster board and post-it notes and do the same thing. Have index cards and make use of a bulletin board. Another option is to hang

> The more opportunities to talk about books this way allows for more opportunities for readers to discover books either vetted by a reader's advisor or a peer – and a peer may be just as strong a reader's advisor as a librarian, teacher, or other gatekeeper.

wire or string from the ceiling or the tops of book shelves and allow readers to attach recommendations (or have readers give them to you to attach). Make use of window space or door space to do the same thing.

- Highlight a book trailer once a week (or more or less) either through social media or in the library or classroom.

- Develop your own memes to entice readers. Create something like "First Line Friday," and share the first line of a book over your social media, along with the bibliographic information, to get readers curious about new books.

- Combining the ideas of in-book read alike lists with the value and influence of peer suggestions: allow readers to include a small book review when they finish the book, either through a note attached inside the book or a bookmark inserted in the book. The more readers, the more opportunities to influence other readers, not only because of peer recommendations, but also because this sort of recommendation can be a wealth of information for a reader's advisor, as well.

- Use your social media to share current reads and reviews from teens themselves.

Reviews from readers can give insight into what it is about a book that's hooking them or not hooking them. This information is invaluable in determining reader appeal for a title. It is also useful for thinking about read alikes of other titles and whether there are similar appeal factors or not.

All of these suggestions, while passive, take time. They take the time of the reader's advisor and sometimes the part of the reader. Sometimes, the things you try won't be very effective. Other times, you will try things that are wildly successful. The key is being willing to experiment and to allow for these failures and successes.

The biggest reason different techniques are worth trying is because not all readers want or need the same things. Some may be hooked by book lists while others may not find themselves interested in advisory until they see a shelf talker next to the book they love and have read many times already.

Just like every book has a different set of appeal factors for readers, so do means of reader's advisory. Offer a variety, keep it fresh, and continue to experiment.

Active Reader's Advisory

Active reader's advisory requires actual interaction between reader and advisor, either through physical or digital, one-on-one or one-to-group, means. It involves a real-time investment on the part of the reader and the advisor. This can happen at a reference desk in a library, in a classroom between the teacher and the students, in a bookstore between seller and customer, or in any other situation where one person is offering advisory

---

There's a difference between a book talk and a book summary, and that comes through the method of delivery. A book talk should include a book summary, but it should be more than that:

Book Summary	Book Talk
• Entirely about the plot – it describes what the book is about quickly and succinctly.	• Highlights the summary, but focuses on appeal factors of the book.
• Emphasizes strengths of the book in and of itself.	• Plays up the book's strengths in terms of what it is a reader wants.
	• Gives an idea of the "feel" of a book, rather than simply what it is about.

to another reader.

Active advisory is the act of hand selling a book.

While there are a number of methods of delivering active RA, the most popular method is book talking. Book talking *is* hand selling a title. It's delivered through a script either written and practiced prior to presentation or developed on-the-spot. Book talking can happen in an individual setting or can be done in a group.

Every book can be sold multiple ways. That's why reading critically and thinking about appeal factors are so important.

For contemporary realistic fiction in particular, book talking is critical for selling a title to a reader. This is partially because contemporary fiction doesn't have the splash factor that other genres do, though it's more largely due to the fact that contemporary fiction can be book talked to highlight so many different appeal factors. Those who are good book talkers can make a contemporary book fit into any reader's advisory session, doing so both on the merits of the book at hand and by thoughtfully comparing it to titles that may be popular outside the genre, too. It all comes back to teasing out the appeal factors and making them the selling points of the book.

Because of how widespread a method of RA book talking is, there are scads of resources available for those who are unsure where to begin. While this book does not seek to reinvent the wheel, part of the goal is to offer a basic guide to the elements of successful book talking.

A Roadmap to Book Talking

Though it can sound intimidating at first, book talking becomes easier and more natural the more it's done. Book talking is nothing but selling the book to readers, but the trick comes in figuring out how much to say, how to say it, and how to cater that book talk to the readers so that their interest in the title is piqued.

You aren't going to connect every book to every reader, nor should that be the goal. The goal should be making a connection between a book and a reader: how you talk the book and what it is you choose to highlight are key to putting the book in the hands of the right reader.

The most important aspects of a book talk are:

- A quick overview of salient and exciting plot points

- An emphasis on who the book appeals to.
  Use references to books, television, movies, video games, or any other sort of pop culture hat compare to the book at hand.

Laying out the plot gives readers an idea of what's inside – much like a book review would – and the appeal factors are what "sells" the book. Pair up the elements of critical reading with those

---

Get Beyond the Easy Reach

While it can be helpful to make comparisons among books during a book talk, it's important to remember the value of good reader's advisory over ease and the easy reach. In other words, not every book is like a John Green book. Despite his immense popularity, he has certain appeal factors that work for readers that are not apparent in every other contemporary realistic novel. Throwing his name out as a means of appealing to readers does a disservice to both the reader and the book being compared.

While a book like Jesse Andrews's *Me & Earl & The Dying Girl* (Abrahms, 2012) features cancer at the center of the story, it is not necessarily a strong read alike to Green's *The Fault in Our Stars* (Dutton, 2012), unless what the appeal factor a reader wants is a cancer story. Rarely is what a reader wants that easy or that simple, though. Green's book is more serious in tone and execution, with a stronger emotional tug for readers than Andrews's, which instead is a bit more light-hearted and humorous. The narratives and the characters are not easily compared, despite the large topic at the heart of both stories.

The easy reach is not always the best fit.

Evaluating Book Trailers

It takes watching many book trailers to tease out the things that do and do not work, and like books themselves, different book trailers will appeal to different readers. There are times when the trailer may appeal to a reader, even though the book itself actually doesn't. That could be because the trailer offers something visually appealing that the book doesn't provide textually. But generally, there are features to think about with book trailers:

- Short length: Trailers that go on too long run the risk of boring the viewer, as much as they run the risk of not telling anything about the book itself. They may also tell too much. Choose shorter trailers to keep your audience's attention.

- Careful use of text: One problem trailers run into is that they can become too dependent upon text to visually convey the story. Trailers that are most successful either use the text as a means of enticing the reader into the visuals or use it sparingly. A trailer that is a minute of pure text with background music isn't effective. It's demanding on the part of the viewer to figure out what the story is about, rather than enticing the reader with the story itself.

- Interesting visuals: There are trailers that are a narrative in and of themselves, where there is a singular story told within it. There are also trailers which string together a variety of interesting sounds and images to convey the story. Neither type of trailer is superior to the other. What matters, though, is the trailer makes sense in and of itself. Does it tell you what the book is about? Can a reader watch it and be engaged with it? Does it look sloppy? The key is that the visuals make sense and engage the viewer.

- Appropriate audio: Not all trailers will include an audio element, but those that do should incorporate it purposefully. A trailer may have a theme song which could lead the viewer through the visuals, or the trailer may use a single sound or two to grab attention. What's important to think about is the level of sound the audio has and whether or not it overwhelms the viewer or the trailer itself. If the audio is reading the words scrolling through the trailer, does the trailer serve a purpose at all?

If a trailer delivers on these elements and captures your attention, it's worth thinking about including it to supplement book talking and reader's advisory more broadly. Trailers can be particularly useful in situations where you haven't read the book personally, but you know via reviews or other readers that it has something appealing to it.

factors that make a book a read alike to others.

Making comparisons among books during a book talk is a strength of the book talk, not a weakness. If there are books within the talk that complement one another, mentioning that heightens appeal factors and strengthens the talks for both.

By no means, though, does a book talk need to include only books that are similar to one another. In fact, a book talk where the books are wildly divergent from one another may actually help showcase appeal of each book. In some cases, it's possible that a book talk consisting of very different types of books may help in discovering appeal factors that *do* link the books to one another by some means, further strengthening an RA program, as well as your critical reading skills (not to mention your teens' reading skills).

Shake Up Your Book Talks

Because everyone has different listening and learning preferences, sometimes it's best to mix things up and offer book talks that feature more than simply you standing in front of a room and talking. This takes pressure off you, too, in that it allow you to maximize the range of books talked. If you haven't read a title and want to sell it to readers, you can instead use other tools out there to talk the book for you.

It's easy to incorporate audiobook snippets to capture a

reader's attention while book talking. This can be effective for readers who prefer listening to their books, but even more than that, it can be a way to draw new readers into a book that may otherwise not grab their attention visually via the cover or aurally via a book talk. Hearing the words from the book may be the key for some readers.

As part of marketing and publicity of a book, many publishers and authors develop videos wherein the author talks about his or her book, either discussing the plot or talking about some of the elements of the story that are favorites. Incorporating these videos can also be a way of hooking a reader into a title in a different way.

Consider also including book trailers into your book talks. Book trailers, which are like movie trailers developed to sell a book, can often supplement or stand in for more polished and prepared book talks. Trailers, though, are a double edged sword, with plenty of positives and negatives to them. The ease comes because trailers can be easy to find; however, it's challenging to find trailers that are actually compelling and offer readers a real glimpse into the book. If the goal of reader's advisory is to home in on appeal factors of a book, that should also be the goal of a book trailer.

Throughout the book lists portion of this book, strong examples of book trailers have been included. This is to serve as a means of supplementing annotations and appeal factors.

Tying It All Together

Reader's advisory is the act of bringing together the elements of reading critically with the books themselves and then selling those books to readers based on appeal factors. It's a skill constantly under construction. There aren't easy outs in reader's advisory, which is why it is a skill that not everyone has and it's one that is regularly strengthened through experience. Anyone can recommend a book, but it's when that recommendation comes through a sharp and savvy eye does it become advisory.

It's important when advocating for contemporary realistic fiction and the readers who want these stories that you not go for the easy reach. While so often contemporary fiction is lumped together as novels tackling problems or as novels that are dark, that's not true. Contemporary fiction spans so many different arenas and takes on so many different stories, voices, situations, settings, and tones. By not parsing it out and considering the books on an individual level, no favors are done for the reader. The same goes for not considering what it is that readers want as individuals.

Incorporating contemporary fiction into a regular reader's advisory program makes understanding the genre, as well as its readers and potential readers, easier. Include contemporary fiction in assigned reading. Include it as read alikes to classics. Include it in displays, in book lists, and in book talks. Use guides like the ones in the back of this book to discuss larger and important themes present within a variety of different contemporary realistic titles. These are themes that are present not just in the books, but in the real everyday lives of today's readers.

Part 2
Real Reads

Significant contributors to contemporary YA fiction can be easy to spot. There's John Green with *Looking for Alaska*, *Paper Towns*, and *The Fault in Our Stars*. There's Maureen Johnson with *Suite Scarlett* and *The Bermudez Triangle* (retitled as *On the Count of Three*). There's Ellen Hopkins with her dark and gritty verse novels, such as *Identical* and the *Crank* trilogy and Sarah Dessen with her stories about family, friendship, and the value of interpersonal relationships, including *The Moon and More*, *Along for the Ride*, and *Just Listen*.

Elizabeth Scott, Susane Colasanti, and Deb Caletti have published a number of contemporary titles in the last decade, making names for themselves because of their own strong writing but also because of how nicely their books pair with those like Sarah Dessen. Of course, contemporary YA is also home to Laurie Halse Anderson, Walter Dean Myers, Chris Crutcher, Stephanie Perkins, Gayle Forman, and Lauren Myracle – all authors whose names stand out to readers because of their honest, realistic portrayals of teen lives.

But the ultimate purpose of this section isn't to reintroduce well-known or big-name authors. It's to go beyond them and explore the wealth of voices writing contemporary YA for today's teens.

It's not easy to figure out how to organize, categorize, and summarize book titles. Rarely does a book ever touch only on one topic or theme, and placing books within any given category is a game of subjectivity. Even more challenging is selecting which titles to annotate – with so much contemporary fiction published over the last few years, narrowing down the annotations to 150 proved challenging. Choosing which books not to include in annotations was equally difficult.

The following book lists span ten broad topics, and within each list are fifteen unique annotations. These annotations include a concise book summary, at least four appeal factors, and a selection of read alikes. At the end of each annotated book list are additional titles which fall within the scope of that category.

Note that annotated titles are those which are less likely to be found in other resources outside this book. There are not annotations for the authors listed above because finding information about those titles is easy. Appeal factors span a range of topics, including the gender of the main character, themes explored in the book, noteworthy settings, and other elements which may pique a reader's interest. These may also prove helpful for reader's advisory, as discussed in Part I. Read alikes for each annotation provide next picks for readers and give a sense of who the readership for the annotated title may be.

Sit back and enjoy exploring the wide world of contemporary YA fiction.

Chapter 6

The Arts: Music, Photography, Film, Dance, and More

The students in my classroom run the gamut of genre preferences, but I find the ones who love realistic fiction are often searching for answers to life's dilemmas. In order to provide them with that opportunity to seek those answers, I supply my classroom with a great deal of contemporary titles. I want my students to feel like the books they are reading are relevant to their own life experiences. – Beth Shaum, middle school English and literature teacher

There is something about creation, be it painting, music, acting, or writing, that appeals to YA readers. Contemporary fiction is in a unique and exciting position to highlight the value of creativity and the arts in one's life because of its setting in the real world. Even more than that, creative expression is sometimes the way through the toughest challenges in a reader's life. This is reflected and observed through realistic literature for that very reason. The creative arts showcase the value of passion that exists within teen lives and reminds readers that pursuing passion – in whatever form or output necessary – is part of a full life.

Although not all of these books focus specifically on the mechanics of the arts, some do. Those that do not, though, use some form of arts to propel the story or the character forward in a way that's noteworthy.

Andrews, Jesse. *Me & Earl & The Dying Girl*. Amulet, 2012. 304p. $16.95. 978-1-4197-0176-4. $7.95 Trade pb. 978-1-4197-0532-8.

Greg's always been a bit of a social outcast. He and best friend Earl enjoy spending their free time creating films that only they will ever watch. These movies stink. But when Greg's mom forces him to befriend Rachel, a former member of his church youth group, when she's diagnosed with cancer, Greg's once social-outcast-and-proud status changes. It's not because he's hanging out with someone popular or because he's doing something altruistic. In fact, Greg hates that he has to see Rachel. But over the course of forced friendliness, Greg realizes it might be his talent for filmmaking that helps Rachel through the challenges of her own diagnosis. Not to mention, it helps him out quite a bit, too.

Appeal Factors

- Filmmaking
- Friendship
- Humor
- Illness

- Male main character
- People of color
- Pittsburgh

Read Alikes

- The *Stupid Fast* series by Geoff Herbach for the humor, the strong-voiced male main characters, the exploration of male friendship, and passion for personal interests. Both stories also feature strong secondary plots about interracial friendships and romance.

- The humor, the male-female relationships, and social aspects – especially the questions whether it's better to be a loner or to try to fit in – make Brent Crawford's *Carter Finally Gets It* series another strong read alike.

Crowley, Cath. *A Little Wanting Song*. Ember, 2011. 288p. $8.99. 978-0-375-85449-1.

Charlie Duskin wants nothing more than to fit in with the other people her age in the small town where she's forced to spend her summers. She's no one but Charlie Dorkin to those people. Even being known as the girl with the good singing voice can't help her make the friends she needs. This summer, Rose, one of the girls who once taunted and teased Charlie, realizes that Charlie may be key to her own dreams of getting out of this small town and into a bigger, better life in the city. Through her own selfish needs in choosing to spend time with Charlie, Rose realizes that Charlie is exactly the kind of person she really needs as a friend. This book is told in alternating perspectives, showing the desire in Charlie and in Rose's voices for two very different things.

Appeal Factors

- Australia
- Dual points of view
- Female main characters
- Foreign setting
- Friendship
- Music
- Quieter read
- Singing
- Small town setting
- Summer story

Read Alikes

- Fans of Sarah Dessen's writing style and the way she develops interpersonal relationships – romantic and friendly – will find Cath Crowley's style and characters similar.

- Because of the use of flashbacks to reflect upon prior summers and events, this is an excellent read alike to Jandy Nelson's *The Sky is Everywhere*. Crowley doesn't explore grief in quite the way Nelson does, but the writing styles and means of unfolding story make these two a worthwhile pairing.

Flack, Sophie. ***Bunheads***. Poppy, 2011. 294p. $17.99. 978-0-316-12653-3. $9.99 Trade pb. 978-0-316-12654-0.

Hannah is a nineteen-year-old member of the prestigious Manhattan Ballet Company, an honor for anyone who wants to make dancing his or her livelihood. She balances her practice schedule with an outside social life as much as she can, especially as being a part of the Company sometimes means dealing with other ballerinas who aren't always interested in being friendly. The world of ballet can be cutthroat. Dancers must be willing to go the distance in order to make it and shine. But when Hannah meets Jacob, she finds herself falling in love, and she enjoys the idea of being a part of a real romantic relationship. It's something she's never experienced before because she's devoted so much to her art. Maybe even more challenging for Hannah is that she finds herself questioning whether ballet is the future she really wants or not. Can she give up the dream she's always wanted, especially with the knowledge that she's got a rare opportunity that so many other people want but will never have?

Appeal Factors

- Ballet
- Dance
- Female main character
- New York City
- Peer relationships
- Post-high school setting
- Private/boarding school
- Romance

Read Alikes

- Stasia Ward Kehoe's *Audition* will appeal to fans of Flack's book because of the setting at a private dance academy, the budding romance between the main character and a male (in Kehoe's book, it's between two dancers, whereas in Flack's novel, it's between a dancer and an "outsider"), and the internal conflict that emerges in the mind of the dancer about whether or not devoting her future to her art is what she really wants to do.

- Readers interested in the idea of following a passion to the extreme will want to try Suzanne Supplee's *Somebody Everybody Listens To*, wherein the main character chooses to pursue her dream of singing country music by leaving home and heading to Nashville with little to go on except her desire to achieve.

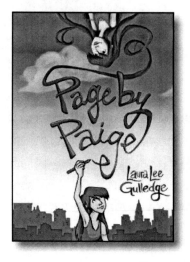

Gulledge, Laura Lee. *Page by Paige*. Amulet, 2011. 192 p. $18.95 978-0-8109-9721-9. $9.99 Trade pb. 978-0-8109-9722-6.

It's hard enough to move half way through Paige's high school career, but what makes it harder is that she thinks everyone at her new school seems to know exactly who they are and what it is they want to do with their lives. These are cool city kids who seem so together. Paige, on the other hand, feels like she'll never know, and it makes her retreat into herself a bit, rather than try to socialize. She pours the feelings she's bottling up into her notebook and into her art. It doesn't take long for people at her school though to notice what talent she has. By accident – and okay, maybe a little on purpose – Paige begins to discover that she can make friends in her new school. All it takes is for her to accept that being an artist and creating art is part and parcel of who she is and to share that with others.

Book Trailer

http://youtu.be/_djoaooRcE4

Appeal Factors

- Art
- Changing schools
- Drawing
- Friendship
- Graphic novel

- Female main character
- Making new friends
- Moving
- New York City

Read Alikes

- Siobhan Vivian's novel *Same Difference*, which follows a girl starting at an art academy for the summer and who finds herself having trouble making the kinds of friendships she was hoping to make, is a natural pick for readers who enjoyed Gulledge's story. Both books delve into what it means to be an artist, what it is to create art, and what it means to take ownership of both one's sense of self as an artist, as well as one's art.

- Try Liz Gallagher's *My Not-So-Still Life* for the story of a young female artist coming to grips with her talent and interest in creating art.

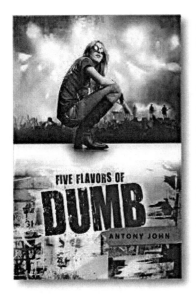

John, Antony. *Five Flavors of Dumb*. Dial, 2011. 352p. $16.99. 978-0-8037-3433-3. $9.99. Trade pb. 978-0-14-241943-4.

When Piper arrives at school one day, Dumb is playing their set in front of a crowd of adoring fans. The band is hugely popular. Piper, though, is equal parts disgusted by the group and intrigued. But what can she tell about a band that's won a couple of studio sessions and a little buzz at her high school when she's deaf? It's not like she can hear them play. Piper doesn't let this get in her way: she offers Dumb a challenge, saying she can get them a paying gig and become their manager. Even though Dumb doesn't believe a word of it – she can't even hear them – they accept the challenge. Can a girl who doesn't hear the music have what it takes to bring the band to the next level? Piper's hoping to get a lot more out of this than simply winning a bet.

Appeal Factors

- Bands
- Deafness
- Disabilities
- Family relationships
- Female main character
- Friendship
- Music
- Seattle

Read Alikes

- The setting and the use of music as a means of working through a physical or mental challenge makes Tara Kelly's *Harmonic Feedback* a great read alike. Drea, the main character in Kelly's book, suffers from ADHD and Asperger's, and her desire to not be defined by them mirrors Piper's commitment to getting Dumb a gig. Both books are also set in or around Seattle, infusing them with similar settings and similar musical history.

- Readers who enjoy this setting and the musical history underlying John's book will want to read Conrad Wesselhoeft's *Adios, Nirvana*.

Joseph, Danielle. *Pure Red*. Flux, 2011. 240p. $9.99. Trade pb. 978-0-7387-2743-1.

Cassia's father is a well-known local artist and whenever he's painting, he's "in the zone." Cassia herself is a little bit of a weird girl – she's got an artistic streak, but more, she finds meanings in every color around her. The problem is she's not particularly passionate about anything, and this causes concern for her from the school guidance counselor. As she falls for a boy she believes is out of her reach, can Cassia overcome her social status and her own beliefs about herself in order to go after him? It may be art that helps her gain the confidence she needs to go for what she really wants. Perhaps finding her passion won't be an impossible task.

Appeal Factors

- Art
- Basketball
- Family relationships
- Female main character
- Friendship
- Quieter read
- Romance

Read Alikes

- Because of the use of art and the use of color throughout the book as means of self-discovery and gaining of self-confidence, this is a great read alike to Liz Gallagher's *My Not-So-Still Life*.

- Although Paige is more self-aware than Cassia, Laura Lee Gulledge's *Page by Paige* would be a strong read alike, as both stories explore what it means to have a passion.

Kelly, Tara. *Amplified*. Henry Holt, 2011. 304p. $16.99. 978-0-8050-9296-7.

Jasmine is seventeen, and even though she has all the privilege in the world, the last thing she wants to do is follow the path she's expected to – go to college, get a good job, and have the textbook life. Instead, she wants to strike out on her own and make a name for herself with her music. Her father doesn't like the plan, so he kicks her out, and now Jasmine's left to build a life by herself in Santa Cruz. When she has the opportunity to try out for a band, she tells a little lie about her music experience. It turns out that little lie might come back to haunt her during her performances, leaving Jasmine and her band mates to wonder if she's really cut out for the music life or if she is best to follow the path her dad prefers. But Jasmine might not be ready to give up on her dream.

Appeal Factors

- Bands
- Female main character
- Gritty
- Guitar player
- Music
- Post-high school setting
- Romance
- Santa Cruz

Read Alikes

- Kelly's edgy and gritty style will appeal to fans of Ellen Hopkins. Likewise, more reluctant readers who like Hopkins's style and pacing will find much to appreciate in Kelly's book.

- Readers who haven't yet read Kelly's first novel, *Harmonic Feedback*, will want to go back and visit this story about a girl struggling with ADHD and Asperger's who has a passion for music and sound design. The pacing, pulse, and memorably-voiced main character make them good read alikes for one another.

LaCour, Nina. ***The Disenchantments***. Dutton, 2012. 336p. 978-0-525-42219-8. $8.99 Trade pb. 978-0-14-242391-2.

Colby and Bev made a pact. After graduation, they would go on a road trip with Bev's band, The Disenchantments, as it performs shows in the Pacific Northwest. Then, Colby and Bev would travel around Europe together for a year by themselves before deciding whether or not they would attend college. This pact is thrown for a loop though when, after Colby follows through his end of the bargain, he's informed by Bev that she'll be attending college in the fall. She never actually believed in the pact with Colby; she thought it was just for fun. Now that Colby's already on the road with The Disenchantments, he can't escape her or how she betrayed him. Nor can he escape the fear, frustration, and humiliation he feels about not having a plan ready for when this adventure ends.

Book Trailer

http://youtu.be/iI8bpvmNpvE

Appeal Factors

- Bands
- Friendship
- Male main character
- Pacific Northwest
- Post-high school setting
- Road trip
- Travel

Read Alikes

- For the road trip as self-discovery aspect of LaCour's novel, there are plenty of read alikes. Try Antony John's *Thou Shalt Not Road Trip* for the male main character and the struggles he has with a female friend who forces him to examine the choices he's made in the past as a way to guide himself toward better choices in the future. Although Bev offers little to Colby in LaCour's book in terms of the great "what next" question, she is the impetus for his self-exploration and understanding of the importance of making choices for himself.

- Hilary Weisman Graham's *Reunited* and Jessi Kirby's *In Honor* both feature road trips where the main character follows a favorite band. In Graham's story, the three girls had not been friends for quite some time, and it's through the trip that they learn the ways friendships stay together or fall apart. In Kirby's story, the trip is about remembering a brother and understanding the impact he had on other people. These two books also explore the interpersonal politics of being with other people for an extended period of time on the road with music as a uniting force.

- The post-graduation travel aspect will make Kirsten Hubbard' *Wanderlove* a strong follow-up read.

Marcus, Kimberly. *Exposed*. Ember, 2012. 272p. $8.99 Trade pb. 978-0-375-86591-6.

Liz is the girl behind the camera. She loves to take pictures. But this isn't just Liz's story: this is the story of best friend Kate and Liz's brother Mike. Kate is a dancer, and Mike is in college and a former high school athlete. After a wicked fight between Kate and Liz during one of their sleepovers, a secret slips out about a relationship between Kate and Mike. It's not the kind of secret Liz wants to hear: her brother might be assaulting her best friend. Not only does it make her uncomfortable, it puts her smack in the middle of a problem confronting two people she loves. She can't choose sides or decide who is right or wrong, even though she knows how she *should* feel.

Appeal Factors

- Family relationships
- Female main character
- Friendship
- Photography

- Sexual violence
- Siblings
- Verse novel

Read Alikes

- Because of the topic of sexual violence at the center of the novel, this is a natural read alike to Carol Lynch Williams's *Glimpse*, which is also written in verse. Williams's novel, like Marcus's, tackles what happens when a sibling must confront the sexual choices – or non-choices – of a brother or sister. Williams's *Waiting*, while not about sexual violence, does confront sexuality of a sibling, and it, too, would make a good read alike. It is also written in verse.

- One of the themes in Marcus's novel is justice for victims, making it a great read alike to Daisy Whitney's *The Mockingbirds*, especially as both books tackle the challenges of sex, blame, and responsibility.

- In terms of style, readers who enjoy Ellen Hopkins's raw and gritty verse will find Marcus's book a good next read. Those readers who haven't tried Hopkins will want to do so after *Exposed*.

Smith, Hilary T. *Wild Awake*. Katherine Tegen, 2013. 400p. $17.99. 978-0-06-218468-9.

Kiri's parents have left her alone at home for the summer while they're on a cruise. She's using the time to practice piano – she's one of the best pianists around. She's also using the time to practice for a series of "Battle of the Bands" shows with bandmate/friend/crush Lukas. But a phone call from a stranger opens what Kiri thought was a long-closed case: the mystery surrounding her sister's death years ago. The accident she was told caused Sukey's death may have been anything but an accident. Kiri wants to know the truth of the matter, even if it means sacrificing the time she has for practice and performance. Along the way, Kiri will meet a boy who might change her mind entirely about Lukas, and she will struggle with a mental illness she can't easily ignore.

Appeal Factors

- Bands
- Grief
- Female main character
- Mental illness
- Music
- Mystery

- Piano
- Romance
- Siblings
- Summer story
- Urban setting

Read Alikes

- This voice-driven novel will appeal to readers who like stories with strong and memorable main characters. Those who have enjoyed the film *Juno* will find Kiri has a similar voice, sense of humor, and vivacity to her, despite the circumstances of her life.

- Readers looking for a grief novel that explores the depths of sibling relationships may want to try Jandy Nelson's *The Sky is Everywhere*. Although Nelson's book is quieter and slower-paced than Smith's, there are similarities in voice, in the desire to make sense of death, and in the relationships that develop between the main character and the characters who were a significant part of their dead siblings' lives.

Spalding, Amy. *The Reece Malcolm List*. Entangled Select, 2013. 352p. $9.99. Trade pb. 978-1-62061-240-8.

When Devan's father dies, she's sent from her home in Missouri to her mom's home in Los Angeles. Devan's never met her mom before, despite knowing she is the infamous author Reece Malcolm. As she adjusts to life with her mom, it's not all bad – Devan's enrolled in the local school for the performing arts and she's able to thrust herself into her passion for musical theater full-throttle. It doesn't make getting to know her mother easier, but it does allow Devan to stand up and take the stage using her own talents.

Appeal Factors

- "Clean" read
- Female main character
- Friendship
- Humor
- Los Angeles
- Making new friends
- Moving
- Musical theater
- Non-traditional families
- Private/boarding school
- Romance

Read Alikes

- Fans of musical theater or who are fans of television shows like *Glee* will find the performance elements, as well as the interpersonal drama of theatrical life appealing. There are fewer social dramatics in Spalding's novel than in the show, but it's the thrill and the passion for performance that resonate.
- The humor in this novel will appeal to fans of Meg Cabot or Sarah Mylnowski.
- *Dramarama* by E. Lockhart will appeal to readers for the performing arts storyline, as well as the spots of humor and the passion behind the main characters' interests.

Telgemeier, Raina. *Drama*. Graphix, 2012. 240p. $10.99 Trade pb. 978-0-545-32699-5.

Callie knows her singing chops aren't strong enough to score a part in her middle school's show "Moon Over Mississippi." But she still wants to be involved in the production, so she takes part in the stage crew and hopes to create the most amazing set. The problem is that there's virtually no budget and her dreams are much bigger than the money she's been allotted. Also complicating things a bit is that she knows almost nothing about building, the ticket sales for the show are not promising, and there is a lot of tension among the crew members. Not to mention that there are a couple of boys that Callie finds herself attracted to, and she has no idea which one she really should pursue. Can she make the best of the tools she has while also finding the perfect guy to call her first real boyfriend?

Book Trailer

http://youtu.be/ysWrqAMktc0

Appeal Factors

- "Clean" read
- Female main character
- Graphic novel
- Humor
- LGBTQ

- Middle school setting
- People of color
- Romance
- Theater
- Theatrical stage crew

Read Alikes

- Readers who are interested in the stage crew side of theatrical productions will find much to enjoy in Allen Zadoff's *My Life, The Theater, and Other Tragedies.*

- Even though Amy Spalding's *The Reece Malcolm List* explores musical theater from the front-and-center side of the stage and it's geared at a slightly older readership (though there are no content issues to consider in Spalding's title), the way that the romantic relationships play out in each book is similar. In both cases, the relationships are full of awkwardness, shyness, but they are ultimately sweet and authentic. Readers get to see not only the theatrical side of the main character, but their personal, interior sides as well.

- Older readers – or those ready for more challenging titles – who are interested in the value of self-acceptance and self-discovery through theater will find David Levithan and John Green's *Will Grayson, will grayson* and Lili Wilkinson's *Pink* worth picking up.

Ward Kehoe, Stasia. *Audition*. Viking, 2011. 458p. $17.99. 978-0-670-01319-7.

Sara won a coveted scholarship to study ballet at an academy her junior year of high school. Even though she knows this means she has to sacrifice everything about her life as it is, she's excited for the chance to devote herself to dance. While she's lonely living away from friends and family, it's not too long before twenty-something Remington catches her eye – and she catches his. But is he really interested in her romantically or is he interested in her only as his muse and artistic inspiration? And what happens when Sara discovers that maybe ballet doesn't light her heart on fire the way she thought it did? Can she give up her dream and explore something new or is she stuck to following this path?

Appeal Factors

- Ballet

- Dance

- Female main character

- Moving

- Private/boarding school

- Romance

- Verse novel

Read Alikes

- *Audition* and Sophie Flack's *Bunheads* traverse a lot of similar territory in terms of the ballet world. Both delve into the ever-present pressure to compete and become elite through whatever means possible, as well as what it means to discover that your love for performance can shift and alter depending upon relationships made with other people and with other forms of creative expression.

- Readers will find the struggle Sara has over loneliness and devotion to her art similar to that of Emily in Siobhan Vivian's *Same Difference*. There are also similarities in the way both girls attend focused academies for their art and the way they work through the tricky social worlds within these schools.

Wealer, Sara Bennett. *Rival*. HarperTeen, 2011. 336p. $16.99. 978-0-06-182762-4.

Brooke and Kathryn do not get along. Both senior girls are highly involved in their school choir and both have the chance to perform at the Blackmore Young Artists Contest. Aside from the prestige and recognition of the competition, the winner of the contest earns a huge check. For Kathryn, that check would be her way into college and studying music. Money is tight in her family. For Brooke, the check would mean proving to her family that she has talent and that she is worthy of their support. But will the rivalry between the two girls ruin the chances either of them has to perform at her best? Maybe even worse is knowing that their rivalry might only get worse if one girl walks away the winner at Blackmore and not the other.

Appeal Factors

- Choir

- Competition

- Dual points of view

- Family relationships

- Female main characters

- Friendship

- Rivalry

- Socioeconomic class

- Singing

Read Alikes

- Fans of television shows like *Glee* will appreciate Wealer's weaving of competition and singing together. The social dynamics will resonate, as well.

- For the high stakes competition angle, Sara Zarr's *The Lucy Variations* is an excellent next read. Exploration of socioeconomic class, privilege, and the value of familial support and acceptance when it comes to the performing arts are similar.

- Because a significant portion of the book revolves around the dissolving relationship between Brooke and Kathryn, this could make an interesting pairing with Leila Sales's *Mostly Good Girls*. Both books magnify the events that can pull girls apart, as well as the things that can bring their friendships back together.

Zarr, Sara. ***The Lucy Variations***. Little, Brown, 2013. 320p. $18. 978-0-316-20501-6.

    Lucy chose to quit piano. For someone with her reputation and talent – she's a prodigy and lives a life of privilege – this stuns not only the performing world, but it causes a rift between her and her family. But it was her family and their inability to see how important the world outside piano was to her that forced Lucy to make the decision. In the wake of quitting, Lucy's left to deal with grief of not only stopping but also that of losing her grandmother. In the wake of her decision, Lucy struggles to figure out who she is without her reputation. But when her little brother gets a new piano teacher and he takes a shine to Lucy, will she change her mind about quitting all together? Can she ever find the spark again? Lucy must come to terms with what it means to pursue something because she genuinely loves it, rather than because she feels she has to do it in order to live up to the expectations of others.

Appeal Factors

- Family relationships
- Female main character
- Grief
- Literary writing
- Musical performance
- Piano

Read Alikes

- While there is not a rivalry in Zarr's story, the pressure of performance and competition at the expense of human relationships makes it a read alike to Sara Bennett-Wealer's *Rival*.

- Although Zarr's book is not entirely a grief novel, Lucy's decision to leave piano causes her to mourn the loss of a huge part of what made her who she was. This same exploration of grief when it comes to loss of self-understanding shines through in Anna Jarzab's *The Opposite of Hallelujah*. Both books also tackle family relationships, the change in family dynamics, and both are examples of literary fiction with much depth to them.

- Readers who are interested in a story about another musical prodigy will be satisfied with Jessica Martinez's *Virtuosity*.

■ More Books Featuring the Arts

Theater and Performance

Adler, Dahlia. *Behind The Scenes*. Spencer Hill Contemporary, 2014. 360p. $9.95 Trade pb. 978-1-9393-9297-8.

Bjorkman, Lauren. *My Invented Life*. Henry Holt, 2009. 240p. $17.99. 978-0-8050-8950-9.

Calin, Marisa. *Between You & Me*. Bloomsbury, 2012. 256p. $16.99. 978-1-59990-758-1.

Calonita, Jen. *Broadway Lights*. Poppy, 2011. 384p. $8.99. Trade pb. 978-0-316-03066-3.

Flores-Scott, Patrick. *Jumped In*. Square Fish, 2014. 320p. $9.99 Trade pb. 978-1-2500-05398-5.

Green, John, and David Levithan. *Will Grayson, will grayson*. Speak, 2011. 336p. $9.99 Trade pb. 978-0-14-241847-5.

Horner, Emily. *A Love Story Starring My Dead Best Friend*. Dial, 2010. 272p. $16.99. 978-0-8037-3420-3.

Leveen, Tom. *manicpixiedreamgirl*. Random House, 2013. 256p. $16.99. 978-0-3758-7005-7.

Lockhart, E. *Dramarama*. Hyperion, 2008. 320p. $9.99 Trade pb. 978-0-7868-3817-2.

Martin, C. K. Kelly. *The Lighter Side of Life and Death*. Random House, 2011. 256p. $9.99 Trade pb. 978-0-375-84589-5.

Rennison, Louise. *A Midsummer Tights Dream*. HarperTeen, 2012. 256p. $17.99. 978-0-06-179936-5. (First in the "Misadventures of Tallulah Casey" series)

Schmidt, Gary D. *Okay for Now*. Houghton Mifflin Harcourt, 2012. $6.99 Trade pb. 978-0-544-02280-5.

Strahler, David. *Spinning Out*. Chronicle, 2011. 288p. $17.99. 978-0-8118-7780-0.

Voorhees, Coert. *Lucky Fools*. Hyperion, 2012. 304p. $16.99. 978-1-4231-2398-9.

Wilkinson, Lili. *Pink*. HarperTeen, 2012. 320p. $9.99. Trade pb. 978-0-06-192654-9.

Zadoff, Allen. *My Life, the Theater, and Other Tragedies*. EgmontUSA, 2011. 288p. $16.99. 978-1-60684-036-8.

Music

Amato, Mary. *Guitar Notes*. EgmontUSA, 2013. 320p. $8.99 Trade pb. 978-1-6068-4503-5.

Anthony, Jessica and Rodrigo Corral. *Chopsticks*. Razorbill, 2012. 304p. $19.99 Trade pb. 978-1-59514-435-5.

Boles, Philana Marie. *Glitz*. Viking, 2011. 256p. $16.99. 978-0-670-01204-6.

Briant, Ed. *I Am (Not) the Walrus*. Flux, 2012. 288p. $9.95 Trade pb. 978-0-7387-3246-6.

Cronn-Mills, Kristin. *Beautiful Music for Ugly Children*. Flux, 2012. 262p. $9.99 Trade pb. 978-0-7387-3251-0.

Dionne, Erin. *Notes from an Accidental Band Geek*. Dial, 2011. 288p. $16.99. 978-0-8037-3564-4.

Echols, Jennifer. *Dirty Little Secret*. MTV Books, 2014. 288p. $11.00 Trade pb. 978-1-4516-5804-0.

Eulberg, Elizabeth. *Take a Bow*. Scholastic, 2013. 288p. $9.99 Trade pb. 978-0-545-33476-1.

Huntley Parsons, Mark. *Road Rash*. Knopf, 2014. 352p. $16.99. 978-0-3857-5342-5.

Joseph, Danielle. *Indigo Blue*. Flux, 2010. 231p. $9.95 Trade pb. 978-0-7387-2059-3.

London, Kelli. *Uptown Dreams*. K-Teen, 2011. 256p. $9.99 Trade pb. 978-0-7582-6128-1.

Love, Maia. *DJ Rising*. Little, Brown, 2013. 304p. $8.99 Trade pb. 978-0-316-12189-7.

Marchetta, Melina. *The Piper's Son*. Candlewick, 2012. 336p. $7.99 Trade pb. 978-0-7636-6062-8.

Martinez, Jessica. *Virtuosity*. Simon Pulse, 2012. 320p. $9.99 Trade pb. 978-1-4424-2053-3.

Ostow, Micol. *So Punk Rock: And Other Ways to Disappoint Your Mother*. Flux, 2009. 264p. $9.99 Trade pb. 978-0-7387-1471-4.

Roy, Jennifer. *Mindblind*. Amazon, 2012. 254p. $9.99 Trade pb. 978-1-4778-1712-4.

Sales, Leila. *This Song Will Save Your Life*. Farrar, Straus, Giroux, 2013. 288p. $17.99. 978-0-374-35138-0.

Skovron, Jon. *Struts and Frets*. Amulet, 2011. 304p. $7.95 Trade pb. 978-1-4197-0028-6.

Supplee, Suzanne. *Somebody Everybody Listens To*. Speak, 2011. 304p. $16.99. 978-0-525-42242-6.

Vega, Denise. *Rock On*. Little, Brown, 2012. 296p. $17.99. 978-0-316-13310-4.

Wenberg, Michael. *Stringz*. Westside, 2010. 216p. $16.95. 978-1-934813-33-1.

Wesselhoeft, Conrad. *Adios, Nirvana*. Graphia, 2012. 240p. $9.99 Trade pb. 978-0-547-57725-8.

Whitaker, Alecia. *Wildflower*. Poppy, 2014. 320p. $18.00. 978-0-3162-5138-9.

Dance

Colbert, Brandy. *Pointe*. Putnam, 2014. 352p. $17.99. 978-0-3991-6034-9.

Bavati, Robyn. *Dancing in the Dark*. Flux, 2013. 336p. $9.99. Trade pb. 978-0-7387-3477-4.

Ferrer, Caridad. *When the Stars Go Blue*. St. Martin's Griffin, 2010. 336p. $9.99. 978-0-312-65004-9.

Lundgren, Jodi. *Leap*. Second Story, 2011. 217p. $11.95. Trade pb. 978-1-897187-85-2.

McKayhan, Monica. *Ambitious*. Kimani, 2011. 240p. $9.99. Trade pb. 978-0-373-22996-3.

Padian, Maria. *Jersey Tomatoes Are the Best*. Ember, 2012. 352p. $9.99 Trade pb. 978-0-375-86563-3.

Schabas, Martha. *Various Positions*. Farrar Straus Giroux, 2012. 336p. $17.99. 978-0-374-38086-1.

Venkatraman, Padma. *A Time to Dance*. Nancy Paulson Books, 2014. 320p. $17.99. 978-0-3992-5710-0.

Wilkins, Ebony Joy. *Sellout*. Scholastic, 2010. 272p. $17.99. 978-0-545-10928-4.

Art

Chen, Justina. *North of Beautiful*. Little, Brown, 2010. 384p. $16.99. 978-0-316-02505-8.

Davis, Tanita. *Happy Families*. Alfred A. Knopf, 2012. 240p. $16.99. 978-0-375-86966-2.

Gallagher, Liz. *My Not-So-Still Life*. Ember, 2012. 192p. $7.99 Trade pb. 978-0-375-84155-2.

Hubbard, Kirsten. *Wanderlove*. Delacorte, 2012. 352p. $17.99. 978-0-385-73937-5.

Madigan, L. K. *Flash Burnout*. Houghton Mifflin, 2010. 336p. $16. 978-0-547-19489-9.

Printz, Yvonne. *All You Get Is Me*. HarperTeen, 2010. 288p. $16.99. 978-0-06-171580-8.

Sandall, Lisa Ann. *Map of the Known World*. Scholastic, 2011. 288p. $8.99. Trade pb. 978-0-545-06971-7.

Vivian, Siobhan. *Same Difference*. Scholastic, 2010. 304p. $8.99. Trade pb. 978-0-545-00408-4.

Chapter 7

This Diverse World: Every Ethnicity, Every Setting, Every Experience

I work with teens in a juvenile detention facility in Austin, Texas. The teens we serve often don't see themselves as readers, and many are called "non-readers" by their teachers in school. When they come to the detention center – whether it's for a week, a month, or a year – they quickly discover that a lot of the other options that they had "in the free" are no longer available to them. No Facebook. No TV. No video games. They quickly discover that the library is one of the few places where they are allowed to pick out something to do for fun. The library is the place they can go to pick out something that they have an interest in. They are the master of their own destiny again – in this one small way, they can be free. I work with kids who haven't picked up a book since elementary school. The teens who fill out my reading surveys tell me that they didn't read at all when they were outside the facility. So my first duty, when a new kid is assigned to a unit, is to find out what kind of stuff they like. I don't ask them what kind of books they like – because honestly, the answer might be Judy Moody, because that's the last book they read five years ago. No...what kind of stuff do they like... sports, video games, hip hop, or rap? Then I get them to tell me more... more about what kind of sports/video games/rap music. And then I get them to tell me why. What do they like about it? What are they looking for? A lot of times, the answer I get is that they like rap music because it's real. Because it tells about a life that is true for them, that is a mirror to their reality. And I am happy to work with that. I'll steer them right towards the bookshelf in my library dedicated to urban fiction. Not your mama's urban fiction: this is urban fiction selected specifically for my urban, minority teen audience. They'd like the older, raunchy stuff if I could get it, but I can't and even if I could...that's not really what they're after. They're after stories of addiction, abuse, gangs, violence, and death. And a lot of times, they're also after stories about love.

Sometimes, adults have a hard time understanding why these topics are of interest, and I'll admit, if I were in their shoes, it seems like the last thing I'd want to read is more of the same about the rough life I had on the outside. But here's where things get interesting... because the reason they want to read about all those things, is that it both validates their existence, and simultaneously gives them the comfort of a known reality. A corrections environment for juveniles is a lot different than one for adults in one fundamental way: the system hasn't given up on these kids yet, and they are doing everything they can to rehabilitate them. So every day for my kids is a kind of reverse-brainwashing to help them see how their distorted worldview has had a negative impact on their lives and the lives of those around them. That's got to be pretty surreal – having people tell you all day that everything you thought was real suddenly isn't. And urban fiction books give them a point of reference, something to hold onto. It's something that they can look at and say "Yes, that's what it's like out there...that's real... I didn't imagine it...and that's what I've got to learn to deal with before I go back out there." And that is motivation enough to help them pick up a book for the first time in five years... to struggle through it page by page, until slowly, reading isn't so hard anymore. Until it's actually kind of fun. To go from being a non-reader to a voracious one, to one who can recommend more books than the so-called expert librarian. To be so hungry for reading by the time they've finished everything on the urban fiction shelf, that they just can't help themselves and they start picking up books from the other shelves – fantasy, horror, sci fi, thrillers, and nonfiction. I don't have a single story to tell you about the kids I work with who found their love of reading at a juvenile justice center – I have dozens. I've had kids stop a staff member on the street and say – "Hey! You! Miss, you changed my life..." And there are hundreds of kids we serve every day, and will continue to serve, by finding the right book, at the right time, for that reader.
– Kathleen Houlihan, youth services librarian

When it comes to diversity in contemporary YA fiction, it's hard to deny that there is a lack of it. It's not impossible to find, but it is not as quick to locate on shelves as other realistic fiction. Part of this may be because many stories that feature diverse characters don't feature their character's skin color or ethnic background as the primary theme of the story. Rather, it's a part of who the character is, instead of the whole of the character's story. Part of it also may be that we're finally recognizing there might be a problem in YA fiction, where there are too few stories reflecting the diverse realities of today's world.

There are a number of contemporary series featuring diverse characters or characters of color. Some are written for more reluctant readers and some are written specifically to highlight diversity and/or reach a readership mirrored in the books themselves. Often, these books are categorized as urban fiction. There are publishers such as KimaniTru who release many titles per year featuring characters of color and primarily set in urban areas. Saddleback is another publisher to be aware of for diverse titles catering to more reluctant readers.

The following list showcases the variety of voices, styles, settings, and characters present in diverse contemporary fiction. These stories have little unifying them except for the fact they do feature characters of color or characters from countries outside of the United States and Canada. Of course, this list is not all-inclusive. In fact, this is only a subset of titles that are not highlighted among this book's other book lists.

As we become more vocal about the lack of diversity in YA fiction and in contemporary fiction, hopefully we'll see even more authentic stories featuring characters of color and characters from a wide range of ethnicities.

Booth, Coe. ***Bronxwood***. Push, 2011. 320p. $17.99. 978-0-439-92534-1.

Sixteen-year-old Tyrell's family has never been the picture of perfection. It's been Tyrell's job to be in charge: he's the one who has to keep them afloat since his mom is of no use, dad's locked up, and his brother is in foster care. Life in the inner city isn't helping him out much, either. Tyrell just wants to make it out alive, not get caught up in drugs, and he wants to keep it real with the girl he likes. But when his father is released from jail and wants to step back in as man of the house, things become more tense than they've ever been before. Not to mention things may not be so smooth with Tyrell's girlfriend, if she's even really his girlfriend. Tyrell's faced with a host of tough choices and now he has to stand up and be the man in making the right decisions for himself, as well as for his whole family.

Appeal Factors:

- Bronx
- Drug culture
- Family relationships
- Foster care
- Male main character
- New York City
- Peer relationships
- People of color
- Socioeconomic class

Read Alikes

- B. A. Binns's *Pull* would make a good read alike to Booth's novel, as both stories tackle what it means to be an urban teen faced with the responsibilities of keeping a broken family together as best as possible. Both are gritty in their treatment of life in the inner city, as well as the struggles of families who are far from perfect. Booth and Binns depict real teens speaking in authentic urban voices.

Series Alert

Bronxwood is the third book in a series, though it can be read as a stand-alone. Readers who want more back story should check out the other two installments:

Booth, Coe. *Kendra*. Push, 2010. 304p. $8.99 Trade pb. 978-0-439-92537-2.

Booth, Coe. *Tyrell*. Push, 2007. 320p. $8.99 Trade pb. 978-0-439-83880-1.

Cent, 50. *Playground*. Razorbill, 2011. 320p. $17.99. 978-1-59514-434-8.

It's by accident that thirteen-year-old Butterball becomes a bully. He hates that he no longer gets to live with his dad in the city and is instead stuck living with mom and starting at a new school in the suburbs. He's overweight and picked on for that, among other things. Worse, though, is having to deal with a therapist who doesn't get what it's like to be him. The more his therapist digs to uncover what caused Butterball to end up in detention and send a peer to the hospital, it becomes clearer what events in his own life made Butterball react the way he did. Maybe he's not a true bully – maybe he just made a poor choice. It's possible Butterball can be redeemed before it's too late.

Appeal Factors

- Bullying
- Family relationships
- Illustrations
- Long Island

- Male main character
- Middle school setting
- People of color
- Suburban setting

Read Alikes

- 50 Cent's novel is a nice introduction to many of the topics present in Sherman Alexie's slightly more mature title, *The Absolutely True Diary of a Part-Time Indian*. Both are written in a similar style, using illustrations to enliven the stories that delve into issues of prejudice, of challenging family and cultural lives, and bullying.

- Readers looking for a challenge and who are interested in a similarly-styled novel mixing narrative with illustrations will want to try Andrew Smith's *Winger*. Bullying is a theme in Smith's novel, though the consequences and outcomes of his story are more brutal than in *Playground*.

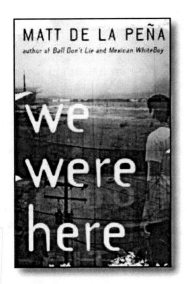

de la Pena, Matt. *We Were Here*. Delacorte, 2010. 368p. $9.99 Trade pb. 978-0-385-73670-1.

Sixteen-year-old Miguel did something bad. Real bad. He's sentenced to a year in a group home, but along with Mong and Rondell, he manages to break out and the three of them make a journey south to Mexico and toward real freedom. Miguel isn't just living it though; he's journaling the trip and experiences, too. The runaway adventure is only one part Miguel's story. The rest lies in what he shares about what his original crime was, why his mother's angry with him, and whether or not he's really ready to make the commitment of leaving his country and the only cultural identity he's ever known.

Appeal Factors

- Alternative format
- Biracial characters
- Crime
- Family relationships
- Friendship
- Gritty
- Homelessness
- Juvenile delinquency

- Male main character
- Multicultural
- Mystery
- People of color
- Road trip
- Runaways
- Travel

Read Alikes

- Readers who haven't read other novels by de la Pena will want to pick up *Mexican Whiteboy* as a follow-up, particularly if they are interested in the challenges of being biracial. Both explore being part-caucasian and part-Mexican, specifically.

- For the story of juvenile delinquency, readers will want to try Gordon Korman's *The Juvie Three* or Walter Dean Myers's *Lockdown* next. Though not an ideal read alike, if it's the juvenile delinquency that appeals to readers here, pass along Steve Watkins's *Juvie*.

Draper, Sharon M. *Panic*. Atheneum, 2013. 272p. $17.99. 978-1-4424-0896-8.

Diamond and her best friend go to the mall one afternoon to kill some time before dance practice. While her best friend tries something on, Diamond finds herself in a conversation with an older man. He asks her what some of her dreams and goals are, and when she mentions she'd love to get more into performance, he says he can hook her up with a spot in an upcoming movie. Since Diamond's role in the school performance of *Peter Pan* is a small one, she considers this offer. The guy checks out by her standards, since he seems to know what he's talking about. He doesn't seem to be leading her on in a creepy way. But when she ditches her friend and decides to follow the man, she realizes things might not be what they seem. After he drugs her drink and she finds herself being forced to do things with a stranger, she learns that not only is he not a good guy, but he's making money off videos he's forcing her to film. Videos that make her uncomfortable and use her in ways she never imagined.

Appeal Factors

- Abuse
- Bullying
- Dance
- Female main characters
- Kidnapping

- Male main characters
- Multiple points of view
- People of color
- Sexual violence

Read Alikes

- Readers who are taken in with the story of a girl who is abducted and held captive will want to read April Henry's *Girl, Stolen*. Though Henry's story is told through a single voice, the abuses that the main character endures are written in a manner that's similar to Draper's.

- Though Draper's main character only mentions Stockholm Syndrome once, readers who want stories featuring girls who are abducted and then find themselves sympathizing with their captor will want to pick up Lucy Christopher's *Stolen* and Liz Coley's *Pretty Girl-13*. Both novels delve further into the psychological realm than Draper's story does and both are more graphic.

Farizan, Sara. *If You Could Be Mine*. Algonquin, 2013. 256p. $17.95. 978-1-61620-251-4.

Sahar has loved her best friend Nasrin for a long time. It's not just the kind of love between best friends, though; Sahar loves her in a romantic way, and Nasrin has reciprocated those feelings. But because the girls live in Iran, their relationship is illegal and the kind of thing that could get them severely punished. When Nasrin's hand is offered to an older man in marriage by her family, Sahar's world falls apart. She doesn't think she'll ever be able to let Nasrin go like that, and she knows Nasrin can't be happy to be married off, either. Through Sahar's cousin, Sahar meets a woman who she finds to not only be one of the most beautiful people she's ever seen, but someone who also happens to be transsexual. In Iran, it's acceptable for people to go through the procedure to change their sex. Now Sahar wonders if going through such a procedure would allow her and Nasrin to be together in the way she thinks they should be.

Appeal Factors

- Female main character
- Foreign setting
- Grief
- Iran
- LGBTQ

- Multicultural
- People of color
- Romance
- Transgendered of transsexual characters

Read Alikes

- There are few books set abroad, much less set in the middle east, that tackle sexuality, particularly within the confines of a country's cultural norms and legal systems. This may be the only book of date tackling the notion of changing one's sex in order to be with a romantic interest as a means of skirting the law. Despite this, readers who are curious about stories where characters question their sexuality and are curious about stories told from a trans- point of view will want to try Cris Beam's *I Am J*, Kristin Elizabeth Clark's *Freakboy*, Kirstin Cronn-Mills's *Beautiful Music for Ugly Children*, and Julie Anne Peters's *Luna*.

- Although not contemporary per se, the graphic novel *Persepolis* by Marjane Satrapi is set in Tehran, Iran, and readers who are curious about the setting or cultural norms present there, particularly for women, should find this a good next read.

Ferrer, Caridad. ***When the Stars Go Blue***. St. Martin's Griffin, 2010. 336p. $9.99. Trade pb. 978-0-312-65004-9.

Soledad Reyes's entire life is devoted to dance. She attends an arts academy in Miami and spends every waking moment she can perfecting her art. When she gets the chance to audition for a lead role in *Carmen* as part of a traveling bugle corps and scores the role, her life is going to change significantly. And it's not just because she's doing something she loves and winning over crowds. It's because the boy who told her about the gig is the boy she wants. This sultry book explores the lines of art and romance and the passions underlying both of them.

Appeal Factors

- Bugle corps
- Dance
- Fast pacing
- Female main character
- People of color

- Performing arts
- Private/boarding school
- Romance
- Summer story

Read Alikes

- For the steamy and pulsing romance, along with the quick pacing, this is a natural pick for fans of Simone Elkeles's *Perfect Chemistry* series. Likewise, the Latino/a characters in Ferrer's story will draw Elkeles fans in further.

- Because the underlying story in Ferrar's book is a retelling of the classic *Carmen*, Walter Dean Myers's *Carmen* may be a strong read alike.

Fichera, Liz. *Hooked*. Harlequin Teen, 2013. 368p. $9.99 Trade pb. 978-0-373-21072-5.

Fredricka Oday – Fred for short – has the chance to be the only girl on her high school's all-boys golf team. She's got a killer swing and the coach knows she's the addition they need. Aside from the problem of being the only girl in boy territory, Fred faces the challenges of being one of the few Native Americans at her school and one of the poorest in a school where other students have much more privilege than she does. Ryan, whose best friend was kicked off the golf team to make room for Fred, can't deny that Fred is good at the game. And despite the fact he's hurt for his friend, he also can't help falling for this girl from a world entirely different than his own. But are their cultural differences too much to make a relationship happen?

Appeal Factors

- Dual points of view
- Family relationships
- Female main character
- Golf
- Interracial relationships
- Male main character

- Multicultural
- People of color
- Socioeconomic class
- Sports
- Romance

Read Alikes

- Those who are interested in the romance elements of this story and how those elements interact with a passion for athletics will want to try Miranda Kenneally's "Thousand Oaks" series, starting with *Catching Jordan* and *Stealing Parker*.

- Another series readers will want to try if they're looking for the marriage of sports and romance is Simone Elkeles's *Wild Cards*. Elkeles's novel is also told in dual points of view, from the male and female sides of the emerging relationship.

Series Alert

Hooked is the first in a series by Fichera. The second book, titled *Played*, will be published in 2014 and feature two different lead characters.

Gurtler, Janet. *If I Tell*. Sourcebooks Fire, 2011. 256p. $9.99. Trade pb. 978-1-4022-6103-9.

Jasmine Evans – who goes by Jaz for short – considers herself a "mistake" as a half-white, half-black girl. Her parents are nothing to brag about, with a really young mom and a dad who wants nothing to do with either her or her mother. To make things tougher, Jaz's small town is close-minded and doesn't accept her. Her classmates tease her and Jaz begins to believe the things she hears about herself being little more than a stain on the world. One bright spot in Jaz's life is her mom's boyfriend Simon; he's good to both her and her mother. But when Jaz sees Simon kissing her best friend, she questions what to do. Does she out them? If she does, she could lose not only her best friend and her potential step father, but she could lose the respect and trust of her own mother, too.

Appeal Factors

- Biracial characters
- Family relationships
- Female main character
- Friendship
- Non-traditional families

- People of color
- Prejudice and racism
- Romance
- Small town setting

Read Alikes

- Gurtler's first novel, *I'm Not Her*, is a worthwhile read alike for those who appreciate the family storyline present in this novel. Both books delve into what comprises a family, as well as the secrets that can bind them or tear them apart.

- A read alike in terms of a story about a biracial main character working through the prejudice she regularly endures, in addition to the challenges of a family falling apart, is Joan Steinau Lester's *Black, White, Other*.

Johnson, Angela. *A Certain October*. Simon & Schuster, 2012. 176p. $16.99. 978-0-689-86505-3.

Scotty doesn't think she's all that exciting, but she likes her friends and she adores her younger brother Keone, who has autism. But a train accident puts her little brother in a coma and causes the death of one of Scotty's classmates, Kris. Kris stayed on the train past his stop to help Scotty out with Keone, out of the kindness of his heart. Now, Scotty's suffering with not only immense grief, but guilt as well. Her friends try to comfort her, but ultimately, Scotty has to determine her own route to happiness and over-coming these feelings about Kris and Keone – and that might come in the form of a boy and a dance.

Appeal Factors

- Accidents
- Autism
- Family relationships
- Female main character

- Grief
- People of color
- Siblings
- Sparse writing

Read Alikes

- For readers who have yet to read Johnson's *Heaven* trilogy, the series would make a good next read for its sparse writing style and exploration of relationship dynamics among friends, family, and even strangers.

- Though not necessarily similar in writing style, fans of *A Certain October* will want to try reading anything by Sharon Draper.

McCall, Guadalupe Garcia. *Under the Mesquite*. Lee & Low, 2011. 224p. $17.95. 978-1-60060-429-4.

Lupita lives in Eagle Pass, Texas, right on the Mexican border. While her mother battles cancer, she's responsible for helping raise her brothers and sisters while balancing school and her passions for acting and poetry. The novel is told in verse, the medium through which Lupita writes. When her mother's illness becomes more severe and the outlook seems less and less positive, Lupita has to focus on her family. Is it possible for her to jug-gle taking care of her family, her future, and work through the challenges of her mother's illness in the way she needs to?

Appeal Factors

- Artistic expression
- Cancer
- Family relationships
- Female main character
- Health and well-being
- Immigrant families
- People of color
- Rural setting
- Verse novel

Read Alikes

- *Illegal* by Bettina Restrepo is an excellent next read for both the story of the struggles of being an immigrant from Mexico in America, but also for working through the loss of a family member.

- Readers who are interested in the struggles of being a child of an immigrant family and how to balance fitting into a new culture with the traditions of an older culture will want to read *What Can('t) Wait* by Ashley Hope Perez. In both Perez's story and in McCall's, the main characters are eager to further their education, which sometimes puts them in precarious positions when it comes to family responsibilities.

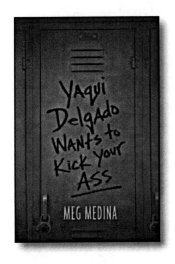

Medina, Meg. *Yaqui Delgado Wants to Kick Your Ass*. Candlewick, 2013. 272p. $17.99. 978-0-7636-5859-5.

When Piddy and her mom move into a new apartment, Piddy's forced to go to a new high school away from her best friend. As bad as that is, it's made worse when she hears that Yaqui Delgado wants to kick her ass. Piddy doesn't even know who Yaqui is and has no idea why someone she doesn't know would want to hurt her. But it doesn't matter what she knows or doesn't know. Yaqui is out to get her because she believes Piddy is making inroads toward stealing her boyfriend. The day the fight breaks out, Yaqui follows through on her promise, and the video of Piddy being beaten up, stripped, and tormented goes viral at school. Combined with learning the truth about who her father is, this might be the worst year of Piddy's entire life.

Appeal Factors

- Bullying
- Family relationships
- Female main characters
- Friendship
- Losing a friend
- Making new friends
- Moving
- New York City
- People of color

Read Alikes

- Pair Medina's novel with Rita Garcia-Williams's *Jumped*, a story about bullying told through multiple points of view. Where in Medina's novel we get Piddy's side of the story only and we are left to wonder what she did to enrage Yaqui, in Garcia-Williams's, we get to see the story from every angle and discover what small things can set a person off. Both portray the effects and consequences of bullying in urban environments.

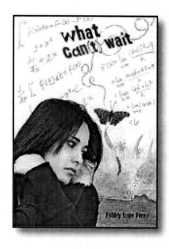

Perez, Ashley Hope. *What Can('t) Wait*. Carolrhoda, 2011. 234p. $17.99. 978-0-7613-6155-8.

Marisa's feeling pressure from everyone. Her mother and father came to Houston, Texas from Mexico, and they've got expectations for their daughter to not only help the family out now, but to find a good boy, marry him, then start her own family. They want her to keep the tradition of family being the core of a solid future. At school, Marisa's teachers pressure her to do well in class, especially her calculus teacher, who thinks if she does well on her AP test, she has a real shot at getting into the engineering program at the University of Texas. As things at home become rockier, and Marisa isn't able to seek the support and help she needs from her family, her boyfriend, or her best friend, can she figure out what it is *she* wants, without feeling like she's letting anyone at home or at school down with her own choices?

Appeal Factors

- Family relationships
- Female main character
- Houston

- Immigrant families
- People of color
- Romance

Read Alikes

- This is a strong read alike to Guadalupe Garcia McCall's *Under the Mesquite,* which also follows a girl struggling to choose between following in the footsteps of her own Mexican cultural heritage or pursuing a more American cultural path toward higher education. Both stories explore that feeling of retaining cultural traditions while remaining open minded to opportunities afforded in a new country.

- Readers curious about the immigration experience will want to read Bettina Restrepo's *Illegal*, which follows the journey of a girl and her mother from their small impoverished Mexican town to a new life in Houston, Texas. Although Perez's story is about a girl who has been in America her entire life, both main characters experience similar cultural challenges. Both stories are set in Houston, as well.

Stella, Leslie. *Permanent Record*. Amazon, 2013. 282p. $17.99. 978-1-4778-1639-4.

Iranian-American Badi is starting at a private Catholic school, following a series of incidents involving him and other students at his public school. He was the target of relentless bullying, and this is his chance to begin fresh. But he's not just going to be starting as a new student. He's getting a new name, too. He's now going to be known as the more "American" Bud Hess. Although Badi is not thrilled about the changes, he finds himself pretty excited to get to know Nikki, the first girl he meets at his new school. Soon after, he meets Reggie, a guy who may or may not be the kind of person Bud wants to make friends with, depending on his relationship to Nikki – are Reggie and Nikki just friends or are they something more serious? When a series of anonymous letters begin showing up in the school newspaper that call out certain student organizations for getting a bigger chunk of funding than others, everyone suspects Badi is the anonymous writer. Part of it is because he's the new kid and part of it is because he's already been causing a stir by refusing to take part in the school's annual chocolate sale. It takes very little time before Budi becomes a victim of bullying yet again. But the question remains whether or not he *is* the one behind the letters.

Appeal Factors

- Bullying
- Chicago
- Depression and anxiety
- Friendship
- Making new friends
- Male main character
- People of color
- Romance

Read Alikes

- Although Prudence Shen and Faith Erin Hicks's *Nothing Can Possibly Go Wrong* is a graphic novel, there are a number of interesting parallels between these two titles. Both are about students who feel that certain student organizations are receiving an unfair allocation of activity money and want to see more equal distribution between sports and other interest groups. Both stories feature the extremes to which students are willing to defend their positions on issues that impact them personally and the entire school population more broadly.

- Stella's book is homage to Robert Cormier's classic *The Chocolate War*, and even one of the teachers considers using Cormier's text as a potential class read. Readers who haven't yet read Cormier's classic will want to after reading this book.

Stevenson, Sarah Jamila. *The Latte Rebellion*. Flux, 2011. 312p. $9.99 Trade pb. 978-0-7387-2278-8.

What started out as a money-making idea turns into a nightmare for Asha Jamison. When she was called a "towel head" at a party last summer, Asha and her friend Carey decide they're not going to stand for the insult. They're going to take ownership of their cultural backgrounds and sell T-shirts promoting what they call the "Latte Rebellion," a club meant to raise awareness of and for those students who are mixed race. It's not for a real cause or club, though. The shirts are just for the girls to raise money for themselves. But soon, their idea for a "Latte Rebellion" becomes a huge hit across the country and other teens are creating actual student organizations to raise awareness of being of mixed heritage. Now Asha cannot keep up with how much demand she's seeing for her shirts and for advice from other students. Her grades begin to fall and her friendship with Carey is growing weaker and weaker. Worse, though, is Asha finds herself facing actual punishment for what she's done when her scheme to make a little money turns more violent.

Appeal Factors

- Biracial characters
- Female main character
- Friendship
- Multicultural
- People of color
- Prejudice and racism
- Social justice

Read Alikes

- Though Asha's intentions for starting the "Latte Rebellion" were not for the purpose of raising awareness of racial issues or to begin an organization for mixed-race students, this is what ultimately ends up happening in the story. Because of this, Stevenson's novel makes a strong read alike to two other stories about students raising awareness for social injustices in their own schools: E. Lockhart's *The Disreputable History of Frankie Landau-Banks* and Daisy Whitney's *The Mockingbirds* and *The Rivals*.

Walker, Brian F. *Black Boy, White School*. Harper Teen, 2012. 256p. $16.99. 978-0-06-191483-6.

Anthony, or Ant for short, lives in a not-so-nice part of East Cleveland, and he is all too aware of what happens in his neighborhood. More often than he'd like, Ant knows the people who are victims of crime and violence. To make matters tougher, his family isn't very stable either. His mother wants nothing more than for Ant to get out of this place and on to a much brighter future. Lucky for him, that future comes in the form of Belton Academy, where Ant's been given a scholarship and an opportunity for a completely fresh start. Belton's deep in rural Maine, so this will be a huge culture shock. Ant's used to being among people who look just like him, but now he feels what it's like truly being a minority. While much of what he feels is real, much of what he's feeling is something he's created in his own mind because he worries he's not good enough to be here. Ant's holding himself back from achieving in the ways he should be able to at Belton. Can he figure out how to let the past go in order to push forward into a bright and promising future?

Appeal Factors

- Cleveland
- Family relationships
- Fast pacing
- Friendship
- Grief
- Male main character
- Moving
- People of color
- Private/boarding school
- Prejudice and racism
- Rural setting

Read Alikes

- The parallels between Walker's book and Sherman Alexie's *The Absolutely True Diary of a Part-Time Indian* are hard to overlook. Both explore what it means to be a cultural minority and given an opportunity to experience the possibilities afforded to those in a majority culture, particularly when it comes to education. There are social and peer expectations on both sides of the coin – those from home (in Walker's case, Cleveland, and in Alexie's case, the Reservation) and those from outside the home (in both cases, a more academically-rigorous school setting).

- Matthew Quick's *Boy21* would make for a strong read alike. Quick's novel follows as "Boy21" starts at a new school and must learn not only to fit in with new peers, but how to grieve and move forward following tragic events in his past. This novel is also fraught with racial tension throughout, even if it is not always blatant, which is similar to how Walker tackles the issues of prejudice and racism.

◼ More Titles Featuring Diversity

Abawi, Atia. *The Secret Sky: A Novel of Forbidden Love in Afghanistan*. Philomel, 2014. 304p. $17.99. 978-0-3991-6078-3.

Alegria, Malin. *Border Town #1: Crossing the Line*. Scholastic, 2012. 192p. $8.99. Trade pb. 978-0-545-40240-8. (First in the *Border Town* series).

Barakiva, Michael. *One Man Guy*. Farrar, Straus and Giroux, 2014. 272p. $17.99. 978-0-3743-5645-3.

Chambers, Veronica. *The Amigas: Fifteen Candles*. Hyperion, 2010. 208p. $9.99 Trade pb. 978-1-4231-2362-0. (First in the *Amigas* series)

Colbert, Brandy. *Pointe*. Putnam, 2014. 352p. $17.99. 978-0-3991-6034-9.

Flake, Sharon. *Pinned*. Scholastic, 2012. 240p. $17.99. 978-0-545-05718-9.

Goo, Maurene. *Since You Asked*. Scholastic, 2013. 262p. $17.99. 978-0-545-44821-5.

Jordan, Dream. *Bad Boy*. St. Martin's Griffin, 2012. 208p. $9.99 Trade pb. 978-0-312-54997-8.

_____. *Hot Girl*. St. Martin's Griffin, 2008. 214p. $10.99 Trade pb. 978-0-312-38284-1.

LaMarche, Una. *Like No Other*. Razorbill, 2014. 352 p. $17.99. 978-1-5951-4674-8.

Maldonado, Torrey. *Secret Saturdays*. Puffin, 2012. 208p. $7.99 Trade pb. 978-0-14-241747-8.

Quick, Matthew. *Boy21*. Little, Brown, 2012. 250p. $17.99. 978-0-316-12797-4.

Restrepo, Bettina. *Illegal*. Katherine Tegen, 2011. 272p. $16.99. 978-0-06-195342-2.

Reynolds, Jason. *When I Was The Greatest*. Atheneum Books for Young Readers, 2014. 240p. $17.99. 978-1-4424-5947-2.

Sharif, Medeia. *Bestest Ramadan Ever*. Flux, 2011. 312p. $9.95 Trade pb. 978-0-7387-2323-5.

Vigilante, Danette. *The Trouble with Half a Moon*. Putnam, 2011. 196p. $16.99. 978-0-399-25159-7.

Whitman, Sylvia. *The Milk of Birds*. Atheneum, 2013. 384p. $17.99. 978-1-4424-4682-3.

Chapter 8

Families Great and Small

I am influenced by contemporary characters that feel so real you'd swear you could know them. Carly from Kirsty Eagar's Raw Blue, *who is pulled out of her pain by a mad Dutch word and action leaps off the page. I'm influenced by Morgan from* The Sky Always Hears *salsa dancer and a boy with synesthesia. Or Melina Marchetta's Jonah Griggs, whose every* Me: and the Hill Don't Mind *[by Kirstin Cronn-Mills], a girl I can picture as she screams dirty words that echo through the hills. These are the kind of characters I strive to create with my own writing—the ones that grab you on page one and never really let you go.*

I write contemporary YA because I'm much more interested in examining the aches and pains of the real world than I am with escaping it. I'm interested in how teenagers love and hate, and how frustrating the world can be when you're sixteen. I write contemporary YA because teens need to know that what they're feeling—bad or good—is okay. That they're not alone. I write contemporary YA because I remember. – Trish Doller, author of *Something Like Normal* and *Where The Stars Still Shine*

Families come in all shapes and sizes, all orientations and combinations. As such, the stories that are told about families and the ways in which family can impact an individual are dynamic and unique. There are stories of strong sibling bonds, of adapting to a new blended family, stories of parents and teens who don't get along on any level. There are stories that introduce teens to families they didn't know they had and stories of how one family member's struggles can impact the entire unit.

This book list spans all types of families – the traditional to the non-traditional – and offers a diverse range of stories about what it means to make and to be part of a family. Even when it seems like adolescence is a time of moving away from family, of pushing against the people who have always been a part of one's life, these stories prove that sometimes, it's those family ties and stories which have the most significant impact on the lives and futures of teens.

Arcos, Carrie. *Out of Reach*. Simon Pulse, 2012. 256p. $16.99. 978-1-4424-4053-1.

A cryptic message two weeks ago rattles Rachel's conscious. Her brother Micah disappeared and the letter she got gave the warning that he might really be in trouble. She wants to find out where he is and get him the help he needs. Of course, it won't be easy; as a meth addict, he's found himself in trouble plenty of times before. With Micah's best friend Taylor by her side, Rachel takes a trip a couple hours south of her home to find her brother on the streets of the last known place he was spending time. This novel explores the ways in which drug addiction can impact not only the person dealing with the consequences, but how that addiction can rattle an entire family.

Book Trailer

http://youtu.be/v7XQJ-TAzUU

Appeal Factors

- Drug addiction
- Family relationships
- Female main character
- Homelessness
- Methamphetamine
- Mystery
- Siblings

Read Alikes

- While Arcos's story focuses on the way that drug addiction impacts a family – though we do not get any information from Micah's side of the story – readers who enjoy this book will want to check out Amy Reed's *Clean* and Blake Nelson's *Recovery Road* for characters sharing their sides of the story and how addiction impacts them personally. Both Reed and Nelson offer insight into the ways addiction affects families, but through the skewed perspective of the addicts themselves.

- Readers who are interested in the street life aspect of this story will want to try Blake Nelson's *The Prince of Venice Beach*, a story told from the perspective of a character who is a runaway living on Venice Beach. Though this story is lighter in tone, it still delves into the reasons why kids choose street life and what costs some may go to in order to protect the choices of their friends.

Davis, Tanita. *Happy Families*. Alfred A. Knopf, 2012. 240p. $16.99. 978-0-375-86966-2. $9.99 Trade pb. 978-0-375-87170-2.

Twins Ysabel and Justin Nicholas have always had a fairly comfortable and supportive family life. Ysabel loves designing jewelry and she's managed to make inroads in the art world, and Justin's above-average intelligence mean he's on his way to a top-ranked college. But things change suddenly when their father breaks a secret to the family that none of them could have ever imagined: he's transgendered. It's not just that he's transgendered, he's also planning on moving out of the house so he can fully embrace and live his true life more openly. Can Ysabel and Justin not only accept their father's lifestyle but also come to understand why it is he needs to leave them? Is family still family, even if they don't all live under the same roof?

Appeal Factors

- Artistic expression
- Dual points of view
- Family relationships
- Female main character
- Male main character
- Siblings
- Spirituality and religion
- Transgendered or transsexual characters

Read Alikes

- There are a few books that explore trans characters, but they happen to be the teen main character in the story, rather than the adult in the story, including Kristin Elizabeth Clark's *Freakboy*, *Beautiful Music for Ugly Children* by Kirstin Cronn-Mills, and Cris Beam's *I Am J*. Readers who are interested in that element of Davis's book will want to explore those titles to see the experience of trans choices and decisions.

- Readers taken with the story of how teens come to terms with a parent's admission of sexual identity that differs from the experience they've always seen will want to read Jo Knowles's *Pearl*, where the mother of the main character admits to being a lesbian. It's emotional and powerful for the main character Bean, much in the way that Ysabel and Justin's understanding of their father's confession is to them.

Doller, Trish. *Where the Stars Still Shine*. Bloomsbury, 2013. 352p. $17.99. 978-1-61963-144-1.

When she was young, Callie was taken from her family by her mother, who has been on the run. Callie's never known a true home, never known what it's like to go to a real school, and she's never had any idea what normal could or should feel like. But when Callie's mother is arrested and charged for kidnapping her, she's sent to live with her father and his family in Florida. The transition won't be easy, especially as she continues to be plagued by nightmares of what happened when she was held captive by her mother. Can she ever find a way to fit in again? Or can she ever learn to trust herself to maybe even fall in love?

Appeal Factors

- Abuse
- Family relationships
- Female main character
- Kidnapping
- Non-traditional families
- Romance
- Sexual violence

Read Alikes

- This is a near-perfect read alike to Emily Murdoch's *If You Find Me*, which is a story of two sisters who had been kidnapped and raised deep in the secluded woods by their unstable mother. Like Callie in Doller's novel, the girls are sent to live with their father, where they must acclimate to a new blended family, to a normal school life, and even to figuring out how to initiate friendships and romances with new people. Both stories also feature main characters haunted by the sexual abuse they sustained via the boyfriends of their mothers.

Griffin, Adele. *All You Never Wanted*. Alfred A. Knopf, 2012. 240p. $17.99. 978-0-375-87082-8.

Thanks to their mother's new husband Arthur, who happens to be one of the richest men around, sisters Alex and Thea look like they have it all. But while it may be that the girls have access to any of the material things they could possibly want, money might be what tears them apart as sisters. Alex always had popularity – she's the older sister, the one who always succeeds without trying. Life with Arthur as step father, though, isn't making her happy. Even with all of his connections and his ability to get her a high-level internship in her dream field, Alex finds herself withdrawing, especially after a mortifying incident on the job that reminds her she didn't earn this job herself. Younger sister Thea, on the other hand, thrives in this new life. Or at least, she thinks she thrives. When mom and Arthur are out of town, Thea wants to throw the biggest party Greenwich has ever seen. But what Thea really wants to get out of the party is the boy she shouldn't even be going after: her sister's boyfriend. So what happens when Thea throws the party and now she has to face the boy she wants, the sister who won't accept her choice to throw the party, and the classmates who aren't really interested in befriending her? Maybe money doesn't buy anything at all.

Appeal Factors

- Depression and anxiety
- Disordered eating
- Dual points of view
- Female main characters
- Greenwich
- Non-traditional families
- Peer relationships
- Rivalry
- Romance
- Siblings
- Socioeconomic class

Read Alikes

- This is a slower-paced, character-driven narrative which challenges some of the assumptions readers may have about female characters and about peer, sibling, and family relationships. This isn't a story about mean girls or about how privilege is damaging; it's about how those things can impact and define relationships in unexpected ways. Readers who enjoy Griffin's novel will want to pick up books by Sara Zarr or Siobhan Vivian for similarly strong and challenging writing and characters. Zarr's books will appeal to those readers hungry for more stories about family relationships and Vivian's will appeal for their focus on friendship, feminism, and social pressures foisted upon girls.

Jaden, Denise. *Losing Faith*. Simon Pulse, 2010. 400p. $9.99 Trade pb. 978-1-4169-9609-5.

Brie is at a party when she gets the call from her father to get to the emergency room as soon as possible. It's her sister, Faith. She's dead and the circumstances are suspicious – just who were these friends Faith spent so much time with anyway? Why was she so devoted to them and their beliefs? Brie wants to move forward, but the way her parents are grieving and the way that her friends and boyfriend avoid her because they're unsure how to behave around her, makes the grieving process even tougher.

Book Trailer

http://youtu.be/pP63Oiqlg8c

Appeal Factors

- Cults
- Family relationships
- Female main character
- Grief

- Mystery
- Siblings
- Spirituality and religion
- Romance

Read Alikes

- *Hold Still* by Nina LaCour is a strong read alike for the mysterious and painful circumstances surrounding the death of a loved one. Both stories also feature lead characters who pursue closure despite not always having the support for it that they'd like to have.

- Readers who are interested in the cult aspects of the story and want to read books featuring a religious or spiritually based cult will want to read *The Right and the Real* by Joelle Anthony or Carol Lynch William's *The Chosen One*.

Jarzab, Anna. *The Opposite of Hallelujah*. Delacorte, 2012. 464p. $16.99. 978-0-385-73836-1.

When Caro's older sister Hannah returns from an eight year stay at contemplative convent, Caro's far from excited. But worse is that Hannah is just weird: she never eats, never interacts, and she always looks sullen. Much as Caro wants to ignore her sister completely, she can't. She wants to know why Hannah is so withdrawn. Hannah's behavior isn't simply a matter of her being devoted to a higher power. She's broken over the death of her best childhood friend eight years ago – the death in which she believes she played a role. But has turning to God helped her grieve properly? And what about Caro? Has having her sister return home after so many years caused her to mourn the loss of her independence as an only child? It might be Caro's desire to figure out her sister's inner demons that leads the two of them into the sort of strong relationship they never thought they'd have.

Appeal Factors

- Disordered eating
- Family relationships
- Female main character
- Grief
- Mental Illness

- Mystery
- Post-traumatic stress disorder
- Siblings
- Spirituality and religion
- Romance

Read Alikes

- For the focus on family relationships, personal loss, and on the aspects of faith and spirituality intersecting with each, readers will want to try Sara Zarr's *Once Was Lost* (in paperback, retitled as *What We Lost*).

Keplinger, Kody. *A Midsummer's Nightmare*. Poppy, 2012. 304p. $17.99. 978-0-316-08422-2. $9. Trade pb. 978-0-316-08421-5.

Whitley's parents are divorced and she splits her time with them, spending school years with mom and summers with dad. Whitley loves those summers with dad: he has a great condo, and he's a reprieve from her mother, whom she can find annoying. But this summer isn't what Whitley hoped for when she hears that dad has not only sold his condo, but he's also got a new woman and step kids in his life. And to make matters more awkward? One of those kids happens to be the boy that Whitley may have hooked up with at one of the big end-of-school-year parties. Maybe this won't be the fun summer she hoped for after all.

Appeal Factors

- Cyber bullying
- Family relationships
- Female main character
- Non-traditional families
- Post-high school setting
- Romance
- Step siblings
- Summer story

Read Alikes

- In terms of writing, those who appreciate Keplinger's unflinching look at teens who party, who drink, and who engage in sex will want to read Kristin Halbrook's *Nobody But Us*. Not only are the writing styles similar, but both books explore what happens when a romantic or intimate relationship doesn't work out as planned.

- Because this book tackles the effects of divorce on a teenager, a solid read alike might be K. M. Walton's *Empty*, which follows a teen girl as she grieves the loss of her once happy family when her mother and father divorce. Even though Keplinger's book takes place years after her parents were divorced, it's the introduction of a new family and new set of rules and circumstances that reflect the experience of growing up as the teen of divorce.

- For those readers who have yet to read Keplinger's first novel, *The DUFF*, it makes for a strong read alike in terms of writing style, in voice, and in the way that Keplinger allows her characters to make authentic teen decisions, even if sometimes they aren't the most likable or desirable ones to make.

Knowles, Jo. *Pearl*. Henry Holt, 2011. 224p. $16.99. 978-0-8050-9207-3.

Bean – whose real name is Pearl – lives with her mother Lexie, who she doesn't like, as well as her grandfather Gus, who she does like. Bean resents her mother for the way she treats Gus, even though it's clear from the start that there's deep-seated resentment between Lexie and Gus. When Gus dies, secrets begin to spill out, and Bean's mother spends more and more time with her old friend Claire. Though they act more like teenagers than adults when they're together, Bean is convinced her mother and Claire are behaving this way because Lexie lost her own teenage years to being a young mother. Now that Gus is gone, this is her mother's way of grieving his loss and grieving the loss of her own childhood. However, it's through observing this relationship that Bean untangles some of the secrets of her own birth. That maybe she herself was born because of her mother's relationship with Gus. That her mother may have had reason to be angry and bitter toward Gus. That Claire and her mother were maybe much more than just good friends.

Appeal Factors

- Family relationships
- Female main character
- Friendship
- Grief
- Intergenerational stories
- LGBTQ
- Quieter read
- Slower pacing

Read Alikes

- For a story about a secret ripping a hole in a family told through quiet prose and a quiet main character, try Alyssa B. Sheinmel's *The Lucky Kind*. Even though Sheinmel's novel is told through a male point of view, this story focuses on what happens to a teenager who learns that a parent has been harboring a life-altering secret for his whole life. Both books are on the shorter side, and they're both slower paced.

- There are a number of similarities between Knowles's novel and Sarah Ockler's *Fixing Delilah*, where family secrets spill before the characters and ultimately force a change in perception. Both stories are written with a bit of restraint, allowing the reader to become invested in the characters and be challenged in their own understanding of good and bad. The main characters in each story are forced to figure out who they are and what they stand for in the midst of everything being pulled out from underneath them.

Leavitt, Lindsey. *Sean Griswold's Head*. Bloomsbury, 2012. 304p. $9.99 Trade pb. 978-1-59990-911-0.

Payton begins seeing a school counselor, despite not wanting to – she's not convinced that she's the one who needs help. It's her family's decision to keep dad's diagnosis of multiple sclerosis a secret that made her feel the way she does; it's their fault, not hers. She's only reacting to how anyone would when that sort of news is sprung on them. When the counselor suggests that Payton keep a focus journal in order to reframe her thinking and help align her emotions, Payton finds the idea appealing. She likes to be organized and she's a perfectionist, so having a reason to study and focus on one thing obsessively is something she can get into. But when Payton chooses the back of her classmate Sean Griswold's head to be her focus item, she doesn't realize the impact it could have not only on helping her through the highs and lows of her father's illness, but it could lead her to discovering that Sean Griswold himself is sort of a guy she'd like to know more about. He may be the person she needs to be by her side through this tough time for her and her family.

Appeal Factors

- "Clean" read
- Family relationships
- Female main character
- Friendship
- Health and well-being

- Humor
- Multiple sclerosis
- Romance
- Therapy

Read Alikes

- Fans of Sarah Dessen, particularly *Along for the Ride*, will find Leavitt's story to be a great next choice. Both tackle family relationships and the sweetness of a new, budding romance.

- Payton's a younger teen main character at fifteen years old, and this book will appeal to younger teen readers who are looking for books that aren't necessarily angsty but do tackle tougher issues. Even though Jenny Han's book *Shug* is geared more toward middle grade readers than young adult readers, it makes for a strong read alike. It's sweet without being saccharine, and it tackles issues of friendship and romance between a male and female character. It's less about family relationships than Han's *The Summer I Turned Pretty* series, which would also make for good read alikes to Leavitt's title.

- Readers who haven't read Phyllis Reynolds Naylor's *Alice* series would likely find those books as good picks for fans of Leavitt's book.

Maldonia, Kristen Paige. *Fingerprints of You*. Simon & Schuster, 2012. 272p. $17.99. 978-1-4424-2920-8

.Lemon's life was never stable. Her mom Stella always uproots them and Stella cycles through men like they're candy. But this isn't her mom's story; this is Lemon's story. When Lemon decides to sleep with a local tattoo artist, her life is changed forever – she becomes pregnant. Lemon's not sure she's ready for having a baby because she's not even sure who she is herself. She's going to find out though, and she knows exactly how: a cross-country road trip by bus with her best friend Emmy to California, where she's going to hunt down her real dad and make a connection with the man she never got to know. Along the way, Emmy cuts her trip short, and now Lemon's left on her own in an unfamiliar city, pregnant and looking for her father. When she finds her father, she discovers he's got his own family now. Lemon has to make a decision about how to build a relationship with her father and has to decide what she's going to do with her baby.

Appeal Factors

- Family relationships
- Female main character
- Friendship
- Grief
- Literary writing
- Miscarriage
- Non-traditional families
- People of color
- Road trip
- Romance
- San Francisco
- Teen pregnancy

Read Alikes

- In many ways, this book mirrors what happens in Carrie Arcos's *Out of Reach*, in that both stories are about the search for lost family members. Both are also set in California, though neither depicts the romanticized image of beach retreats and partying. Both stories are about the ways in which families are made and broken.

- There are interesting parallels between Maldonia's novel and both Emily Murdoch's *If You Find Me* and Trish Doller's *Where the Stars Still Shine* in terms of how a main character comes to live with a long-lost father after a life with a mother who isn't stable or nurturing. Readers will see how some blended families can work not from the perspective of knowing of a father's remarriage and being a part of it, but rather, from the perspective of the main character being a child introduced to the new family.

Murdoch, Emily. *If You Find Me*. St. Martin's Griffin, 2013. 256p. $17.99. 978-1-250-02152-6.

Carey and Janessa grew up in the woods. Younger Nessa's been there her entire life, though Carey's had a taste of the world outside the trees. Their mother originally brought them to this place in the woods to protect them, but mom is never around. She's always out, looking for food and for ways to keep the girls alive. But when the authorities show up and take Carey and Nessa from the only home they've ever truly known and they're handed off to their father, stepmother, and a new stepsister, they're left to learn how to adjust to life in a new world with new and strange people. Moreover, they're left to wonder if they'll ever see their mother again. The memories of the struggles they experienced in the woods haunt Carey profoundly until she finally can't keep it tucked away any longer.

Appeal Factors

- Abuse
- Drug addiction
- Family relationships
- Female main character
- Kidnapping
- Non-traditional families
- Romance
- Rural setting
- Sexual violence
- Siblings
- Step siblings

Read Alikes

- Although told in prose, rather than verse, the lyrical quality of Murdoch's writing reads almost like verse. That, coupled with the story of an intense sibling relationship rocked by secret histories and an abusive home life make this an excellent read alike to Carol Lynch Williams's *Glimpse*. Both stories touch upon a history where the main character has been used as a sexual object in order to make ends meet for their families.

- For readers eager to read another story about a girl escaping an unstable home life with a mother who used her to make money, Trish Doller's *Where the Stars Still Shine* makes an excellent read alike. Both stories also feature strong father-daughter relationships and the challenges of fitting into a new family that acquaints the main characters with a biological father and with new step parents. The dynamics of the new blended families are done well in both Murdoch and Doller's books.

Ockler, Sarah. *The Book of Broken Hearts*. Simon Pulse, 2013. 368p. $17.99. 978-1-4424-3038-9.

Jude's last summer before college isn't relaxing like the summers before that her three sisters got to experience. This summer, Jude's staying at home and close to her father, who is suffering from early onset Alzheimer's disease and weakening quickly. One of the things she's decided to help her dad with is getting his old motorcycle fixed up. As it turns out, the mechanic who takes on the job of re-building the old bike is none other than Emilio Vargas, of the infamous Vargas boys. They're the boys that Jude's sisters have warned her about – they're off limits. Even though she finds herself falling a little bit for Emilio, especially because he treats her ailing father with such respect and care, Jude wrestles with her promise to her sisters of staying away from him. But at what point does she need to choose for herself, rather than follow the words of her sisters? It's not like they're around and know Emilio is different than his brothers.

Appeal Factors

- Alzheimer's disease
- Family relationships
- Female main character
- Health and well-being
- People of color

- Post-high school setting
- Romance
- Significant pets or animals
- Siblings
- Summer story

Read Alikes

- A near perfect read alike to Ockler's novel is Morgan Matson's *Second Chance Summer*, which follows a family in the last summer prior to the death of a father from cancer. Both stories explore the ways in which people grieve for a family member – in both cases, a father – who doesn't have much longer before he passes. Both novels also tap into the ways that friendships and romances can be impacted when family needs to be made a priority.

Polisner, Gae. *The Pull of Gravity*. Square Fish, 2013. 224p. $9.99 Trade pb. 978-1-250-01933-2.

Nick's family is having it rough right now, especially since his dad decided he needs to "go for a walk." This is a walk of life, as well as a walk in the more physical sense. He needs to figure out what he wants from life and he needs to lose weight. In other words, dad's heading out and won't be back any time soon. It's at the same time when Nick's close friend and neighbor Scooter becomes sicker and sicker from the disease that's slowly been taking its toll for years. Nick can't wrap his head around losing both his father and his best friend at the same time. When Nick meets Jaycee who knows Scooter, too – something Nick never knew – he learns that Scooter was keeping more than just his friendship with Jaycee a secret. Scooter had another secret: his dying wish was to deliver a first edition of John Steinbeck's *Of Mice and Men* to the father who walked out on him many years ago. Together, Jaycee and Nick are going to make Scooter's wish come true. On their quirky road trip, though, Nick may learn more about his own relationship to his father and family, too.

Appeal Factors

- Family relationships
- Friendship
- Grief
- Health and well-being

- Humor
- Male main character
- Road trip
- Romance

Read Alikes

- It's always a little lofty to compare a novel to anything written by John Green, but many of the elements of Polisner's book are why it is an excellent Green read alike. First and most importantly are the way relationships between teenagers showcase intelligent, mature interactions and dialog. In terms of characterization, Jaycee is reminiscent of many of the female characters in Green's books, particularly the way they're viewed through the eyes of the male main character as quirky, fun, and worth pursing for reasons that aren't primarily physical.

- Hand Antony John's *Thou Shalt Not Road Trip* to readers who enjoy the road trip element of Polisner's book, in addition to the way that the relationship between Jaycee and Nick develops and challenges each of them to think about what it is they need out of their relationship with each other and with other people more broadly.

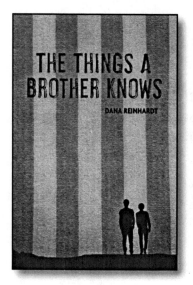

Reinhardt, Dana. *The Things a Brother Knows*. Ember, 2011. 256p. $8.99 Trade pb. 978-0-375-84456-0.

Most people would be excited to hear that their brother is coming home from war, but Levi isn't. He is not sure where he and his brother Boaz even stand – things weren't always happy between them and with Levi unsure of his own place in life and what it is he wants, he can't be certain Boaz will make it any better. When Boaz returns, though, he retreats to his room and refuses to interact with any of his friends or family members. This raises flags for Levi, who now wants to know why it was his brother decided to enlist in the first place, as it seems his return has been anything but exciting. Even as Boaz makes small journeys outside his room, it's clear something is really wrong with him, and now, despite his reservations in his relationship with Boaz, Levi wants to know how it is he can help his brother readjust to home and civilian life, if readjusting is even a possibility.

Appeal Factors

- Boston
- Family relationships
- Health and well-being
- Jewish characters
- Male main character

- Mental illness
- Post-traumatic stress disorder
- Siblings
- War

Read Alikes

- Post-traumatic stress disorder as it relates to teens and those slightly outside of their teen years has been making a more regular appearance in YA fiction, particularly as it becomes part of the reality of today's teenagers who are stepping into combat. Readers taken with Reinhardt's story as it relates to a brother coming to understand what happened to his sibling in war will want to read E. M. Kokie's *Personal Effects*. Kokie's book explores the effects of war through the lens of grief and unraveling the mysteries of the life of a deceased brother, and the commonalities in how the sibling relationships play out in both stories, especially as neither are easy relationships, have many parallels.

- For readers who are interested in the impact of post-traumatic stress disorder on a teen who has served in combat, try Trish Doller's *Something Like Normal*.

- In terms of writing style, readers will want to try Donna Freitas's novels for similar execution and voice. Though Freitas's novels have primarily been through the voice of a female main character, both Freitas and Reinhardt write with a literary edge to them, and both have strong crossover appeal to adult readers.

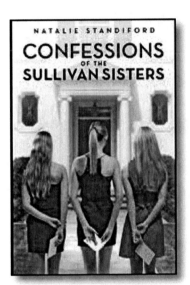

Standiford, Natalie. *Confessions of the Sullivan Sisters*. Scholastic, 2012. $9.99 Trade pb. 978-0-545-10711-2.

It all begins when Grandma "Almighty" Beckford, the matriarch of the Sullivan family, tells her granddaughters that someone has done something wrong – something so terrible – she cannot keep the family in her will any longer. Everyone is surprised to hear this, but the Almighty makes a suggestion: If the person who did the crime fesses up, then maybe she'll reinstate the family into her will. When sisters Norrie, Jane, and Sassy admit to the bad things they've done, which of the girls will be the one who has to apologize for her crimes against the family? And even if one of them does own up to disgracing the family, the Almighty's mood changes may mean she never follows through on her end of the deal.

Appeal Factors

- Baltimore
- Family relationships
- Female main characters
- Humor
- Intergenerational stories

- Multiple points of view
- Quirky
- Romance
- Siblings
- Socioeconomic class

Read Alikes

- The quirky humor and writing is a cornerstone of Standiford's contemporary YA books, and readers who appreciate the story will want to check out *How to Say Goodbye in Robot*. It takes the strange but enjoyable characters and explores how a girl and a boy can become good friends. Family relationships play a significant role into how that friendship evolves, as well.

- An older title with a similarly humorous premise and voice is Robin Benway's *Audrey, Wait*.

- Readers who like Standiford's writing will also want to check out Sarah Mylnowski's books.

■ More Titles Featuring Families

Brody, Jessica. *52 Reasons to Hate My Father*. Square Fish, 2013. 352p. $16.99. 978-0-374-32303-5.

Brown, Jennifer. *Perfect Escape*. Little, Brown, 2012. 368p. $17.99. 978-0-316-18557-8.

Cousins, David. *Fifteen Days without a Head*. Flux, 2013. 312p. $9.99. Trade pb. 978-0-7387-3642-6.

Cronn-Mills, Kirstin. *The Sky Always Hears Me: And the Hills Don't Mind*. Flux, 2009. $9.95 Trade pb. 978-0-7387-1504-9.

Dessen, Sarah. *The Moon and More*. Viking, 2013. 384p. $19.99. 978-0-670-78560-5.

_____. *What Happened to Goodbye?* Viking, 2011. 416 p. $17.99. 978-0-670-01294-7. $9.99 Trade pb. 978-0-14-242383-7.

Eulberg, Elizabeth. *Revenge of the Girl with the Great Personality*. Point, 2013. 272 p. $17.99. 978-0-545-47699-7.

Gelbwasser, Margie. *Pieces of Us*. Flux, 2012. 336 p. $9.95 Trade pb. 978-0-7387-2164-4.

Kirby, Jessi. *Moonglass*. Simon & Schuster, 2012. 256 p. $9.99 Trade pb. 978-1-4424-1695-6.

Kokie. E. M. *Personal Effects*. Candlewick, 2012. 352 p. $16.99. 978-0-7636-5527-3.

Leavitt, Lindsey. *Going Vintage*. Bloomsbury, 2013. 320 p. $16.99. 978-1-59990-787-1.

Marchetta, Melina. *The Piper's Son*. Candlewick, 2011. 336 p. $17.99. 978-0-7636-4758-2. $7.99 Trade pb. 978-0-7636-6062-8.

Matson, Morgan. *Second Chance Summer*. Simon & Schuster, 2012. 480 p. $17.99. 978-1-4169-9067-3.

McCahan, Erin. *I Now Pronounce You Someone Else*. Arthur A. Levine, 2010. 272 p. $16.99. 978-0-545-08818-3.

Ockler, Sarah. *Fixing Delilah*. Little, Brown, 2011. 336 p. $9.99 Trade pb. 978-0-316-05208-5.

Pearce, Jackson. *Purity*. Little, Brown Books, 2012. 218 p. $17.99. 978-0-316-18246-1.

Perez, Ashley Hope. *What Can('t) Wait*. Carolrhoda, 2011. 234 p. $17.99. 978-0-7613-6155-8.

Scheidt, Erica Lorraine. *Uses for Boys*. St. Martin's Griffin, 2013. 240 p. $9.99 Trade pb. 978-1-250-00711-7.

Sheinmel, Alyssa. *The Lucky Kind*. Ember, 2012. 224 p. $8.99 Trade pb. 978-0-375-86608-1.

Spalding, Amy. *Ink is Thicker than Water*. Entagled, 2013. 320 p. $9.99 Trade pb. 978-1-62266-040-7.

_____. *The Reece Malcolm List*. Entagled, 2013. 352 p. $9.99 Trade pb. 978-1-62061-240-8.

Stein, Tammar. *Spoils*. Knopf, 2013. 272 p. $17.99. 978-0-375-87062-0.

Williams, Carol Lynch. *Glimpse*. Simon & Schuster/Paula Wiseman, 2012. 512 p. $9.99 Trade pb. 978-1-4169-9731-3.

_____. *Miles from Ordinary*. St. Martin's Griffin, 2012. 208 p. $9.99 Trade pb. 978-1-250-00260-0.

Wylie, Sarah. *All These Lives*. Farrar Straus Giroux, 2012. 256 p. $17.99. 978-0-374-30208-5.

Zarr, Sara. *How to Save a Life*. Little, Brown, 2012. 368 p. $8.99 Trade pb. 978-0-316-03605-4.

Zielin, Lara. *The Waiting Sky*. Putnam, 2012. 224 p. $17.99. 978-0-399-25686-8.

Chapter 9

From Best Friends to Casual Acquaintances

My mind was blown the first time I read The Chocolate War *by Robert Cormier. It's an amazing litmus of what I'll call The Boy Experience. Cormier dips his pen into the minds of multiple male characters and paints an unflinching portrait of the issues they face—violence, peer pressure, sexuality—with nuance and honesty. I was so impressed with how much he was able to highlight without the book feeling cluttered or heavy-handed. The villains didn't get the big come-uppance they deserved, heroes weren't celebrated, problems weren't solved, justice definitely wasn't served. But is there anything more realistic than that? It was such a brave choice for Cormier to make, and it honored and respected both his story and the lives of his readers to be so unflinchingly truthful about how messy and unsatisfying the battles we fight in life can be.* – Siobhan Vivian, author of *The List, Not That Kind of Girl,* and *Same Difference*

Friends and peers have a significant influence on teens, so it's no surprise that stories about them take up a lot of shelf space in contemporary YA. And just like in the real world, the stories about friends and about peers range from being healthy and supportive to being challenging, to being nasty and downright awful. But it's those interactions and experiences that guide individuals through their social lives and help them figure out what it is they need from their friends and their peers.

The stories here include awkward and uncomfortable tales of forging friendships with new people and stories of friends who've had a falling out. There are tales of what it means to cross the line between friend and romantic interest, as well as what it means to be shunned and frozen out completely by peers and those who seemed to be friends or allies. There are stories of solid and strong friendships that weather the toughest moments, of peer acceptance, and of how friendships can and do influence individuals to become better people. These books explore the wide and diverse range of experiences that happen on a daily basis when it comes to developing and engaging in relationships with others.

Backes, M. Molly. *The Princesses of Iowa*. Candlewick, 2012. 464p. $16.99. 978-0-7636-5312-5.

At the end of last school year, Paige and her two best friends Nicky and Lacey were in a car accident after a late night drinking party. Paige's mom, queen of making sure their family has a pristine reputation in their small town, ships her daughter away to au pair for the summer in France. Getting her out of town should ensure that when the new school year rolls around, the incident is forgotten and behind everyone. That way, Paige can maintain her image as pretty, popular, and perfect. But it's not that simple. When Paige returns, Nicky and Lacey want nothing to do with her and neither does her boyfriend Jake. All three were hurt after the accident – in physical and emotional ways – and Paige can't just expect forgiveness, especially since she had the chance to get away from it all for three months with no repercussions. They had to live with the consequences every day. What will it take for Paige to earn forgiveness from her friends and to establish relationships with new friends? Maybe more importantly, what will it take for her to own up and accept responsibility for the events that changed the lives of everyone in her small town?

Appeal Factors

- Accidents
- Bullying
- Creative writing
- Family relationships
- Female main character
- Friendship

- LGBTQ
- Making new friends
- Peer relationships
- Romance
- Rural setting

Read Alikes

- Readers who are interested in the mean girl angle of this book would do well picking up Lauren Oliver's *Before I Fall*. Even though it's not contemporary (there is a fantastical element to it), Oliver's book features an unlikeable female character who makes choices that impact her friendship and peer relationships.

- The mean girl/bullying appeal factors for Backes's novel would also make *Some Girls Are* by Courtney Summers a worthwhile read alike.

- For the mean girls/bullying aspect with an element of homophobia, try Hannah Harrington's *Speechless*. All three books in this read alike list are told from the point of view of the popular girl who finds herself fallen from that position and wants nothing more than to climb back on top of the social ladder.

Brown, Jennifer. *Hate List*. Little, Brown Books, 2010. 224p. $8.99 Trade pb. 978-0-316-04145-4.

It was Valerie's boyfriend Nick who shot the gun in school. He even hit her on his rampage as she tried to save someone who was in the line of fire. Though Nick committed the heinous crime, Valerie finds herself in trouble. She's cast out by her peers because of her role in the matter: she and Nick drafted a list of people they hated together. It was from that list Nick picked his targets. In the eyes of everyone around Valerie, she's at fault, too, despite not taking part in the actual shooting. She's guilty by association. Now with summer ending and her seclusion from her peers over, Valerie has to figure out how to fit back in at school, how she can make friends again, and how she can ever move on from Nick's behavior.

Book Trailer

http://youtu.be/KWNGIRTU2u4

Appeal Factors

- Bullying
- Crime
- Family relationships
- Female main character
- Friendship
- Grief
- Peer relationships
- School shooting
- Therapy

Read Alikes

- This sort of story, similar to so many real-life events in the news, lends itself to a non-fiction read alike in David Cullen's *Columbine*. Cullen's book explores what went on during the real life events of Columbine and offers a portrait of what the perpetrators must have been feeling socially. It's not entirely sympathetic toward them or their actions, much as Valerie is not in Brown's story. Another non-fiction title worth giving to readers interested in the elements of bullying that lead teens to extremes is Emily Bazelon's *Sticks and Stones*.

- Jennifer Brown's writing style is reminiscent of Susan Vaught's, and this book would make for a strong read alike to Vaught's *Going Underground*, which follows a male character as he deals with the repercussions of being caught sexting. He didn't do it maliciously, but because of how laws toward sexting are, he's given a punishment that causes him to question whether or not he is a good or bad person, much in the way Valerie does, too. He's outcast by his peers and knows he won't have the chance to fit in. These feelings and the way they're worked through are quite similar to Brown's novel.

Chappell, Crissa-Jean. *Narc*. Flux, 2012. 288p. $9.95 Trade pb. 978-0-7387-3247-3.

When seventeen-year-old Aaron gets pulled over for speeding, it's his little sister who is caught with a bag of weed. He takes the blame for it in order to keep her out of trouble. But the officer makes Aaron a deal: he can get off the hook for this incident if he will play the role of narc, locate the source of drug distribution at his high school, and report back as soon as he has a good lead. Happy to not face the consequences of a charge for possession, Aaron agrees. Over the course of his duty, Aaron befriends Morgan and Skully, who are known for being into the school's drug culture and who may have ties to the person or people who sell. Aaron has the source within his reach and when he's ready to spill to the police, he finds himself unable to go through as planned – some of these people he's about to narc on became his friends and the last thing he wants to do is get them in trouble now.

Appeal Factors

- Crime
- Drug culture
- Family relationships
- Friendship
- Gritty

- Male main character
- Miami
- Peer relationships
- Siblings

Read Alikes

- Two other recent novels tackle the teen-turned-drug-informant idea, so readers who are taken with Chappell's novel will want to read Alissa Grosso's *Ferocity Summer* and Allison van Diepen's *Takedown*.

Graham, Hilary Weisman. *Reunited*. Simon & Schuster, 2012. 336p. $16.99. 978-1-4424-3984-9.

Alice, Summer, and Tiernan were best friends and their love of the band Level3 kept them together. That is until the band broke up; that's when the girls also found their friendship in shatters, as they discovered they had less in common with one another than they thought. Alice was always a bit of a book worm, while Summer always wanted to fit in with the popular kids, and Tiernan liked being a bit rebellious. But Level3 is getting back together for one night only and on a whim, Alice buys three tickets. Can she convince the other girls to join her on this spontaneous road trip to see their favorite band once again? More importantly, can this road trip help them all see each other eye to eye and reestablish the bonds they once had before they all graduate high school?

Book Trailer

http://youtu.be/N3mmS6nA0Ls

Appeal Factors

- Female main characters
- Friendship
- Humor
- Multiple points of view

- Music
- Post-high school setting
- Road trip
- Summer story

Read Alikes

- The post-high school setting via road trip, the following of a band, and the way that relationships are made or broken therein may make this a good read alike to Nina LaCour's *The Disenchantments*. LaCour's novel is more literary in structure and execution, with less humor, than Graham's title, but readers will likely enjoy it as as next pick.

- Jessi Kirby's *In Honor* is another novel that features a road trip to see a musical act, and like Graham's novel, part of the story takes place in Texas. In Kirby's book, the main character travels with her now-deceased brother's friend, making for a road trip that is, at times, as uncomfortable as the one among the three girls in Graham's novel. Kirby's book doesn't have the humor of Graham's, but it should be a similarly-enjoyable read for the road trip, music, and relationship aspects.

Griffin, N. *The Whole Stupid Way We Are*. Atheneum, 2013. 368p. $16.99. 978-1-4442-3155-3.

Dinah's rescuing her best friend Skint from detention yet again, this time because he's been sentenced for sketching pictures someone found offensive. From there, the story follows this ragtag best friend duo to a donkey show at a local church, then through their commitment to helping get food to a family who lives in the most rural part of their small town. Maybe most importantly, it follows the pair on their never-ending quest to be good people. Dinah and Skint are tight friends, even though they don't always share everything openly with one another; but it's when Dinah can't be there for the hurt Skint feels in his life that the basis of their friendship, trust, and reliance upon one another is called into question. The thing is, it's never about Dinah not being there when Skint's father's dementia hits a critical point. It's about what happens when she is there in the way he and his father need.

Appeal Factors

- Abuse
- Dementia
- Dual points of view
- Family relationships
- Female main character

- Friendship
- Health and well-being
- Male main character
- Rural setting
- Socioeconomic class

Read Alikes

- This is an excellent example of a story that seems fairly rare: friendships between a male and female character without any hint of romance or sex between them. Even though the possibility of something else lurks beneath the surface in Angela Johnson's *A Certain October*, it would make a worthwhile read alike to Griffin's title. In both books, the story is a bit fragmented, and neither book dwells in back story. Both are character-driven and focus on friendships and what happens when the kindness of one person impacts another significantly. They are very different stories from their settings, but the execution and the view from a moment in time are quite similar.

- Another potential pairing for Griffin's book might be Alyssa B. Sheinmel's *The Beautiful Between*. Both are quieter stories of friendship (though it's arguable Sheinmel's story goes down the path toward romance), and the family situations in both books help the friends bond.

Hubbard, Kirsten. *Like Mandarin*. Delacorte, 2011. 320 p. $17.99. 978-0-385-73935-1. $9.99 Trade pb. 978-0-385-73936-8.

Fifteen-year-old Grace is bored in her small town of Washokey, Wyoming. Nothing happens here, she's got no real way out until college, and she definitely doesn't want to be stuck in nowhere Wyoming any longer than she has to be. This town eats people alive. The only reason she's here is because of her mother, who is obsessed with her little sister's pageant career. There is something in Washokey for Grace though, and that's seventeen-year-old Mandarin. She is everything Grace is not: edgy, worldly, experienced, sexy. But when the girls get to know one another better thanks to a school project, Grace begins to wonder if what she once thought about Mandarin is who she is at all. Sure, Grace is completely taken with Mandarin and she wants nothing more than to be as cool and carefree as her, but Mandarin uses these qualities to manipulate people, including Grace. Where Grace once saw Mandarin as the girl who had it all and the kind of person she'd like to get to know, now that she sees Mandarin for who she really is, maybe she isn't worth knowing at all.

Book Trailer

http://youtu.be/PYpRRnJKMrc

Appeal Factors

- Family relationships
- Female main character
- Friendship
- Rural setting
- Sexuality

Read Alikes

- Mandarin encompasses a lot of the qualities that Paige does in M. Molly Backes's *The Princesses of Iowa*. She's a bit of a mean girl and she's manipulative about getting the things she wants to in her small town. Readers will see many similarities between the two books in that regard, as well as in their small-town settings. There are also interesting connections between Paige's family in Backes's story and Grace's family, right down to the image-conscious and pageant-obsessed mothers.

- The friendship and relationship tensions between Grace and Mandarin is reminiscent of what happened between Adrienne and Dakota prior to Dakota's disappearance in Lauren Strasnick's *Then You Were Gone*. Strasnick's story is much shorter than Hubbard's, but the way both pairs of girls develop in their friendship and closeness – then ultimate distance – makes them strong read alikes.

- There are also some striking similarities between the relationship in Hubbard's book and the relationship between Gia and Lida in Erin Saldin's *The Girls of No Return*, especially when it comes to tracing the lines between what it is to be friends with someone and what it means to take that friendship to a more romantic level. Both tiptoe into questions about sexuality.

Jackson, Corrine. *If I Lie*. Simon Pulse, 2012. 288p. $16.99. 978-1-4424-5413-2.

In her small military town of Sweethaven, North Carolina, Quinn becomes the center of a scandal when a photograph of her and Blake emerges. They're not a couple. In fact, Quinn's boyfriend Carey is serving overseas and he's just gone missing in action. No one is afraid to tell Quinn how they feel about her cheating and about how much disrespect she's brought not only her boyfriend, but the whole town. As punishment, her father forces Quinn to volunteer at the local veteran's hospital, where she makes fast friends with George. The thing is, Quinn isn't being disrespectful, nor is she cheating. Quinn is the only person who knows Carey's biggest secret: he's gay. Beyond suffering bullying and cruelty, Quinn has to work through losing Carey, as well as the possibility of losing the one person who has been a true friend to her through it all – George.

Appeal Factors

- Bullying
- Female main character
- Grief
- Intergenerational stories
- LGBTQ

- Military
- Romance
- Small town setting
- War

Read Alikes

- *Something Like Normal* by Trish Doller and *In Honor* by Jessi Kirby are strong read alikes to Jackson's book for their explorations of grieving and loss and how those are tied to military service and combat. All three titles also explore the changes in social dynamics as they relate to war and service.

- Readers interested in the themes of military service and grief who are also interested in the challenges of being gay while serving will want to read *Personal Effects* by E. M. Kokie.

Keplinger, Kody. *The DUFF: Designated Ugly Fat Friend*. Poppy, 2011. $8.99 Trade pb. 978-0-316-08424-6.

Bianca and her best friends Casey and Jessica like to hang out at the local under-21 club, but it's the day when Wesley – one of the guys in their class – calls her "Bianca the DUFF" that things change. Bianca demands an explanation for what the word "DUFF" means, and he tells her it means she's the designated ugly fat friend of their clique. If a guy can be nice to someone "like her," then he's kind of guy a girl would want to date because he's shown sensitivity. Bianca doesn't really believe her friends would use her like that. They're close. But with things at home start getting a little rocky and she becomes desperate for a person to turn to, Bianca approaches Wesley, who ends up being a much better listener than she ever thought. Maybe he's someone she can see herself spending more than a little time with, despite what he said to her before. Then there's the question that hangs over her still: Are Casey and Jessica really her friends or are they using her?

Appeal Factors

- Body image
- Family relationships
- Female main character
- Friendship
- Humor
- Romance

Read Alikes

- In terms of writing and the romantic tension in Keplinger's novel, this would be a great read alike for fans of Simone Elkeles and vice versa.

- Even though Bianca stumbles a bit in her own vision of herself, her voice and the ultimate overarching struggle of body-image and self-acceptance are reminiscent of what Susan Vaught achieves in *My Big Fat Manifesto*. Jamie is much more confident in herself than Bianca, but she has the same tone and vision for social acceptance that Bianca does.

- For a broader picture of the beauty myth, consider pairing Keplinger's book with Siobhan Vivian's *The List*, as there are girls within the story (both on the pretty list and ugly list) who work through much of what Bianca works through, not only in terms of self-image and acceptance, but even in broader familial and peer relationships.

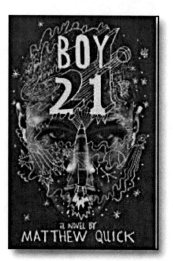

Quick, Matthew. *Boy21*. Little, Brown, 2012. 250p. $17.99. 978-0-316-12797-4. $9 Trade pb. 978-0-316-12796-7.

Finley loves basketball and he's really good at it, despite the challenges he faces being the only white kid on the team. When he dedicates, he dedicates. Finley's best friend/girlfriend Erin is also a huge basketball player. But Finley's devotion to the game is such that during the season, he tells Erin they can't be together. He cannot lose focus. This changes, though, when Finley's coach shows up to his house one day and informs Finley that he'll be responsible for showing new kid Russell the ropes. Playing the role of ambassador to Russell isn't Finley's idea of a good time, especially as he discovers how weird Russell is. There's nothing normal about him at all. Not to mention he's a threat to Finley's own role on the school's team, since Russell is one of the country's top college basketball recruits. Slowly, as the boys spend more time together, Finley learns that Russell's got game, despite being afraid to show it on the court. Russell's deeply hurting, much in the way Finley is, even though neither willingly shows it. It's a shared love of basketball and a hope for humanity that draw these two closer than they could have imagined.

Book Trailer

http://youtu.be/iBbbaUgGQZk

Appeal Factors

- Basketball
- Family relationships
- Friendship
- Grief
- Male main character
- People of color
- Prejudice and racism

Read Alikes

- Readers not already familiar with Quick's *Sorta Like a Rock Star* will want to read it if *Boy21* resonates. Both stories feature characters who are good of heart but stuck in challenging situations. They make the best of what it is they have and in neither case, do these characters rely on fantastic, unbelievable solutions when working toward fulfilling their emotional needs.

- Because of the story's execution, the smart dialog between teens, and the male voice, fans of John Green's style will find much to enjoy here. There is something hopeful and redemptive in Quick's characters, much as there are in Green's.

Reed, Amy. *Over You*. Simon Pulse, 2013. 320p. $16.99. 978-1-4424-5696-9.

When Sadie is kicked out of her father's house for drinking too much and she's sent to live on her mother's farm in rural Nebraska, Max comes along with her. Max is Sadie's best friend, sometimes-girlfriend, and confidante. Max is always willing to do what it takes to be there for Sadie. When the girls get to Nebraska, they realize that summer on the farm isn't as quaint as they imagined. It's work, and the girls are living together in a tiny trailer with no amenities. But when Sadie comes down with a terrible virus which forces Max to take residence in one of the farm's yurts in order to avoid becoming sick herself, there is a seismic shift in their friendship. Part of it has to do with the fact that Max chooses to spend more time with Dylan, one of the only people on the farm anywhere near her age. His good looks don't hurt either. More than that, Max realizes that all of this alone time away from Sadie has forced her to think about the things she likes and enjoys for herself. When Sadie's mother begins to dote on her daughter – as does another younger girl on the farm – Max understands the friendship was never one she benefitted much from anyway. It was one-sided. Now Max must make one of the hardest decisions of her life: how to break up with someone she thought was her best friend. Like working on the farm, it won't be easy and Dylan might complicate things more than necessary.

Appeal Factors

- Farm setting
- Female main character
- Friendship

- LGBTQ
- Rural setting
- Summer story

Read Alikes

- The relationship between Sadie and Max is reminiscent of the relationship that develops between Grace and Mandarin in Kirsten Hubbard's *Like Mandarin*. In both books, the story is narrated from the point of view of the girl feeling as though she's getting a lot out of the friendship because she's able to be near someone who many others consider "cool" or "exotic." In both stories, the girls come to realize their friends are not quite the people they imagined them to be and instead, they're better off not holding tight to these unhealthy relationships. Additionally, both stories also blur the lines between friendship and romance. Where Hubbard's is more restrained, Reed is outright in exploring how Sadie and Grace had more physical, romantic interactions.

Saldin, Erin. *The Girls of No Return*. Arthur A. Levine, 2012. 352p. $17.99. 978-0-545-31026-0.

Lida arrives at the Alice Marshall School for Girls after a "very bad incident" happened. The school, set in the sprawling and remote woods of Idaho, is meant to help girls work through their problems, which they are taught in therapy to call their Things. Lida has no idea what her Thing is, but she goes through the motions in order to get through the program and back home again. But what's really worrying Lida is less what her own Thing is and more what the Things are of the girls she's living with. She's not sure these girls are stable or safe to be around. When one of the girls Lida comes to trust exposes what Lida's Thing is that the story spirals into an exploration of depression, of self-injury, and many other dark secrets clouding Lida's past. It's possible the girls Lida first came to fear are the exact girls she needs on her side to work through her Thing. They might not be so scary after all.

Appeal Factors

- Depression and anxiety
- Female main character
- Friendship
- Peer relationships

- Rural setting
- Self-injury and self-harm
- Sexuality
- Therapy

Read Alikes

- Readers will be sucked into the relationship that develops between Lida and Gia, the newest girl at Alice Marshall. Because of the questions surrounding whether or not their relationship will become romantic or remain platonic, this makes a great read alike to Kirsten Hubbard's *Like Mandarin*. Another read alike exploring friendship and the way it can be troublesome or damaging is in Jo Knowles's *Lessons from a Dead Girl*.

- For the setting in a remote facility that involves girls struggling with a host of mental health issues, readers will do well in picking up Nora Price's *Zoe Letting Go*.

- For those fascinated with the self-harm and self-injury angles of this story, in conjunction with other mental health challenges, Ilsa J. Bick's *Drowning Instinct* is a strong read alike, as are Patricia McCormick's classic *Cut* and Julia Hoban's *Willow*.

Sales, Leila. *Mostly Good Girls*. Simon Pulse, 2011. 368p. $9.99 Trade pb. 978-1-4424-0680-3.

Violet and Katie have been best friends for a long time, and they attend an all-girls school near Boston. Both are the kinds of girls who have a lot of goals in front of them and they set off to achieve them. They're nothing if not driven. Up until this year, neither was particularly interested in any boys, but all of that changes when Katie starts dating Martin. This is after Katie earns perfect test scores and could get into any college she wants. Martin didn't go to college, and he's perfectly happy living a life as a barista. Violet tries not to be judgmental, but she can't help it – she thinks Katie deserves something more in a boyfriend and that she's lowered her standards. Can their friendship be broken over a boy?

Appeal Factors

- Boston
- Female main character
- Friendship
- Humor
- Private/boarding school
- Romance
- Vignette writing style

Read Alikes

- The humor in this book makes it a strong read alike for authors such as Meg Cabot and Ally Carter. Readers may also want to try Louise Rennison's *Georgia Nicholson* series.

- In terms of the friendship angle, Sales's novel is reminiscent of Siobhan Vivian's *Same Difference* and *A Little Friendly Advice*.

Shen, Prudence. *Nothing Can Possibly Go Wrong*. First Second, 2013. 288p. $11.99. Trade pb. 978-1-59643-659-6.

Charlie is captain of the basketball team, boyfriend of the super hot and popular cheerleader Holly, and the unlikely best friend of Nate, president of the school's robotics team. When Holly dumps Charlie, Nate drops the news that the student activities funding, which could be spent either on a national robots convention for his group or on new uniforms for the cheerleaders, is being left in the student council's hands. So now, Nate wants to run for student council president in order to delegate the money for his own group. Charlie panics. He knows Holly will reel him into this scheme, despite their relationship being over, and he's right. She's making him run for student council president, too, in order for him to delegate the money toward the cheerleaders. Now it's friend against friend in a race to student council president – an honor which neither of them really wants.

Appeal Factors

- Basketball
- "Clean" read
- Friendship
- Graphic novel

- Humor
- Male main characters
- Peer relationships

Read Alikes

- Shen's book, illustrated by Faith Erin Hicks, is a strong read alike for readers who love Raina Telgemeier's *Drama*, though Shen's book is set in high school rather than middle school. Both stories take place almost entirely within the walls of their respective schools and feature a wide range of characters who defy stereotype. These books show teens in their element and both offer not only visually interesting stories, but also tight and realistic dialog rapt with humor. As important, both are explorations of peer relationships and the pressure there is in keeping and maintaining those.

Standiford, Natalie. *How to Say Goodbye in Robot*. Scholastic, 2010. $9.99 Trade pb. 978-0-545-10709-9.

It's senior year and Bea is the new girl at school. She's hoping that despite the fact she's had to move at about the crummiest time she could, she can make some solid friends who will help her through this final year of high school. Her luck won't be so good, as she's seated beside Jonah, who everyone refers to as Ghost Boy because he's a loner and has not made friends in school. Bea can't contain herself, and she wants to get to know him, even though he is not the easiest person to get to know. He's gloomy and withdrawn. There's something going on beneath his surface and Bea wants to know what it is. But it won't happen easily nor will it happen in any sort of expected manner – the two of them forge their relationship through a late-night call-in radio show. What Bea discovers about Jonah and the challenges he faces on a daily basis at home makes her love him and appreciate the friendship they forge even more. It's intimate and emotional, but it's not a romance.

Appeal Factors

- Baltimore
- Family relationships
- Female main character
- Friendship
- Grief
- Making new friends
- Moving
- Quirky

Read Alikes

- Even though Rainbow Rowell's *Eleanor and Park* is not a contemporary novel, as it's purposefully set in 1986, the relationship between the two main characters is reminiscent of Bea and Jonah's. Where Eleanor and Park do find themselves falling into more romantic love than platonic love, the weaving of the strong back stories into their mutually understanding of one another makes this a strong novel to hand to those who liked Standiford's and vice versa.

- For another exploration of the way a friendship develops between a male and a female – even if there are underpinnings of longing from one of the characters – readers would do well trying Laura Buzo's dual-voiced *Love and Other Perishable Objects*. Having two voices allows both Amelia and Chris to give insight into how they grow to need and appreciate one another. Likewise, both Standiford's book and Buzo's are less about a significant event happening and more about a slice of life. They're character-driven narratives.

Vivian, Siobhan. *Not That Kind of Girl*. Push, 2011. 336p. $9.99 Trade pb. 978-0-545-16916-5.

Natalie's driven. She's the girl who worked hard to become class president since the minute she got into high school. She's the girl who will graduate at the top of her class and the girl who will go on to a top college. She's not the kind of girl who will ruin her life by getting involved with any boys. But it's not just *her* mission: Natalie wants to make sure no other girls hurt themselves by becoming "victims" of relationships with boys. Her best friend Autumn was burned to the point she's earned a terrible nickname she can't shed, and Natalie can't let others have that happen to them. When Natalie stops a freshman named Spencer from exposing herself too much at school, all Spencer wants to do is act the opposite of Natalie's warning. She wants to be around and near boys – and she wants to be around Natalie because they not only share a little bit of history, but because Natalie is the kind of girl that Spencer might aspire to be in terms of success, recognition, and power at school. What happens when Natalie's world comes crumbling down because she meets Conner? After her insistence that boys are worthless and not to be fussed with in high school, it's possible she needs to reevaluate her stance and allow good boy Conner to become part of her life. Despite her insistence on knowing what's best for herself and every other girl, Natalie may come to learn that being a strong, independent girl isn't about swearing off other people but rather, allowing herself to see what it is anyone can bring to a relationship.

Appeal Factors

- Female main character
- Friendship
- Peer relationships

- Romance
- Sexuality

Read Alikes

- Feminism and the definition of what it is to be a strong girl are themes that Vivian explores in all of her titles, and these themes are explored in light of what it means to be and to have a friend in *Not That Kind of Girl*. For readers who haven't explored Vivian's other titles but like what she does in this book would be well-served by reading her other contemporary titles. Her books challenge the notion that there is only one way to be right or one way to be a girl.

- Even though Natalie swears off boys initially, her voice is reminiscent of Jessica Darling. Readers who haven't read Megan McCafferty's series, beginning with *Sloppy Firsts*, would find these strong novels to follow Vivian's.

- In terms of voice, style, and depth of character, as well as the development and exploration of interpersonal relationships, readers would find Vivian's novels strong read alikes to Sarah Dessen and Jenny Han.

Vivian, Siobhan. *The List*. Push, 2012. 336p. $17.99. 978-0-545-16917-2.

Every year at Mt. Washington High School during Homecoming week, an anonymous list is posted that names the prettiest and the ugliest girls in each class (freshman, sophomore, junior, and senior). Getting on the list is a status for these girls, regardless of which side of the list they're found on. What happens to these eight girls differs, but they all share one thing: the way they're treated by everyone else at school changes. More than that, earning a spot on the list ensures the girls will be unable to stop reflecting on themselves and evaluating what it means to be considered the prettiest or the ugliest girl around.

Appeal Factors

- Body image
- Disordered eating
- Female main characters
- Friendship

- Health and well-being
- Multiple points of view
- Peer relationships

Read Alikes

- Kody Keplinger's *The DUFF* is told only through one point of view, but Bianca's voice will be reminiscent of many of the voices in Vivian's novel. Both books home in on what it means to be pretty or ugly and what that status may or may not mean in terms of friends, peers, and romantic relationships.

◼ More Titles Exploring Friendships and Peer Relationships

Avasthi, Swati. *Chasing Shadows*. Knopf Books, 2013. 320p. $17.99. 978-0-3758-6342-4.

Blazanin, Jan. *A & L Do Summer*. EgmontUSA, 2011. 288p. $8.99 Trade pb. 978-1-60684-191-4.

Bock, Caroline. *Before My Eyes*. St. Martin's Griffin, 2014. 304p. $18.99. 978-1-2500-4558-4.

Cameron, Emma. *Out of This Place*. Candlewick, 2013. 416p. $17.99. 978-0-7636-6404-6.

Cartern Caela. *My Best Friend, Maybe*. Bloomsbury, 2014. 352p. $17.99. 978-1-5999-0970-7.

Haas, Abigail. *Dangerous Girls*. Simon Pulse, 2014. 400p. $9.99 Trade pb. 978-1-4442-8660-7.

Halpern, Julie. *Into the Wild Nerd Yonder*. Square Fish, 2011. 272p. $8.99 Trade pb. 978-0-312-65307-1.

Harbison, Paige. *Anything to Have You*. Harlequin Teen, 2014. 304p. $9.99 Trade pb. 978-0-3732-1088-6.

Hassan, Michael. *Crash and Burn*. Balzar & Bray, 2013. 544p. $18.99. 978-0-06-211290-3.

Kantor, Melissa. *The Darlings Are Forever*. Hyperion, 2011. 352p. $16.99. 978-1-4231-2368-2. (First title in *The Darlings* series)

Lange, Erin Jade. *Butter*. Bloomsbury, 2012. 320p. $17.99. 978-1-59990-780-2.

Matson, Morgan. *Since You've Been Gone*. Simon & Schuster, 2014. 400p. $17.99. 978-1-4442-3500-1.

Oates, Joyce Carol. *Two or Three Things I Forgot to Tell You*. HarperTeen, 2013. 288p. $17.99. 978-0-06-211047-3.

Oliver, Lauren. *Panic*. HarperCollins, 2014. 416p. $17.99. 978-0-0620-1455-9.

Philbin, Joanna. *The Daughters*. Poppy, 2010. 275p. $16.99. 978-0-316-04900-9. (First title in *The Daughters* series)

Rapp, Adam. *The Children and the Wolves*. Candlewick, 2012. 160p. $16.99. 978-0-7636-5337-8.

Sales, Leila. *This Song Will Save Your Life*. Farrar, Straus and Giroux, 2013. 288p. $17.99. 978-0-374-35138-0.

Smith, Andrew. *Winger*. Simon and Schuster, 2013. 448p. $18.99. 978-1-4442-4492-8.

Smith, Kirsten. *Trinkets*. Little, Brown, 2014. 288p. $10.00. Trade pb. 978-0-3160-6773-7.

Strasnick, Lauren. *Then You Were Gone*. Simon Pulse, 2014. 272p. $9.99 Trade pb. 978-1-4442-2716-7.

Summers, Courtney. *Some Girls Are*. St. Martin's Griffin, 2010. 256p. $9.99 Trade pb. 978-0-312-57380-5.

Woodson, Jacqueline. *After Tupac and D Foster*. Puffin, 2010. 176p. $9.99 Trade pb. 978-0-14-241399-9.

Zarr, Sara and Tara Altebrando. *Roomies*. Little, Brown, 2013. 288p. $18.00. 978-0-3162-1749-1.

Zeitlin, Meredith. *Freshman Year & Other Unnatural Disasters*. Putnam, 2012. 288p. $16.99. 978-0-399-25423-9.

Chapter 10

Grief, Loss, and Moving Forward

Every year, I challenge my students to read forty books over the course of the school year, a la Donalyn Miller. This elicits a chorus and moans and groans from my high-achieving but math and science-loving students. And causing even more consternation is the fact that I require them to read from a variety of genres. Those who do read usually prefer nonfiction, science fiction, and fantasy. When they see realistic fiction on the list they try to figure out ways to avoid it. For most of my students, realistic contemporary fiction is usually viewed as boring. Or even worse, their parents ask them not to read it because they think it is a waste of their time. For some reason, contemporary YA seems to equal soap opera in their eyes. But I stock my classroom library with plenty of contemporary YA and I book talk great titles each week. Slowly but surely, my students start to connect with contemporary YA.

At the end of the year I survey my students. Last year, when I asked them to list a book that all incoming freshmen should be required to read, I received dozens of suggestions and explanations. But my favorite suggestion said, "I would recommend It's Kind of a Funny Story *[by Ned Vizzini] since Craig's whole storyline, with his depression and almost-suicide, directly relates to the stress that he gained from his attending a highly challenging high school and focusing so much on succeeding. While I don't think our school could stress anyone out enough to want to die, this book sends a good message to not worry so much on grades and at succeeding*

on the Typical Successive Things (enough money, good college, etc.) but to focus more on what makes you happy." Wow! That's what every teacher hopes that a student gets from a book. Contemporary YA lets students connect with characters like themselves or nothing like them. They can safely explore new ideas, new places, and new identities. They can contemplate possibilities beyond their home and their town.
– Sarah Gross, high school teacher

If there's anything about grief that's universal, it's that grief is one of the most non-universal emotions. People experience it on their own terms. Sometimes it's fairly straightforward, with an outward manifestation of sadness and other times, it's anything but obvious. Grief combines sadness and anger, stress and frustration, as well as loss and loneliness in ways that force individuals to work through at their own pace and in their own unique way. Each way of experiencing grief is the right way, as each way pushes an individual to work toward healing and resolve.

The titles in this booklist explore grief differently. There are titles taking it head-on, with grief pouring from characters because of an immediate loss to them, be it of a family member or close friend. Then there are titles where the grieving is not only about loss of another person but also about the loss of something internal and personal. One of the interesting elements that ties many of these books together, though, is that of mystery – why is it someone is gone? These stories feature characters hoping for a solid answer to that question, even if it's a question that can never be answered.

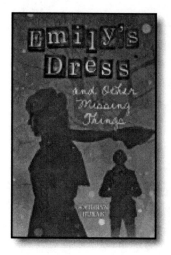

Burak, Kathryn. ***Emily's Dress and Other Missing Things***. Roaring Brook, 2012. 240p. $17.99. 978-1-59643-736-4.

Claire and her father just moved to Amherst, Massachusetts, home of Emily Dickinson. But this isn't a happy move. In the last year, Claire's mother died and her best friend Richie went missing – and Claire may or may not hold the key to his disappearance. This move is meant to help her heal from her losses. It's tough for Claire to adjust to her new life, but one of her teachers is helping her by engaging her in serious discussion of literature and other intellectual challenges. Claire takes sanctuary at the Amherst Museum, among the Dickinson ephemera. Being surrounded by Emily's spirit is calming and comforting. One night, Claire can't help herself and she takes off with one of the museum's dresses. Now she's not only a suspect in Richie's disappearance; she's also a criminal. But it's her teacher who may help her come to grips with the theft and in unlocking the truth to where Richie went.

Appeal Factors

- Female main character
- Grief
- Literary writing
- Moving
- Making new friends
- Mystery
- Romance

Read Alikes

- Mary O'Connell's *The Sharp Time* makes for a strong read alike for the way that both O'Connell's main character and Burak's throw themselves into a new passion to work through the grieving process. Both novels lean more literary, and both tackle losing a mother through the eyes of a daughter.

- Though it doesn't tackle grief in quite the same capacity, Sara Zarr's *The Lucy Variations* contains a number of similar elements to Burak's, including a relationship between a high school student and her teacher. Although both books tiptoe around romance (and whether these are romantic relationships is left to the interpretation of the reader), each explores the mentoring and healing relationship that can evolve between a student and her teacher.

Castle, Jennifer. *The Beginning of After*. Harper Teen, 2011. 432p. $17.99. 978-0-06-198579-9.

Laurel divides her life into two halves: before and after. Before, Laurel's family had just finished a celebratory dinner with David's family. Before, she and David decided that they weren't going to join their families on a trip out for something sweet. But now it's after. After the car accident that took the entirety of Laurel's family and David's family, except for his father. The accident had no discernible cause, and the only person who could offer insight into what happened is David's unconscious father. Now, despite Laurel and David's differences and the years of distance between them, they find the only comfort they have to work through their losses and struggles is through each other.

Appeal Factors

- Accidents
- Family relationships
- Female main character
- Grief
- Romance
- Significant pets or animals

Read Alikes

- Readers who enjoyed Gayle Forman's *If I Stay* will want to try Castle's novel for the devastating and sudden loss of family. While Castle's novel is less cerebral, Forman fans will appreciate and see similarities between Mia and Laurel's grief and acceptance. Both books explore the ugly sides of grief and loss and what happens to relationships that once seemed solid.

Doller, Trish. *Something Like Normal*. Bloomsbury, 2012. 224p. $16.99. 978-1-59990-844-1. $9.99 Trade pb. 978-1-61963-146-5.

Nineteen-year-old Travis, on leave from the Marines, comes home to parents who are on the brink of divorce; an ex-girlfriend who is dating his brother; and Harper, a girl who blames Travis for giving her a reputation which isn't true. Worse, Travis regularly re-lives the pain of watching his best military friend Charlie die. When he has to confront his grief head-on at Charlie's memorial service, he not only has to work through the loss, but he's forced to come to terms with and work through his worsening Post-Traumatic Stress Disorder symptoms.

Appeal Factors

- Fort Myers
- Grief
- Male main character
- Mental illness
- Military

- Post-high school setting
- Post-traumatic stress disorder
- Romance
- War

Read Alikes

- Three recent titles tackling military themes in conjunction with grief and loss that would make excellent next reads include *If I Lie* by Corrine Jackson, *In Honor* by Jessi Kirby, and *Personal Effects* by E. M. Kokie. Even though they share similar topics, the ways in which each book approaches how the characters grieve and work through mental anguish puts them in a unique conversation with one another and highlights the truth that there is no one way to experience loss.

- Readers who enjoy Travis's voice will want to try C. K. Kelly Martin's *I Know It's Over*. Nick, the main character in Martin's novel, is also working through grief, though his is over the ending of a romantic relationship that's made complicated by an unexpected pregnancy. The voice and perspective of Nick rings similarly to Travis's.

- For another story about working through loss from the post-high school male point of view, try Daisy Whitney's *When You Were Here*.

Freitas, Donna. *The Survival Kit*. Farrar Straus Giroux, 2011. 368p. $16.99. 978-0-374-39917-7.

Shortly after her mother dies from cancer, Rose discovers a brown paper bag in her mom's closet labeled "Rose's Survival Kit." She can't bring herself to open it. It's not too long after that Rose's long-term relationship with boyfriend Chris ends. It's not because she can't get over losing her mom; it's just a matter of how relationships fall apart. But in the space following the breakup, Rose discovers Will. For a long time, he was nobody but the boy hired by Rose's family to take care of the yard. Now she can't stop thinking about him. When she and Will bond over shared experiences, including loss, Rose finally has the courage to open the survival kit her mother made for her. In it, Rose finds not only a way to work through her grief, but a way to better understand who she is and where she should go from here.

Appeal Factors

- Cancer
- Depression and anxiety
- Female main character
- Friendship

- Grief
- Hockey
- Music
- Romance

Read Alikes

- Dana Reinhardt's *The Things a Brother Knows* will resonate for the family storyline, as well as tone and story execution.

- Although Freitas's novel doesn't include a road trip, the story of a grieving girl and a boy who may or may not become a boyfriend is reminiscent of Morgan Matson's *Amy & Roger's Epic Detour*. Both Freitas and Matson's stories explore the highs and lows of grief, and both make use of a series of objects and experiences to help the grieving character move forward.

- For the strong female lead who learns to see people differently over the course of her story, readers should try Siobhan Vivian's books for similar characters, including *Same Difference* and *Not That Kind of Girl*.

Harrington, Hannah. *Saving June*. Harlequin, 2011. 336p. $9.99 Trade pb. 978-0-373-21024-4.

Harper's sister June killed herself. June had always been the good sister – she was pretty, had good grades, and made plenty of friends. It doesn't make sense why she'd want to die, especially one week short of her high school graduation. Harper's parents, who are on the brink of divorce, are going to split their deceased daughter's remains, but Harper doesn't see that a fitting end to June's life. Instead, she and best friend Laney decide they're going to drive to California and spread June's ashes in the place she always wanted to go. They won't take this trip alone, though. Jake, a guy who claims to know a secret or two about June, wants to join them. Who is Harper to stop him, especially when he might be able to shed insight into June's choice of committing suicide?

Appeal Factors

- Family relationships
- Female main character
- Grief
- Music

- Road trip
- Romance
- Siblings
- Suicide

Read Alikes

- For those who enjoyed the aspect of dealing with grief via a road trip, *Amy & Roger's Epic Detour* by Morgan Matson is a strong next read.

- Readers taken with Harper's intelligent, curious, and yet vulnerable voice will want to try *And Then Things Fall Apart* by Arlaina Tibensky. Tibensky's main character and Harrington's share similar structures in working through challenging and confusing family issues.

- The suicide aspect of Harrington's story – why June chose to end her own life and the mysteries surrounding that choice – make *Fall for Anything* by Courtney Summers a strong read alike, as well.

Hubbard, Jennifer R. *The Secret Year*. Speak, 2010. 208p. $7.99 pb. 978-0-14-241779-9.

Colt and Julia are from opposite sides of the mountain – literally. Julia is from the top of Black Mountain, where the rich families live, and Colt is from the bottom of Black Mountain, where the less-wealthy reside. Despite their differences and despite the fact Julia has a boyfriend, she and Colt were seeing one another romantically. No one else knew. When Julia dies in a car accident, Colt can't grieve openly, and it tears him apart inside. Especially because he fears he played a role in her death.

Appeal Factors

- Accidents
- Grief
- Gritty
- Male main character

- Romance
- Sexuality
- Socioeconomic class

Read Alikes

- For the romantic aspects of the story – including the secretive elements – as well as both the exploration of social class and the gritty realism, both the *Perfect Chemistry* and *Leaving Paradise* series by Simone Elkeles are strong read alikes.

- Hubbard's second novel, *Try Not to Breathe*, also makes for a good next pick, as it delves into grief, with a hint of romance between a boy and a girl both working through their own losses.

Kokie, E. M. *Personal Effects*. Candlewick, 2012. 352p. $16.99. 978-0-7636-5527-3.

Matt's brother TJ died serving overseas, and now, TJ's personal effects have returned in the form of a couple of footlockers. Matt's father wants nothing to do with them, but Matt can't help himself. When he opens the lockers, Matt's in for more than he expected when he discovers a series of letters signed by someone named Celia, along with photos of a little girl. Now Matt wonders if all he knew about TJ was wrong. Was he married and had a baby before he was called to service? Matt decides to get in his car and make the trip to Madison, Wisconsin, to seek out this mysterious Celia. When he gets there, though, what Matt learns about TJ is far more than what he expects, and it might make the process of healing from his loss even tougher.

Appeal Factors

- Family relationships
- Friendship
- Grief
- LGBTQ
- Male main character

- Military
- Road trip
- Siblings
- War

Read Alikes

- For working through the loss of a brother following his military service, readers will want to try *In Honor* by Jessi Kirby. Though told through the voice of the deceased's sister, the road trip element serves as a means of working through grief in both stories.

- Both *Something Like Normal* by Trish Doller and *The Things a Brother Knows* share the military service elements with Kokie's novel. Each also explores grief and the ups and downs of family relationships, especially as loss settles in.

- Perhaps the biggest element of Kokie's novel is that of TJ's sexuality. Readers curious about the implications of being gay and serving in the military will want to try *If I Lie* by Corrine Jackson.

LaCour, Nina. *Hold Still*. Pulse, 2010. 256p. $8.99. 978-0-14-241694-5.

Caitlin's best friend Ingrid killed herself. She left a diary behind, and for Caitlin, the diary is comforting and a way of seeing into the mind of someone who so desperately wanted to get away that she chose suicide. The letter Ingrid left Caitlin personally inside the diary sheds insight when it proclaims that, no matter how badly she wants to know, Caitlin can and will never learn the truth. Ingrid's mental illness kept her hurting. Armed with a stronger understanding of the depths to which Ingrid suffered mentally, Caitlin is better able to process the loss and be there for others who may need her.

Book Trailer

http://youtu.be/_XYJQa4u2jQ

Appeal Factors

- Artistic expression
- Depression and anxiety
- Female main character
- Friendship
- Grief

- Literary writing
- Mental illness
- Photography
- Suicide

Read Alikes

- *13 Reasons Why* by Jay Asher, *34 Pieces of You* by Carmen Rodrigues, and *I Swear* by Lane Davis all make strong read alikes for the way a surviving character attempts to unravel the reasons behind a departed character's suicide. Each book contains the pieces of a life that are strung back together in an attempt to understand why.

- Readers interested in the emotional complexity of mental disorders, as well as the grieving experience over the loss of a best friend, will want to read *Wintergirls* by Laurie Halse Anderson.

Matson, Morgan. *Second Chance Summer*. Simon & Schuster, 2012. 480p. $16.99. 978-1-4169-9067-3.

Taylor's father has a terminal cancer diagnosis, but her family has decided it's important to spend one last summer together as a whole at their summer home in the Poconos. It's been five years since the last time Taylor was there, and now she wants to patch up the relationships between her former best friend and the boy who may or may not be her boyfriend. More than that, though, this is the summer Taylor has to learn how to accept goodbye as something permanent.

Appeal Factors

- Cancer
- Family relationships
- Female main character
- Friendship
- Grief
- Romance
- Summer story

Read Alikes

- This book is a near-perfect match for Sarah Dessen fans, as Matson's story delves deep into interpersonal relationships. Taylor's voice is reminiscent of many of the voices in Dessen's novels, and the way setting plays a crucial role in character development will appeal to readers.

- Readers who want another story about grief with a strong and memorable setting will want to read Jessi Kirby's *Moonglass*.

Nelson, Jandy. *The Sky Is Eveywhere*. Speak, 2011. 304p. $8.99. 978-0-14-241780-5.

Lennie's older sister Bailey was always the fiery one. She had the boys and the social recognition while Lennie lived more quietly, happy as a bookworm and second clarinet in the school orchestra. When Bailey dies suddenly, Lennie's life is turned upside down. It's not just that she's lost her sister. In the wake of Bailey's death, Lennie's suddenly found herself the interest of two boys, Joe and Toby. Joe's the boy everyone thinks Lennie should pursue, but Toby has her interest more tightly. Toby was Bailey's former boyfriend – at least, that's what everyone thought. The truth is, Toby was Bailey's former fiance and the father to the baby

Bailey never had. It's not romantic companionship Lennie really wants. It's someone with whom to grieve in the honest way she needs.

Book Trailer

http://youtu.be/Yqim02tVu3U

Appeal Factors

- Artistic expression
- Female main character
- Grief
- Literary writing

- Music
- Non-traditional families
- Romance
- Siblings

Read Alikes

- A strong next read might be *Adios, Nirvana* by Conrad Wosselhoeft for the similarities in grieving a lost sibling, as well as the use of poetry by the main character to work through loss.
- Readers who enjoy the way a main character shares and experiences her loss with the significant other of the deceased will want to try *Then You Were Gone* by Lauren Strasnick.

Scott, Mindi. *Freefall*. Simon Pulse, 2010. 336p. $8.99. 978-1-4442-0278-2.

Seth and Isaac always partied, always drank. But this was the time when Isaac drank a little too much, passed out, and never woke up again. Now Seth is rattled with grief and guilt. He should have stopped Isaac sooner, should have known this lifestyle would eventually hurt them. Now that Isaac is dead, Seth has to choose whether to sober up and get his own life together or throw in the towel and let his addictions do to him what they did to his best friend. It's Rosetta, a girl who has her own challenges, who steps in and shows Seth that it is possible to move forward.

Appeal Factors

- Alcohol addiction
- Friendship
- Grief
- Humor

- Male main character
- Music
- Romance
- Socioeconomic class

Read Alikes

- For the strong and memorable male narrator who is working through immense grief, readers will want to try *Adios, Nirvana* by Conrad Wosselhoeft.

- Another worthwhile read alike is *The Spectacular Now* by Tim Tharp for the way the male narrator is voiced, as well as the themes of partying and drinking and their effects on the character's life and decision-making.

Strasnick, Lauren. *Then You Were Gone*. Simon Pulse, 2013. 272p. $16.99. 978-1-4424-2715-0.

It's been two years since Adrienne and Dakota have been best friends, but Dakota's sudden disappearance sends Adrienne into a tailspin. Everyone in town assumes Dakota's rough-and-tumble lifestyle is the reason she went missing and is presumed dead. Adrienne refuses to believe that, though, and she's doing everything within her power to keep the spirit of Dakota alive. If she can channel enough of Dakota's spirit and energy, then maybe, just maybe, Dakota will come back from wherever she went. But is Adrienne's ache enough to make Dakota return? And what role did Dakota's last boyfriend play in all of this?

Appeal Factors

- Female main character
- Friendship
- Grief
- Mystery

- Non-traditional families
- Romance
- Sparse writing

Read Alikes

- Strasnick's novel makes for an excellent read alike to *Like Mandarin* by Kirsten Hubbard, for the intense female friendship theme. Though Hubbard's title doesn't tackle grief, the focus on interpersonal relationships mirrors that in Strasnick's book.

Summers, Courtney. *Fall For Anything*. St. Martin's Griffin, 2010. 224p. $9.99 Trade pb. 978-0-312-65673-7.

Eddie Reeves wants to know why her father, a well-respected photographer and teacher, killed himself. When she meets Culler, one of her father's former students, Eddie can't pull herself away from him, even if the attraction to Culler is dangerous. The further he draws her into his world, one he promises will shed light into her father's life, the more vulnerable Eddie becomes. As Eddie wrestles with her grief, it becomes clear that there's no real answer to her father's death and putting her hope for an answer on someone else might be more risky than she bargained for.

Book Trailer

http://youtu.be/0UNDoouMZd0

Appeal Factors

- Artistic expression
- Family relationships
- Female main character
- Friendship
- Grief

- Mystery
- Photography
- Sparse writing
- Suicide

Read Alikes

- Summers's novel is comparable to *The Sky is Everywhere* by Jandy Nelson for the literary approach to loss. Both Nelson and Summers weave art and the meaning of creative pursuit in the way their characters seek solace.

- Readers who are drawn in by the mystery surrounding unexplained death and suicide will want to read *Saving June* by Hannah Harrington and Nina LaCour's *Hold Still*. All three stories explore whether or not finding an answer to the question of why is worthwhile and whether or not there can be an answer at all.

Wesselhoeft, Conrad. *Adios, Nirvana*. Graphia, 2012. 240p. $7.99 Trade pb. 978-0-547-57725-8.

Jonathan becomes a wreck when his twin brother Telly dies. He can't get himself together and everything he had passion for suddenly becomes uninteresting to him. Last year, Jonathan won the honor of Best Young Poet in Washington. This year, he can hardly show up to class, let alone write poetry or perform music with his guitar. Jonathan's in danger of repeating junior year until his principal intervenes: Jonathan can pass if he writes the life story of David, a local World War II veteran on his last days at the local hospice. Hanging out with a guy on the brink of death is the last thing Jonathan wants to do, but as he embarks on the trip, he comes to better understand the importance of loss and tragedy and how they help in developing a sense of self. It may just give him the courage and knowledge he needs to write and perform once again.

Appeal Factors

- Accidents
- Artistic expression
- Family relationships
- Grief
- Intergenerational stories

- Male main character
- Music
- Poetry
- Seattle
- Siblings

Read Alikes

- A strong read alike for this novel is *The Sky is Everywhere* by Jandy Nelson for tackling the loss of a sibling, as well as the incorporation of writing and poetry as healing art.

- Readers who enjoy the male voice may want to try Mindi Scott's *Freefall*, which also tackles grief and loss, though it's of a friend, rather than a sibling.

- For those readers who are interested in reading backlist titles, it's hard not to compare Wesselhoeft's novel to Rob Thomas's classic *Rats Saw God*. Both feature grief, tackle friendship and growth, and both are infused with music. The male voice of Steve York will resonate with readers who connect with Wesselhoeft's Jonathan.

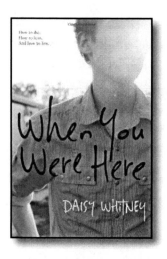

Whitney, Daisy. *When You Were Here*. Little, Brown, 2013. 257p. $17.99. 978-0-316-20974-8.

Danny's mom had one goal before she died: to see him give his valedictorian speech at high school graduation. But she dies before she has the chance. As Danny approaches the podium to deliver that speech without his mom there, he loses his cool, tells everyone that nothing matters, and leaves. At eighteen, he has to choose where to go from here. Without a parent and with an absent half-sister, as well as a girlfriend who dumped him mysteriously, he is entirely free to follow whatever path he chooses. He decides to spend the summer in the family's Tokyo vacation home as a means of determining what's next. While abroad, Danny discovers the secrets of what kept his mother happy in her final days, despite having her final wish unfilled. He also uncovers the truth behind his girlfriend's sudden departure. Armed with the knowledge of both, Danny is able to put himself on a path toward acceptance and the future opening widely before him.

Appeal Factors

- Cancer
- Foreign setting
- Grief
- Male main character
- Japan
- Post-high school setting
- Romance
- Teen pregnancy
- Significant pets or animals

Read Alikes

- Readers interested in exploring grief while abroad, as well as the impact of adventure and new friendships during the healing process, will want to read Tammar Stein's *High Dive*.

- For the emotional – though not out of character – male voice, try *Where She Went* by Gayle Forman. Both Whitney and Forman write about the post-high school boy and how he can struggle with romance in the midst of significant loss.

More Books Exploring Grief and Loss

Ackley, Amy. *Sign Language*. Viking, 2011. 392p. $16.99. 978-0-316-03605-4.

Arcos, Carrie. *There Will Come A Time*. Simon Pulse, 2014. 256p. $17.99. 978-1-4424-9585-2.

Avasthi, Swati. *Chasing Shadows*. Knopf, 2013. 320p. $17.99. 978-0-375-86342-4.

Brown, Jennifer. *Torn Away*. Little, Brown, 2014. 288p. $18. 978-0-3162-4553-1.

Cook, Eileen. *Year of Mistaken Discoveries*. Simon Pulse, 2014. 272p. $17.99. 978-1-4424-4022-7.

Cupala, Holly. *Tell Me A Secret*. HarperTeen, 2011. 304p. $16.99. 978-0-06-176666-4.

Dale, Katie. *Someone Else's Life*. Delacorte, 2012. 464p. $17.99. 978-0-385-74065-4.

Dellaria, Ava. *Love Letters to the Dead*. Farrar, Straus and Giroux, 2014. 336p. $17.99. 978-0-3743-4667-6.

Harmel, Kristin. *After*. Delacorte, 2010. 240p. $16.99. 978-0-385-73476-9.

Horner, Emily. *A Love Story Starring My Dead Best Friend*. Dial, 2010. 272p. $16.99. 978-0-8037-3420-3.

Howard, Leila. *Nantucket Blue*. Hyperion, 2013. 304p. $16.99. 978-1-4231-6051-9.

Howard, J. J. *That Time I Joined the Circus*. Point, 2013. 272p. $16.99. 978-0-545-43381-5.

Hubbard, Jennifer R. *Try Not to Breathe*. Speak, 2013. 256p. $8.99. 978-0-14-242387-5.

Jackson, Corrine. *If I Lie*. Simon Pulse, 2012. 288p. $16.99. 978-1-4424-5413-2.

Jaden, Denise. *Losing Faith*. Simon Pulse, 2010. 400p. $9.99 Trade pb. 978-1-4169-9609-5.

Jarzab, Anna. *The Opposite of Hallelujah*. Delacorte, 2012. 464p. $16.99. 978-0-385-73836-1.

Johnson, Angela. *A Certain October*. Simon & Schuster, 2012. 176p. $16.99. 978-0-689-86505-3.

Johnson, J. J. *The Theory of Everything*. Peachtree, 2012. 334p. $16.95. 978-1-56145-623-9.

King, A. S. *Please Ignore Vera Dietz*. Ember, 2012. 326p. $9.99 Trade pb. 978-0-375-86564-0.

Matson, Morgan. *Amy and Roger's Epic Detour*. Simon & Schuster, 2011. 336p. $9.99 Trade pb. 978-1-4169-9066-6.

McBride, Kristina. *One Moment*. Egmont USA, 2012. 272p. $17.99. 978-1-60684-086-3.

McCall, Guadalupe Garcia. *Under the Mesquite*. Lee & Low, 2011. 224p. $17.95. 978-1-60060-429-4.

McNamara, Amy. *Lovely, Dark and Deep*. Simon & Schuster, 2012. 352p. $16.99. 978-1-4424-3435-6.

O'Connell, Mary. *The Sharp Time*. Delacorte, 2011. 240p. $17.99. 978-0-385-74048-7.

Pixley, Marcella. *Without Tess*. Farrar Straus Giroux, 2011. 288p. $16.99. 978-0-374-36174-7.

Quick, Matthew. *Sorta Like a Rock Star*. Little, Brown, 2011. 355p. $8.99. 978-0-316-04353-3.

Schutz, Samantha. *You Are Not Here*. Push, 2012. 304p. $9.99 Trade pb. 978-0-545-16912-7.

Scott, Elizabeth. *Heartbeat*. Harlequin Teen, 2014. 304p. $16.99. 978-0-373-21096-1.

Sheinmel, Alyssa. *The Beautiful Between*. Ember, 2011. 192p. $7.99 Trade pb. 978-0-375-85473-6.

Skilton, Sarah. *Bruised*. Amulet, 2013. 288p. $16.95. 978-1-4197-0387-4.

Thompson, Holly. *The Language Inside*. Delacorte, 2013. 528p. $17.99. 978-0-385-73979-5.

Wakefield, Vikki. *Friday Never Leaving*. Simon & Schuster, 2013. 352p. $16.99. 978-1-4224-8652-2.

Watkins, Steve. *What Comes After*. Candlewick, 2011. 334p. $16.99. 978-0-7636-4250-1.

Wiess, Laura. *Me Since You*. MTV Books, 2014. 368p. $10.99 Trade pb. 978-1-4391-9397-6.

Williams, Carol Lynch. *Waiting*. Simon & Schuster, 2013. 352p. $9.99. 978-1-4424-4354-9.

Woolston, Blythe. *The Freak Observer*. Carolrhoda, 2012. 202p. $9.95. 978-0-7613-8132-7.

Zarr, Sara. *How to Save a Life*. Little, Brown, 2012. 368p. $8.99. 978-0-316-03605-4.

Chapter 11

Health and Well-Being:
Navigating Physical and Mental Turbulence

I write contemporary YA because I find the real world magical and confusing and frustrating and wonderful. There is so much I want to examine and challenge and admire. For me, the best way to make sense of all the things that puzzle/thrill/horrify me is by exploring them in fiction. – Tiffany Schmidt, author of *Send Me a Sign* and *Bright before Sunrise*

With adolescence comes a particular flavor of physical and mental self-awareness. It's no surprise there is an abundance of books that explore when physical and mental things don't go quite like they're supposed to go. Contemporary fiction delves into those places of discomfort because these are real issues today's teens tackle, be it learning they've been newly diagnosed with cancer and will be enduring chemotherapy just to survive or accepting that they've got an eating disorder and they need help to get through it. But more than simply being stories that are prescriptive or meant to serve as warnings for teens, these stories are about the characters involved. It's about the entirety of their being and their personhood, not just about their diagnosis. These books are important because they're reminders about the very human consequences and triumphs that come with owning and operating a physical body.

The books on this list include mental wellness as much as they include physical wellness. They explore the difficulties and challenges that come through addiction, eating disorders, leukemia diagnosis, life-altering car accidents, post-traumatic stress disorder, and more. Some of these books are tearjerkers, while others aren't. Some of these books push their health and wellness aspects to the foreground while others use it as an impetus to explore other elements in the story, including relationships between friends and family.

Bick, Ilsa J. ***Drowning Instinct***. Carolrhoda, 2012. 352p. $17.95. 978-0-7613-7752-8. $9.95. Trade pb. 978-1-4677-0912-5.

Jenna Lord's given a voice recorder and informed by the detective working on her case that it's now her job to tell the whole story from the beginning. He needs to know how she ended up in the hospital, and she is the only person who can tell him. Jenna's been a student at Turing Academy for the last few months. She was sent there following treatment for the scars and burns covering her body. Some of those marks are her own doing. While attending Turing, Jenna turns her sights onto one of her teachers and he reciprocates. It's not long before suddenly, Jenna's self-injuring is less about the cuts she delivers on her skin and more about the way she seeks solace in the relationship between herself and her teacher.

Appeal Factors

- Abuse
- Depression and anxiety
- Family relationships
- Female main character
- Grief

- Intergenerational stories
- Mental illness
- Self-injury and self-harm
- Sexual violence

Read Alikes

- This is a dark and gritty novel that does not hold back. Readers who appreciate the candid nature of books by Laurie Halse Anderson, Ellen Hopkins, Amy Reed, and Courtney Summers will find much to appreciate here.

- Readers drawn in by the nature of a taboo relationship between a student and a teacher will want to check out Tabitha Suzuma's *Forbidden*, which explores a taboo incestuous relationship. For another story about a student-teacher relationship, try Barry Lyga's *Boy Toy*.

- Because self-injury is a theme in this book, readers will want to check out Erin Saldin's *The Girls of No Return*. Both Bick and Saldin's books also explore how a character removes herself from the self-harm mentally and how she chooses instead to fixate on other objects to release the feelings for which cutting was once used.

Bostic, Megan. ***Never Eighteen***. Graphia, 2012. 204p. $9.99. Trade pb. 978-0-547-55076-3.

Seventeen-year-old Austin has terminal cancer and knows his life is nearing the end. This weekend, along with his best friend Kaylee, Austin plans on doing all of the things on his bucket list, including having the conversations with people he's been meaning to have but keeps putting off. This trip isn't just about making peace with the world around him; it's also about making peace with himself and with his relationship with Kaylee. How will she react knowing his deep-held crush on her, especially with the reality that Austin might not be alive much longer to act upon his feelings toward her.

Appeal Factors

- Cancer
- Family relationships
- Fast pacing
- Friendship
- Grief
- Male main character
- Road trip
- Romance
- Seattle

Read Alikes

- Although Bostic's novel tackles the end of life from the perspective of someone still alive, there are many parallels to Jay Asher's *13 Reasons Why* and Carmen Rodrigues's *34 Pieces of Me*. In Asher and Rodrigues's novels, the last thoughts and comments from someone who committed suicide are explored by those who were connected to the deceased. Readers seeking stories about relationships impacted by death and the moments leading to it will find much in common among these titles. All three also share swift pacing and short time frames through which the story is told, making them page turners.

Cooner, Donna. *Skinny*. Point, 2012. 272p. $17.99. 978-0-545-42763-0.

Fifteen-year-old Ever is fat. Three hundred pounds fat. After losing her mother, Ever turned to food for comfort. It only became worse when her father began a relationship with a new woman and Ever found herself with a new family she never wanted. Ever's weight struggle isn't just about the way she looks on the outside; it's also about the voice inside her head she's named Skinny. That voice tells her all the time she's not good enough nor will she ever be good enough. When Ever decides she can't take it any longer, she makes a big decision: the only way to rid herself of her weight and that voice is through gastric bypass surgery. But will changing how she looks on the outside make Skinny go away? Will surgery make it easier to fit in at school or with the new family she's inherited?

Book Trailer

http://youtu.be/k4rZSAF1qcQ

Appeal Factors

- Body image
- Female main character
- Gastric bypass surgery
- Grief
- Non-traditional families
- Obesity
- Peer relationships

Read Alikes

- Cooner's book delves into the decision a teen makes when it comes to her own body and when it comes to choosing the surgical option of gastric bypass for weight loss. Susan Vaught's *My Big Fat*

Manifesto features an overweight female main character, and her boyfriend, also overweight, who chooses the option of gastric bypass to help him with his weight control.

- Readers who want to get inside the head of an obese character who also struggles with grief and significant changes in family dynamics will find many similarities in K. M. Walton's *Empty*. It's worth mentioning that Walton's novel is much bleaker in resolution than Cooner's.

Hassan, Michael. ***Crash and Burn***. Balzar & Bray/HarperTeen, 2013. 544p. $18.99. 978-0-06-211290-3.

Steve Crashinsky (Crash) is the only person who is able to stop David Burnett (Burn) from holding the entire school hostage. But the boys aren't friends. In fact, it's been a long time since they've even talked to one another, despite the fact they have a long and complicated history and relationship with one another. Both boys suffer an alphabet of mental illnesses between them, but it's their ADD and ADHD which hinder and fuel them and color the world around them. What is it that ultimately drives Burn to back down from his destructive plans when confronted by Crash?

Appeal Factors

- Attention deficit disorder
- Attention deficit hyperactive disorder
- Family relationships
- Friendship
- Male main character

- Mental illness
- Peer relationships
- Romance
- School hostage situation

Read Alikes

- This is a lengthy book, but readers who like Ellen Hopkins and want stories that delve into the inner psyche of aching characters, regardless of style, will find Hassan's novel immensely satisfying. It's gritty and honest, with an authentic, unflinching main character.

- The exploration of the inner workings of the male mind make Stephanie Kuehn's *Charm and Strange* a strong read alike. The way that male characters blame themselves for their mental instability and social frustrations are similar and heartbreaking.

Kuehn, Stephanie. ***Charm & Strange***. St. Martin's Griffin, 2013. 224p. $16.99. 978-1-250-02194-6.

Win is an outcast, even though part of the reason he's at this new school is so that he can escape from his past. This is a fresh start. The problem is Win believes he is a wolf inside and this makes him a too-easy target for bullying at school. Worse, when there's a death near campus, Win is convinced he's the murderer. But when Win meets Jordan – the first person, let alone first girl – to truly listen to him tell his story, she puts together enough pieces of his past to realize that he needs serious psychological help. This book explores depression, post-traumatic stress disorder, and the fear that lingers inside someone who has lost just about everything there is to lose.

Appeal Factors

- Abuse
- Bullying
- Depression and anxiety
- Family relationships
- Friendship
- Male main character
- Mental illness
- Post-traumatic stress disorder
- Private/boarding school
- Sparse writing

Read Alikes

- This book is a perfect title to hand to fans of Blythe Woolston or Adam Rapp's dark, haunting, and psychologically-driven realistic fiction. Kuehn's novel flirts with genre, in that the reader is never entirely sure it's a contemporary novel or paranormal. Likewise, the tight writing style, the focus on characters and their relationships to their internal selves and those around them further appeals to Woolston and Rapp readers.

- The pacing of this book and the rich exploration of mental illness should resonate with readers of Ellen Hopkins who are willing to try a non-verse novel.

Nelson, Blake. *Recovery Road*. Scholastic, 2011. 320p. $16.99. 978-0-545-10729-7.

Maddie's just beginning her time at the halfway house for drug and alcohol abuse when she meets Trish, who is on her way out of treatment. When Trish is gone, Maddie begins a relationship with fellow housemate Stewart. Maddie grows close to Stewart, who has a host of his own demons to work through. At the same time, she maintains ties with Trish, whose transition back into the world has been anything but easy. And now, as Maddie prepares to move back home and readjust to life in high school again – this time not as the party girl, but as the girl who has cleaned up her act – will she be able to succeed? Or will her past addictions continue to hinder her recovery? While Trish and Stewart played significant roles in her time at the treatment center, it's through their own bumpy paths to recovery and sobriety in the real world which may help Maddie in her own.

Appeal Factors

- Alcohol addiction
- Drug addiction
- Female main character
- Friendship
- Grief
- Making new friends
- Romance
- Therapy

Read Alikes

- A near perfect read alike to Nelson's title is Amy Reed's *Clean*, which follows the institutionalization of five teenagers struggling with their addictions. Where Nelson's story is told through Maddie's perspective alone, Reed's offers the perspectives of five different characters, which allow readers some insight into what Nelson's Stewart or Trish may have been troubled with on their own paths to recovery. Both books are honest explorations of what addiction means, not only to the person with the addiction, but to those who are impacted by it as friends and family.

Omololu, C. J. *Dirty Little Secrets*. Walker, 2011. 224p. $8.99. Trade pb. 978-0-8027-2233-1.

Lucy has a secret. Actually, Lucy's mom has a secret: she's a hoarder. It's not that she just keeps receipts or old clothes. She keeps everything, and their entire house is filled with items that don't need to be there. But this isn't a story about Lucy's mom. It's Lucy's story about how she can begin to pick up the pieces of her life now that her mom has died. She struggles with how much she can let other people in and how much she should take on herself. Lucy knows she should call the police, but she doesn't want anyone to know the state of her living conditions, even if it means getting the help she so desperately needs.

Appeal Factors

- Family relationships
- Fast pacing
- Female main character
- Grief

- Health and well-being
- Hoarding
- Mental illness

Read Alikes

- Hoarding has been an underexplored theme in contemporary YA fiction, although a number of adult non-fiction titles have been written on the topic. Readers curious about hoarding and the ramifications it has on family relationships should try Jessie Sholl's memoir about her own mother's hoarding, *Dirty Secret: A Daughter Comes Clean*.

- Omololu's writing and her ability to tackle a heavy topic with care and compassion via Lucy are reminiscent of Elizabeth Scott's ability to write a similarly-challenging topic in *Living Dead Girl*. Both are sparser novels, but both come from the perspective of a teen girl who grew up in a life where she had little control of her own living conditions. Readers may also want to try Liz Coley's *Pretty Girl-13*, the story of a girl abducted at a young age and who stumbles back into her old family life carrying the weight of the secrets and traumatic memories of her past.

Price, Nora. *Zoe Letting Go*. Razorbill, 2012. 288p. $17.99. 978-1-59514-466-9.

When Zoe is admitted to Twin Birch, she can't help but think the other girls at the treatment facility are some of the weirdest, most off-putting people she's ever met. They like to hurt themselves. They don't like to eat. They look like skeletons and require "quiet time" after meals in order to recover. Zoe is definitely not one of those girls. She doesn't even belong here. She should be at home with her best friend Elise instead. Elise and she understood each other and both knew they didn't need any sort of weird "help" like the kind Zoe's subjected to here. But what Zoe doesn't know is that Elise is the reason she's found herself at Twin Birch and the reason why she needs the kind of help that only Twin Birch can provide.

Appeal Factors

- Disordered eating
- Female main character
- Friendship
- Grief

- Mental illness
- Self-injury and self-harm
- Therapy

Read Alikes

- The way Zoe dissociates from her mental state and her eating disorder makes this a read alike to Laurie Halse Anderson's *Wintergirls.* Both also feature an underlying element of grief, as the girls in both Price's and Anderson's stories work through losing a best friend to an eating disorder.

- Zoe's fascination and frustration with the girls in Twin Birch is reminiscent of the way the main character in Erin Saldin's *The Girls of No Return* feels when she, too, is admitted to a treatment facility for her own acts of self-injury.

Reed, Amy. *Crazy*. Simon Pulse, 2012. 384p. $16.99. 978-1-4424-1347-4. $8.99 Trade pb. 978-1-4424-1348-1.

Connor and Izzy met at summer camp and swore they'd keep in touch, even as they went their separate ways at the end of the season. And they do just that, thanks to email. But as Izzy's emails become fewer and farther between, as well as more erratic and filled with pleas for help between the lines, Connor knows something is seriously wrong with his friend. Even though he wants to blame himself and his advances – he does have a crush on her after all – Connor realizes that he is the only person in the position to help her in the way she needs to be helped. She's only ever opened up to him.

Appeal Factors

- Alternative format
- Bipolar disorder
- Depression and anxiety
- Dual points of view
- Epistolary format

- Female main character
- Male main character
- Mental illness
- Seattle

Read Alikes

- For readers who haven't read Reed's books before, they are a great starting place for read alikes in and of themselves for their tight writing, strong pacing, and exploration of issues relating to mental health and illness. *Beautiful*, her first novel, delves into how a young teen fits into a new and popular crowd, and tackles her increasing addiction to medication; *Clean*, as discussed earlier, explores drug and alcohol addiction from teens inside a treatment facility; and *Over You* begins as a story about a teen who has a drinking problem.

- Topically and stylistically (though in prose, rather than verse) Reed's writing is reminiscent of Ellen Hopkins's. Readers looking for a similar writing style in prose would do well with Holly Cupala's writing, and *Don't Breathe a Word* in particular makes a great read alike. Cupala and Reed both set their respective books in Seattle.

Roskos, Evan. ***Dr. Bird's Advice for Sad Poets***. Houghton Mifflin, 2013. 320p. $16.99. 978-0-547-92853-1.

James's sister Jorie was kicked out of the house immediately once her parents learn she was expelled from school. James can't handle that this happened to her because he can imagine no reason why someone as great as Jorie would either get expelled or disappoint her parents so much that she would be banished from home. Now with her out of the house, James's parents have turned their attention to him and not in a good way. James escapes them through the use of his imaginary therapist, Dr. Bird, who takes the shape of a pigeon. He realizes, though, that his depression and anxiety are much worse than he's ever experienced and he knows that his imaginary therapist alone won't help him feel better. So James takes a part time job to pay for the therapy he needs to work through years of abuse at the hands of his own parents – though his greatest healing may come at the hands of helping his sister admit how much she needs help, too.

Appeal Factors

- Abuse
- Depression and anxiety
- Family relationships
- Humor
- Male main character
- Mental illness
- Poetry
- Siblings
- Therapy

Read Alikes

- This book is a near perfect combination of Jesse Andrews's *Me & Earl & The Dying Girl* in terms of its humor; Matthew Quick's *Sorta Like a Rock Star* for its ever-optimistic main character in spite of the challenges lying before him; and Geoff Herbach's *Stupid Fast* series for the way family relationships directly impact the main character's mental health and his humor. Andrews and Herbach's books feature male narrators with strong and memorable voices with strong similarities to James's.

- Even though the subject matter of Stephanie Kuehn's *Charm & Strange* is presented in a much darker manner than Roskos's, both stories explore the way parental abuse can and does impact teenagers, particularly when it comes to their mental health and their fears about repeating the cycle of violence in the future.

Schmidt, Tiffany. *Send Me a Sign*. Walker, 2012. 384p. $16.99. 978-0-8027-2840-1. $9.99 Trade pb. 978-0-8027-3540-9.

Mia's always been the popular girl and the girl who believes in signs. Certain songs, certain sights, and certain objects must mean something. But when she's diagnosed with leukemia, the last thing she wants to do is have any of her friends know about it. She doesn't want to be known as the girl with cancer and she definitely doesn't want the attention for it, so Mia keeps it a secret. But she can't keep it hidden from everyone, and she spills to her long-time best friend Gyver. After undergoing chemotherapy during the summer and dodging questions from friends by explaining her disappearance as spending time with family in another state, Mia develops a strong crush on another boy – the cute and athletic Ryan. He'd never taken a shine to her before, but now, it looks like it might finally be her time. Keeping secrets is getting hard, as is keeping the story straight. Is it even possible for Mia to keep her diagnosis hidden anymore? And what happens when her best friends find out . . . or when Ryan finds out?

Book Trailer

http://youtu.be/BpeibZCgiDM

Appeal Factors

- Cancer
- Family relationships
- Female main character
- Friendship

- Health and well-being
- Leukemia
- Romance
- Significant pets or animals

Read Alikes

- The romantic tension in Schmidt's book will appeal to readers who found the romantic tension in John Green's *The Fault in Our Stars* enjoyable. Despite tackling similar subjects – cancer – the books explore them in very different ways. It is the relationships, though, forged during the characters' respective experiences of illness which will resonate with readers.

- In terms of romance, this book is a surefire win with fans of Jenny Han's *The Summer I Turned Pretty* series. In both Han's and Schmidt's books, there is a choice between two boys who are both likable and flawed. There are no "perfect" boys in either story, and the girl who has to make the choice recognizes and appreciates those flaws for what they are.

- Readers looking for similar writing styles will find Siobhan Vivian and Sarah Dessen to be great read alikes.

Whitney, Daisy. *The Rivals*. Little, Brown, 2012. 352p. $17.99. 978-0-316-09057-5.

After Alex's own positive experience with the Mockingbirds – a society of students at her boarding school that protects and watches over the student body – she's been initiated as the head of the group. It just happens that the case falling into her lap isn't anything small. A prescription drug ring has emerged, and students are using these drugs in order to cheat. It seems like a victimless crime since no one gets hurt, but this drug abuse harms not only those ingesting the pills, but it harms those students getting by on their own abilities without any enhancements. The thing is, it's not easy to bust the ring and it's possible the administration and students at the school would rather ignore the problem than put an end to it.

Appeal Factors

- Drug addiction
- Female main character
- Health and well-being
- Mystery

- Prescription drug abuse
- Private/boarding school
- Vigilante justice

Read Alikes

- *The Rivals*, much like Whitney's *The Mockingbirds*, explores what happens when students choose to investigate the misdoings of other students on their own time and with their own power. Both of these books would make good read alikes to E. Lockhart's *The Disreputable History of Frankie Landau Banks*, as they feature a strong leading female working toward disentangling the underground social structures and problems in their respective schools.

- In terms of writing and in exploration of social constructs, Whitney's book makes an excellent read alike for Siobhan Vivian, particularly *The List*.

Series Alert

This is the companion title to Whitney's debut novel, *The Mockingbirds*. Both stories are set in the same boarding school, with Alex Patrick as the main character. They can be read separately and independently of one another and be understood. Reading *The Mockingbirds* may offer a strong back story to Alex and allow readers deeper insight into her convictions, beliefs, and actions.

Whitney, Daisy. *The Mockingbirds*. Little, Brown Books for Young Readers, 2012. 288 p. $8.99. Trade pb. 9780316090544.

Wylie, Sarah. *All These Lives*. Farrar Straus Giroux, 2012. 256p. $17.99. 978-0-374-30208-5.

Jena and Dani are fraternal twins, and they've been close their entire lives. But when Jena is diagnosed with cancer, both of their lives spin out of control: Jena because of her illness and Dani because she can't work through what it means for her sister to be sick and what it means to be the sister of someone sick. Dani would do anything to make it so Jena was okay, and she doesn't say that lightly. Believing she's been granted nine lives, thanks to a number of near-death incidents in her own past, Dani wishes she could die so that she may spare the pain for Jena. But will dying to save her sister actually save her sister?

Book Trailer

http://youtu.be/jFJSqLlnJQY

Appeal Factors

- Cancer
- Family relationships
- Female main character
- Grief
- Health and well-being
- Siblings

Read Alikes

- Wylie's book is a strong read alike to Janet Gurtler's *I'm Not Her*, which also tells the story of a sibling struggling with how to behave, how to feel, and how to interact with a sister recently diagnosed with major illness.

- Readers interested in similar stories but open to reading books geared toward a slightly younger readership and featuring brothers, rather than sisters, will want to read Jordan Sonnenblick's *Drums, Girls, and Dangerous Pie* and the companion, *After Ever After*.

Young, Janet Ruth. *Things I Shouldn't Think*. Atheneum, 2012. 352p. $8.99. Trade pb. 978-1-4424-5107-0. Original hardcover edition was titled *The Babysitter Murders*. 978-1-4169-5944-1.

Dani's always wanted to be a babysitter, and she's lucky enough to snag a job watching Alex, who she adores. When Dani sees a TV news report about a murder, she rushes Alex out of the room to protect him. But Dani can't wipe the image out of her own mind. In every turn she fixates on the idea of murdering a child. Could she do something so violent? Why would she want to? Of course, she doesn't want to, but she can't let the thoughts go, and she finds herself making sure that any sharp objects around her are hidden so she's not tempted. When Dani can no longer handle the thoughts on her own, she confesses to Alex's mother that she's had these horrible images of killing Alex, even though she knows in a million years she would never actually act upon it. Alex's mother doesn't believe her and cries killer far before it's necessary, leaving Dani to scramble for the help she really needs. She's not criminal – she's suffering from OCD – but now she's been labeled as someone out to do evil.

Appeal Factors

- Family relationships
- Female main character
- Mental illness
- Obsessive compulsive disorder
- Peer relationships
- Vigilante justice

Read Alikes

- It's hard to compare this book with other titles like Heidi Ayarbe's *Compulsion* which also tackles obsessive compulsive disorder (OCD) because this side of OCD is much different. Rather than having compulsions, Dani suffers from obsessions. She is obsessed with the thought of murder, which can sometimes come out in compulsions (while she checks to make sure the knives are hidden, it's of a conscious thought, rather than an obsessive action). Still, readers fascinated with OCD will want to read Ayarbe's title in addition to this one, and they will want to explore other books tackling OCD, such as Lauren Roedy Vaughn's *OCD, The Dude, and Me* and Corey Ann Haydu's *OCD Love Story*.

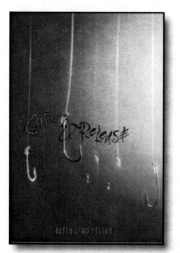

Woolston, Blythe. *Catch and Release*. Carolrhoda, 2012. 216p. $17.95. 978-0-7613-7755-9.

Polly was going to marry Bridger as soon as they finished high school. Then she was going to go to college, get a job, and have kids. Even though it sounds pretty standard, Polly was excited for it. The safety and comfort of this life plan brought her a sense of joy. But all of that changed when she was diagnosed and suffered through a bout of the flesh-eating disease MRSA. It left her ugly and disfigured. It left her without Bridger, too, who ran. While being treated, Polly meets Odd, one of the football players from her school. It wasn't until they were both suffering from MRSA that they ever talked, and it turns out they have much more in common than just this disfiguring disease. When both are released from treatment, Polly wants nothing more than to find out where Bridger disappeared to. It's Odd who will join her on a bizarre road trip to finding out the truth of why Bridger no longer wants the life with Polly that he once did.

Appeal Factors

- Female main character
- Fishing
- Friendship
- Health and well-being
- Literary writing
- MRSA
- Road trip
- Sparse writing

Read Alikes

- Readers who have yet to pick up Woolston's other dark contemporary titles, *The Freak Observer* and *Black Helicopters,* will want to. While *Catch & Release* focuses on the experiences of two teens who have been disfigured by their disease, what makes the story stand out is less the physical manifestations of MRSA and more the internal struggle for identity and place the characters wrestle with *after* the illness. Woolston's other books pull readers in with this same deep psychological struggle of making sense of a world that makes no sense.

- Woolston's dark and minimalist writing style makes her a strong read alike to Adam Rapp.

More Titles Exploring Physical and Mental Health and Well-Being

Andrews, Jesse. *Me and Earl and the Dying Girl*. Amulet, 2012. 304p. $16.95. 978-1-4197-0176-4.

Arcos, Carrie. *Out of Reach*. Simon Pulse, 2012. 256p. $16.99. 978-1-4424-4053-1.

Ayarbe, Heidi. *Compulsion*. Balzar + Bray, 2011. 304p. $17.99. 978-0-06-199386-2.

Brown, Jennifer. *Perfect Escape*. Little, Brown, 2012. 386p. $17.99. 978-0-316-18557-8.

Castrovilla, Selene. *The Girl Next Door*. Westside, 2011. 239p. $9.99. Trade pb. 978-1-934813-59-1.

Cohn, Rachel. *You Know Where to Find Me*. Simon & Schuster, 2009. 224p. $8.99. Trade pb. 978-0-689-87860-2.

de la Pena, Matt. *I Will Save You*. Ember, 2011. 320p. $8.99. Trade pb. 978-0-385-73828-6.

Doller, Trish. *Something Like Normal*. Bloomsbury, 2012. 224p. $16.99. 978-1-59990-844-1.

Ellsworth, Loretta. *In a Heartbeat*. Walker, 2011. 224p. $9.99. 978-0-8027-2234-8.

Green, John. *The Fault in Our Stars*. Dutton, 2012. 336p. $17.99. 978-0-525-47881-2.

Griffin, Adele. *Tighter*. Ember, 2012. 240p. $8.99 Trade pb. 978-0-375-85933-5.

Gurtler, Janet. *I'm Not Her*. Sourcebooks Fire, 2012. 285p. $9.99 Trade pb. 978-1-4022-5636-3.

Haydu, Corey Ann. *OCD Love Story*. Simon Pulse, 2013. 352p. $16.99. 978-1-4424-5732-4.

Jaden, Denise. *Never Enough*. Simon Pulse, 2012. 400p. $9.99 Trade pb. 978-1-4424-2907-9.

James, Brian. *Life is But a Dream*. Feiwel & Friends, 2012. 240p. $16.99. 978-0-312-61004-3.

Jarzab, Anna. *The Opposite of Hallelujah*. Delacorte, 2012. 464p. $16.99. 978-0-385-73836-1.

Kantor, Melissa. *Maybe One Day*. HarperTeen, 2014. 400p. $17.99. 978-0-0622-7920-0.

Kelly, Tara. *Harmonic Feedback*. Henry Holt, 2010. 288p. $16.99. 978-0-8050-9010-9.

Leavitt, Lindsey. *Sean Griswold's Head*. Bloomsbury, 2012. 304p. $9.99 Trade pb. 978-1-59990-911-0.

Le Vann, Kate. *Things I Know About Love*. EgmontUSA, 2011. $7.99. 160p. Trade pb. 978-1-60684-214-0.

McCall, Guadalupe Garcia. *Under the Mesquite*. Lee & Low, 2011. 224p. $17.99. 978-1-60060-429-4.

McDaniel, Lurlene. *Breathless*. Delacorte, 2009. 176p. $7.99 Trade pb. 978-0-440-24016-7.

McDowell, Beck. *This is Not a Drill*. Nancy Paulsen, 2012. 224p. $17.99. 978-0-399-25794-0.

Murphy, Julie. *Side Effects May Vary*. Balzer & Bray, 2014. 336p. $17.99. 978-0-0622-4535-9.

Reed, Amy. *Clean*. Simon Pulse, 2012. 304p. $9.99 Trade pb. 978-1-4424-1345-0.

Saldin, Erin. *The Girls of No Return*. Arthur A. Levine, 2012. 352p. $17.99. 978-0-545-31026-0.

Sheinmel, Alyssa. *The Stone Girl*. Alfred A. Knopf, 2012. 224p. $16.99. 978-0-375-87080-4.

Skilton, Sarah. *Bruised*. Amulet, 2013. 288p. $16.95. 978-1-4197-0387-4.

Stork, Francisco X. *The Last Summer of the Death Warriors*. Scholastic, 2012. 352p. $8.99 Trade pb. 978-0-545-15134-4.

Vaughn, Lauren Roedy. *OCD, The Dude, and Me*. Dial, 2013. 240p. $16.99. 978-0-8037-3843-0.

Vaught, Susan. *Freaks Like Us*. Bloomsbury, 2012. 240p. $16.99. 978-1-59990-872-4.

_____. *My Big Fat Manifesto*. Bloomsbury, 2009. 336p. $9.99 Trade pb. 978-1-59990-362-0.

Verdi, Jessica. *My Life After Now*. Sourcebooks, 2013. 304p. $9.99 Trade pb. 978-1-4022-7785-6.

Walton, K. M. *Empty*. Simon Pulse, 2013. 256p. $16.99. 978-1-4424-5359-3.

Warman, Jessica. *Breathless*. Walker, 2010. 336p. $9.99 Trade pb. 978-0-8027-2174-7.

Williams, Carol Lynch. *Miles from Ordinary*. St. Martin's Griffin, 2012. 208p. $9.99 Trade pb. 978-1-250-00260-0.

Woodson, Jacqueline. *Beneath a Meth Moon*. Speak, 2013. 240p. $8.99 Trade pb. 978-0-14-242392-9.

Chapter 12

Journeys Far and Wide

As far as contemporary YA that I have read that affected my writing, I still think King Dork *is my favorite YA novel. I also loved* Gingerbread *by Rachel Cohn. And* Story of a Girl *by Sara Zarr. If I Stay, How to Say Goodbye in Robot, How We Live Now* also have unique voices. I guess I like the quieter plotted books. I like reality. I feel like I am enriched when smart people describe the real world to me, even if it's fictional. I learn things. I have things I suspected to be true, confirmed by an author I trust.*

I feel like writing about young adults is really a sweet spot for me. I love that time in people's lives, I find it deeply significant. The idea that a forty year old is smarter or wiser or has as much on the line in their daily life as a seventeen year old is ludicrous. Seventeen year olds are way more interesting. They are facing more important choices and decisions. Plus nature equips young people with special abilities, the ability to adapt, the ability to meld with the newest advances in their society. Teenagers' brains are like new cars. They are all potential. They are fresh and clean and ready to take in the newest, most complex realities. Old people's brains get slow. They get bogged down by having too much perspective. They know too much! – Blake Nelson, author of *Recovery Road* and *Paranoid Park*

All contemporary realistic titles can be considered "coming of age" stories. But, as seen through the depths of topics and voices explored throughout this genre, there's always something more within the book than a simple story of getting from point A to point B.

But it's that journey – the moving to and from one place to another – that is in and of itself worth exploring. The journey can take many forms, literal or metaphoric. There are road trips and immigration experiences, spiritual crises, and trips through social or legal justice. Within each of these journeys are stories of what it means to be lost and what it means to be found again; what it means to be a friend; what impact grief can have in making sense of loss; and much more. This list offers a mix of stories, but at the heart of each one is some kind of journey.

Brown, Jennifer. *Perfect Escape*. Little, Brown, 2012. 386p. $17.99. 978-0-316-18557-8.

Kendra's older brother Grayson has suffered OCD her entire life, and she's always felt like she's fallen in his shadow because of it. Her parents dote on Grayson and don't give her the attention she needs. Kendra's felt the pressure to be Miss Perfect because those are the expectations her parents have for her; Grayson's a handful and perfection is something that Kendra can own for herself. But when she does something bad in the name of maintaining that image of perfection, she knows she will find herself in heaps of trouble. When she thinks she's going to get caught and will have to fess up, she grabs the keys to the car, along with her brother, and takes off on the road away from her Midwest home toward the big California fault line. As much as it has to do with the fact that Kendra knows her geology-obsessed brother will love this place, it's more about who she needs to reconnect with at the end of the trip: her former best friend and Grayson's former ex-girlfriend. There was never a reason for her friend's sudden departure to California, and now Kendra wants closure for herself and her brother before she has to face the consequences of all her actions at home.

Appeal Factors

- Family relationships
- Female main character
- Friendship
- Mental illness

- Obsessive compulsive disorder
- Road trip
- Siblings

Read Alikes

- The way Brown explores relationships – both those between siblings Kendra and Grayson and those with strangers, family, and friends along the road – is reminiscent of the way the relationships play out in Sara Zarr's books. Readers will find many similarities, especially in *How to Save a Life* and *The Lucy Variations*.

- The complexities of family relationships in Brown's novel make Sarah Ockler's books natural read alikes, as well. Readers who enjoy the tension between responsibility at home and responsibility to self will want to try Ockler's *The Book of Broken Hearts* in particular.

Forman, Gayle. ***Just One Day***. Dutton Books, 2013. 320p. $17.99. 978-0-525-42591-5.

Allyson's always been a rule-follower, but as her trip through Europe comes to a close and her best friend Melanie decides to go off-course, Allyson makes the bold decision to do something she'd never thought about doing before: break the rules. Rather than spend the final hours with her tour group in London, Allyson instead follows a theater boy named Willem to Paris, where they spend one full day together seeing all of the sights, eating all of the food, and taking in the city together. When she wakes up the next morning, Willem is nowhere to be found. Now Allyson is alone in a city she doesn't know. But when she gets back to London and ultimately, back home to the States, she finds that she misses not only the adventure she took, but she misses the fun and spark of chemistry she'd had with Willem. Now a freshman in college, Allyson is left to wonder if there are any other journeys like this left in her and more importantly, if she can ever reconnect with Willem again.

Appeal Factors

- Boston
- Family relationships
- Female main character
- Foreign setting
- Jewish characters
- London
- Paris
- Post-high school setting
- Romance
- Travel

Read Alikes

- This book fits together with Nina LaCour's *The Disenchantments*, as well as Kirsten Hubbard's *Wanderlove*. Both LaCour and Hubbard set their stories in the immediate time following high school graduation, and both explore what it is that the main character wants to get out of his or her life now that she or he is "free." Of course, nothing is easy to figure out, and like in Forman's book, both LaCour and Hubbard's characters find themselves traveling to seek out some of the answers to the great questions in their minds. Hubbard's novel appeals because it includes a foreign travel element – the story takes place in Central America – where LaCour's novel will appeal to readers of Forman's book because of its emphasis on a relationship seen through the eyes of a character who may or may not find the romance reciprocated.

Halpern, Julie. ***Don't Stop Now***. Feiwel & Friends, 2011. 240p. $16.99. 978-0-312-64346-1.

It's the very first night of freedom from high school and the start of the last summer before college. Lil receives a phone call from her friend Penny, and even though she doesn't answer it, she does listen to the voicemail. All Penny says is "I did it." Penny, who came from a crummy home and has been dating a somewhat abusive boy, has run away. Now Lil's parents, her best friend Josh, and even the police are asking Lil more questions about Penny than she has answers. Rather than sit and wonder where Penny could have gone or what she has done, Lil decides she's going to find her friend. But it's not all about the trip to find Penny – it's also about Lil discovering what side of the friend-boyfriend line Josh falls on, as he joins her on the cross-country trip.

Appeal Factors

- Family relationships
- Female main character
- Friendship
- Humor
- Mystery

- Post-high school setting
- Quirky
- Road trip
- Romance
- Summer story

Read Alikes

- Though this book is not about grief – a little bit of that emerges in regards to the end of high school and what that entails – there is appeal to readers of Morgan Matson's *Amy & Roger's Epic Detour*. Both books explore what can happen in a relationship through a road trip, while also focusing on what it is to make and to be a family. In Halpern's book, we learn a lot about Lil and Josh's respective families along the way, much as we do through Amy's grieving process in Matson's book.

Hoole, Elissa. *Kiss The Morning Star*. Amazon, 2012. 240p. $17.99. 978-0-7614-6269-9.

Anna and Kat are newly graduated and feel like the world is theirs to explore. Kat, who is fanatic about Jack Kerouac's *The Dharma Bums*, suggests they take a cross-country road trip in the spirit of that book, as sort of a way for them to find meaning in their lives and figure out their grand purpose. This trip isn't that simple though. Anna's been dealt a number of significant blows in the last couple of years, including her mother's death and her father's decision to give up his life's calling as a pastor. There's also the question fluttering at the surface for both girls about what their relationship is: Are they friends or are they interested in one another more romantically?

Appeal Factors

- Female main character
- Friendship
- Grief
- LGBTQ
- Post-high school setting

- Road trip
- Romance
- Sexuality
- Spirituality and religion

Read Alikes

- For readers taken with the questions lingering in Anna's mind throughout the story about belief in a higher power and what it is that makes a person good or bad, in addition to the road trip, Antony John's *Thou Shalt Not Road Trip* is a near perfect pairing. The questions of spirituality and interpersonal relationships will resonate.

- As this is a story set post-high school and about what it is the future may hold, there are many other books on this list that make strong read alikes, including Forman's *Just One Day*, Hubbard's *Wanderlove*, and LaCour's *The Disenchantments*. All three have some sort of romantic thread running through them, too.

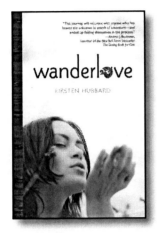

Hubbard, Kirsten. *Wanderlove*. Delacorte, 2012. 352p. $17.99. 978-0-385-73937-5.

Now that she's graduated from high school, Bria's feeling lost and uncertain about her future. Where she was once passionate about art, Bria's now not so sure. After seeing a brochure for the Global Vagabonds program, a travel group exploring Central America, she decides to sign up. This is her chance to travel, to get to know herself, and have no strings attached. When she arrives in Central America, Bria realizes the group isn't what she wanted, so she decides to do what she shouldn't: she ditches the group and chooses to travel on her own. In her exploration, Bria meets up with a group of backpackers who help her understand the value of travel and discovery. It's through these experiences where Bria is able to rediscover the talent and love she has for art.

Appeal Factors

- Art
- Artistic expression
- Backpacking
- Central America
- Female main character
- Foreign setting
- Illustrations
- Post-high school setting
- Romance
- Summer story
- Travel

Read Alikes

- Gayle Forman's *Just One Day* is an excellent read alike to Hubbard's novel, for their characters shared appreciation for travel. The use of romantic relationships in both books to push the main characters toward self-exploration and understanding are similar. The beginning of Forman's novel also takes place in the summer prior to the beginning of college.

- Hubbard's novel is reminiscent of Nina LaCour's *The Disenchantments*, both for the travel elements – though LaCour's is a U.S.-based road trip – as well as the solid writing, the exploration of post-high school life, and the use of art as self-expression. Where Bria uses sketches and identifies as an artist, Colby in LaCour's work is less the musician and more the fanboy of the music makers.

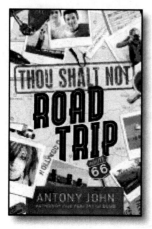

John, Antony. ***Thou Shalt Not Road Trip***. Dial, 2012. 336p. $16.99. 978-0-8037-3434-0.

Sixteen-year-old Luke is a bestselling novelist and his publicist is sending him on a cross-country tour to promote the book. Luke's novel, an inspirational story about faith and belief, has earned him fans all over. The tour kicks off in California, half way across the country from his home in Missouri, and Luke's going to be joined by his older brother and chauffeur Matt. At his first stop, Luke is overwhelmed by reader reception to his book. But it's less about the reception to the book; it's running into a former friend named Fran that sends him swirling. Fran used to be Luke's best friend/girlfriend, but things between them haven't been great for a long time. Imagine his surprise when he learns that Fran will be joining him and Matt on their tour. Now Luke must face the questions he raises in his own book and figure out whether or not the spiritual journey he wrote about is the same one he's about to embark on in real life, too.

Appeal Factors

- Alcohol addiction
- Friendship
- Male main character
- Road trip
- Siblings
- Spirituality and religion

Read Alikes

- John's book explores what happens when Luke – who has lived a fairly sheltered life – must confront the fact his former best friend/girlfriend has a problem with addiction. Luke is forced to consider his own spiritual beliefs in the face of the people in his life who are not always living up to the same sets of expectations he has for himself. This could make an interesting pairing with Melissa Walker's *Small Town Sinners*, wherein the main character is the person questioning the beliefs of others. Walker's story takes the more Fran-approach, in that Lacey asks and explores those tough questions of people who are devout around her. Both novels are careful and thoughtful in their handling of the religious aspects, without laying judgment about whether or not it's right to believe in a higher power.

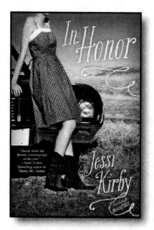

Kirby, Jessi. ***In Honor***. Simon & Schuster, 2013. 240p. $16.99. 978-1-4424-1697-0. $9.99 Trade pb. 978-1-4424-1698-7.

Just days after learning that her brother Finn has died in combat, Honor receives his last and final letter. What she finds inside surprises her: a pair of tickets to see her favorite singer Kyra Kelly. Kyra Kelly happened to be Finn's biggest crush, and in that letter, he tells Honor she should do her best to tell the singer that he was madly in love with her. Now working through the grief of losing Finn, Honor knows she can't *not* try to fulfill her brother's request. But when she tries to leave on her own, she runs into Rusty, the guy who was Finn's best friend before their friendship crumbled. The guy who Honor can hardly stand. And yet, despite the fact they don't get along, Honor and Rusty choose to make the journey from Texas to California in order to see Kyra Kelly together. But it's never about the concert; it's about the two of them working through losing the person who meant a lot to both of them.

Appeal Factors

- Family relationships
- Female main character
- Grief
- Music
- Road trip
- Romance

Read Alikes

- Like Morgan Matson's *Amy & Roger's Epic Detour*, this book uses a road trip as a method of working through grief and loss. Readers who enjoy Kirby's novel will find many similarities thematically, as well as in terms of writing-style. Both books feature a girl on a trip with a boy who she wouldn't consider the kind of guy she'd normally spend time with, but in the end realizes he was the just-right road companion.

- The military angle of this novel and the grief accompanying loss would make E. M. Kokie's *Personal Effects* a strong read alike. Other military-related grief novels readers may want to try after Kirby's include Trish Doller's *Something Like Normal* and Corinne Jackson's *If I Lie*.

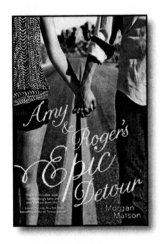

Matson, Morgan. *Amy & Roger's Epic Detour*. Simon & Schuster, 2011. 336p. $9.99 Trade pb. 978-1-4169-9066-6.

Amy's mom and dad were college professors in southern California until the car accident which took Amy's dad's life. Now her mom wants nothing more than to get away. She takes a new position on the east coast, and as soon as their old house sells, Amy will join her mom. But she won't be driving across the country alone – Amy's mom enlists the help of Roger, the son of one of her friends. Mom's made sure to book the hotel rooms and plan the itinerary down to the hour. But when Amy and Roger get on the road, all plans are out the window as Amy works through not only the death of her father, but also the guilt of playing a role in his death.

Appeal Factors

- Accidents
- Female main character
- Grief
- Road trip
- Romance
- Scrapbook-style story telling

Read Alikes

- *Saving June* by Hannah Harrington makes for a strong read alike for the use of a road trip to work through the grieving process. Matson's story is not as heavy in tone, but the physical movement and description of stops along the trip will appeal.

- The sweet romance that emerges between Amy and Roger will work for readers who like Sarah Dessen's romantic stylings.

- *In Honor* by Jessi Kirby uses the road trip to work through grief, while also incorporating a romance. Readers who like both the trip and the budding relationship in Matson's novel will find much to enjoy in Kirby's.

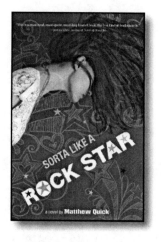

Quick, Matthew. *Sorta Like a Rock Star*. Little, Brown, 2011. 384p. 978-0-316-04353-3.

When Oliver kicks Amber and her mother out of his house, they take up residence in an old school bus. It's not pretty, it's not glamorous, but it's what they have. At least it'll be enough until Amber's mom finds another man to call her boyfriend in exchange for a place to live. But after school one day when Amber comes home to the bus, she discovers mom isn't there. She's not prepared to find out the worst: that mom isn't going to be coming back at all because she died. Now Amber is on her own to figure out how to make ends meet. The thing about Amber is that she's is optimistic, bright, and she's going to find a way to survive, even if every card seems to be stacked against her.

Appeal Factors

- Family relationships
- Female main character
- Friendship
- Grief
- Homelessness

- Mental illness
- Non-traditional families
- Significant pets or animals
- Spirituality and religion
- Socioeconomic class

Read Alikes

- Holly Schindler delves into what it is like to be a teen in charge of both her own life and her mother's in *A Blue So Dark*. Readers who are interested in the way Amber and her mother interact, especially as her mother struggles with a mental illness and with the responsibility of taking care of herself and her child, will find many similarities between these titles.

- *The Sky is Everywhere* by Jandy Nelson is another great read alike to Quick's title, despite the fact the main characters are much different in their attitudes toward grief and loss. The similarities between the characters come through their *processes* of grieving, by way of the use of writing as a coping mechanism and their relationship-building with new people. Both stories are paced slowly and methodically for readers eager for more literary novels.

Restrepo, Bettina. *Illegal*. Katherine Tegen, 2011. 272p. $16.99. 978-0-06-195342-2.

When almost-fifteen-year-old Nora's father left their home in Mexico three years ago to make money in Houston, he promised he'd be back in time for her big quinceñera. Her father's decision is one he has to make, as Nora, her mother, and her grandmother are living in a remote town that poverty continues to destroy. Fortunately, Nora's dad is able to make decent money in Houston and he is good about sending it back to them. That is, until just before her fifteenth birthday. The money stops showing up. Now Nora and her mother wonder if it stopped because he plans on coming back home or if it stopped for other reasons they don't want to think about. When their questions aren't being answered and Nora's father doesn't show up, she and her mother must do something much more drastic. They're going to have to cross the border and find her father when they get to Houston. This journey will be anything but easy for them, as they navigate a challenging system in a country with foreign customs, celebrations, language, and perceptions than the one they left in Mexico.

Appeal Factors

- Family relationships
- Female main character
- Foreign setting
- Grief
- Houston
- Immigration

- Mexico
- Multicultural
- People of color
- Socioeconomic class
- Travel

Read Alikes

- There are few novels that explore border crossing, particularly that done by a teenager. Readers who enjoy this novel, which features a younger teen protagonist, would be well served by reading Will Hobbs's *Crossing the Wire*, which follows a teen boy as he chooses to cross from Mexico into the States in order to make a better life for himself and his family.

- Part of this story deals with coming of age as a minority in the States. Even though the bulk of Restrepo's book focuses on the journey from Mexico to Houston, readers who are taken with Nora's search for self and for fitting in will do well seeking out Ashley Hope Perez's *What Can('t) Wait* and Guadalupe Garcia McCall's *Under the Mesquite*. Both stories also explore the importance of family to those of Mexican heritage, regardless of their current homeland.

Rosenfeld, Kat. *Amelia Anne Is Dead and Gone*. Dutton, 2012. 304p. $17.99. 978-0-525-42389-8.

To celebrate Becca's high school graduation, she and her boyfriend have sex in the back of his car. But it's not a celebration when they're finished. He tells her they're through, and he's moving on with his life. That's the same night when the dead body of a girl shows up on the side of the road. When Becca learns about the body, she finds herself falling apart a little bit more. She always wanted to leave her small town for a bigger adventure, and with her finishing school, the opportunity is there waiting for her. But now she's scared to leave. What was once a safe place no longer feels that way, and she's worried that if she feels this unsettled and disturbed in the place she's always known, how will she ever come to be comfortable somewhere else? With the summer still ahead of her, Becca can consider whether to stay or to leave, and even if she doesn't want to, she finds herself involved in the questions surrounding the dead girl. Who is she and how is she connected to Becca or her ex-boyfriend?

Appeal Factors

- Dual points of view
- Family relationships
- Female main characters
- Friendship
- Mystery
- Post-high school setting
- Romance
- Small town setting
- Summer story

Read Alikes

- While this novel appears to be a murder mystery, it's much more. This is a strong coming-of-age story, with intertwining narratives of Becca and Amelia, the girl who ends up dead on the side of the road. This is also a story about the ways a small town can impact teenagers: can they ever get out? Do they even want to? For those reasons and more, this book appeals to readers who like more literary novels. Even though they don't seem to be strong read alikes on the surface, readers who enjoy Rosenfield's novel will want to explore Blythe Woolston's writing, particularly *The Freak Observer*. The struggles of growing up in a small town, the elusive idea of freedom, and the mysteries tangled in the storylines make them more similar than different.

- Readers interested in the literary writing with a bit of mystery, along with the idea of what a small town setting can do to an individual who yearns for – and yet sometimes fears – freedom, Lauren Myracle's *Shine* is an excellent next read.

Vaught, Susan. *Going Underground*. Bloomsbury USA, 2011. 352p. $17.99. 978-1-59990-640-9. $9.99 Trade pb. 978-1-59990-919-6.

Seventeen-year-old Del made a mistake three years ago that changed the entire course of his life. Even when he turns eighteen, a legal adult, nothing can take back what happened. It will haunt him for life, and he's not being melodramatic in knowing and believing the only job he'll ever be able to have in life is as a grave digger. When Del meets Livia while he's at work in the cemetery, Del forges a relationship in a way he hasn't in the last three years. He's making a friend who is grieving a big loss of her own teen years and her future. When they begin to open up more honestly with one another, Del lets loose the truth of why he has the job he does and why he doesn't believe there's anything for him down the road. He was caught sexting at school and charged for the crime. Though he admits to doing it, as the story unfolds it becomes clearer that he's not an intentional criminal nor someone who was out for any ill intent. He got caught up in a system that unfairly punishes teens for true and honest mistakes. With the help of Livia and his eighteenth birthday on the horizon, can Del find the strength to stand up for himself and his actions again and maybe find a new, more hopeful, path?

Appeal Factors

- Friendship
- Grief
- Legal system
- Male main character

- Romance
- Sexting
- Significant pets or animals

Read Alikes

- Jennifer Brown's *Thousand Words* is another teen's story of being caught for sexting, though her story takes a different turn in terms of how she's prosecuted legally. Where Del is given a harsh punishment and cast out socially, the main character in Brown's book is sentenced to a more reasonable period of community service to make up for her crime.

- Readers compelled by the story of how technology can impact a character will want to read Sarah Darer Littman's *Want to Go Private?*, which follows a high school freshman as she chooses to meet up with someone she met on the Internet. This isn't someone who is out to befriend the main character. Rather, he's an older man who wants to take advantage of the teen's naivety and trust.

- Though they tackle entirely different plots, Matthew Quick's *Sorta like a Rockstar* would make a fascinating read alike to Vaught's story because his main character Amber has the same positive and optimistic outlook in life as Del does, despite luck weighing heavily against them. The attitudes of both characters are part of what makes them so memorable and remarkable.

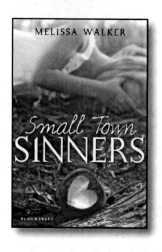

Walker, Melissa. ***Small Town Sinners***. Bloomsbury, 2011. 304p. $16.99. 978-1-59990-527-3. $9.99 Trade pb. 978-1-59990-982-0.

Lacey Anne has always lived in this small town, and one of the biggest parts of her life has been her religion. She's always gone to church and always follows the word of God. She's got two of the most supportive friends in the entire world, too – Dean and Starla Jo – and both of them have big faith. What Lacey Anne dreams of now is within her grasp: playing the role of the abortion girl in her church's Hell House. The Hell House is a tradition in her town and others. It's somewhat like a Halloween haunted house, except instead of meaning to scare people for thrills, it's meant to be a wakeup call for attendees to see different Biblical sins acted out. For Lacey, playing the girl who gets the abortion means she gets to play one of the lead roles, one that is emotionally wrenching not only for the actress, but also for the attendees. She doesn't get the role initially. When secrets begin to spill throughout town and the girl who did get the role finds herself unable to play it, it just may well go to Lacey. When new boy named Ty arrives in town, he challenges every one of Lacey's beliefs, forcing her to reconsider her stances on religion, on belief, and on what makes a person good or bad. It's not that he wants to convert her. It's not that he wants her to give up everything she's ever known. Instead, he wants her to think about whether or not the role of abortion girl is one she really wants and ultimately, consider what makes her so strong in her convictions.

Appeal Factors

- Family relationships
- Female main character
- Friendship
- Hell Houses
- Romance
- Small town setting
- Spirituality and religion
- Teen pregnancy

Read Alikes

- Walker's writing and exploration of what it means to be right and wrong in a religious and/or spiritual sense is reminiscent of Donna Freitas's *This Gorgeous Game*, which follows a well-respected church leader as he intimidates and uses a teen girl in less-than-appropriate ways. Neither of these books is about challenging the belief in religion or a higher power. Rather, both force the main character to consider what it means to share and present a message when sometimes, that message in and of itself isn't always honest or conveyed forthright. Readers will also find a strong read alike in another of Freitas's novels, *The Possibilities of Sainthood*, which also explores the questions of faith and belief.

Zarr, Sara. *What We Lost*. Little, Brown, 2013. 240p. $8.99 Trade pb. 978-0-316-23218-0. Formerly titled *Once Was Lost*, 978-0-316-03603-0.

Despite being the daughter of a pastor, Sam finds herself doubting a lot of things about faith. Her mom is far from perfect, seeking rehab after she was caught driving under the influence. Her dad might be spending more time with those at church than he is with his family who needs him to be there for them. But it's when a girl goes missing in town that Sam's questions about faith, religion, and family come to a head and she can't help but wonder if everything she's been led to believe about them all has been wrong. This isn't a story solely about God or how Sam does or doesn't believe. It's a story about hope and faith in other people and whether or not those are things worth investing in.

Appeal Factors

- Alcohol addiction
- Family relationships
- Female main character
- Grief
- Mystery
- Romance
- Spirituality and religion

Read Alikes

- There are many parallels in Zarr's novel and the work of Donna Freitas, specifically *This Gorgeous Game* and *The Possibilities of Sainthood*. Both grapple with the notions of faith and belief and how people can be imperfect representations of these greater ideas, even if they are themselves figureheads for those beliefs.

- Anna Jarzab's *The Opposite of Hallelujah* offers up a compelling family story with a strong thread of questioning belief and religion within it. Both Jarzab and Zarr weave a mystery into their novels which ultimately question the good of people and faith's role in healing human emotional wounds.

- An interesting, though very different, read alike to this novel might be Elissa Janine Hoole's *Kiss the Morning Star*. In Hoole's novel, one of the main characters is grieving the loss of her mother, and she, too, is the daughter of a church leader. When she is traveling with her best friend/girlfriend on the road, she begins to question her own faith, those who are devout, and her father's devotion to his belief much in the way that Sam does in Zarr's novel.

Zulkey, Claire. *An Off Year*. Dutton, 2009. 304p. $17.99. 978-0-525-42159-7.

Cecily is a rule follower. She did well in high school. She got into the right college. She set herself up on a path for success. But when Cecily shows up at her college, the last thing she wants to do is go. So instead, she turns around and chooses to spend this year at home. Even though there are a million things she could be doing with her year off, Cecily chooses to do nothing. She's not going to travel. She's not going to solve world hunger. Even though this at times means she finds herself deeply depressed, listless, envious of other people, and all-too-willing to lash out at those around her, Cecily finds this year is what she needs in order to move forward. She has time now to think about the things she really wants to do *for herself*, rather than the things she did in order to follow the rules that had always defined her life for her.

Appeal Factors

- Chicago
- Family relationships
- Female main character
- Friendship
- Humor
- Peer relationships
- Post-high school setting
- Quirky

Read Alikes

- Unlike the bulk of stories that follow teens who choose non-traditional paths after high school (such as Jen Violi's *Putting Makeup on Dead People*) or stories where teens have a summer prior to college to sort out what it is they want to do with their lives (such as Gayle Forman's *Just One Day*, Kirsten Hubbard's *Wanderlove*, Nina LaCour's *The Disenchantments*), Zulkey's main character does nothing significant with her time off. In fact, very little happens in the story. But it's Cecily's voice, wit, and ennui which make this book an interesting read alike to any of the above-named titles because it provides an alternate – and yet still realistic – view of what can happen after high school ends. Zulkey's book is for the reader who isn't necessarily thrilled about what the future may hold because the unknown is a scary thing.

■ More Books Featuring Literal and Metaphorical Journeys

Barnholdt, Lauren. *Right of Way*. Simon Pulse, 2013. 320p. $17.99. 978-1-4424-5127-8.

Brown, Jennifer. *Thousand Words*. Little, Brown, 2013. 288p. $17.99. 978-0-316-20972-4.

Dominy, Amy Fellner. *OyMG*. Walker, 2011. 256p. $16.99. 978-0-8027-2177-8.

Forman, Gayle. *Just One Year*. Dutton, 2013. 336p. $17.99. 978-0-5254-2592-2.

Graham, Hilary Weisman. *Reunited*. Simon & Schuster, 2012. 336p. $17.99. 978-1-4424-3984-9.

Halbrook, Kristin. *Nobody But Us*. Harper Teen, 2013. 304p. $8.99. 978-0-06-212126-4.

Harrington, Hannah. *Saving June*. Harlequin Teen, 2011. 336p. $9.99 Trade pb. 978-0-373-21024-4.

Herrndorf, Wolfgang. *Why We Took The Car*. Arther A. Levine, 2014. 256p. $17.99. 978-0-5454-8180-9.

Joseph, Lynn. *Flowers in the Sky*. HarperTeen, 2013. 240p. $17.99. 978-0-06-029794-7.

Kaufman, Sashi. *The Other Way Around*. Carolrhoda, 2014. 288p. $17.99. 978-1-4677-0262-1.

LaCour, Nina. *The Disenchantments*. Dutton, 2012. 336p. $16.99. 978-0-525-42219-8.

Littman, Sarah Darer. *Life, After*. Scholastic Press, 2010. 288p. $16.99. 978-0-545-15144-3.

Maldonia, Kristen Paige. *Fingerprints of You*. Simon & Schuster, 2012. 272p. $17.99. 978-1-4424-2920-8.

Neff, Beth. *Getting Somewhere*. Viking, 2012. 448p. $17.99. 978-0-670-01255-8.

Padian, Maria. *Out of Nowhere*. Alfred A. Knopf, 2013. 352p. $16.99. 978-0-375-86580-0.

Perkins, Stephanie. *Anna and the French Kiss*. Speak, 2011. 400p. $9.99 Trade pb. 978-0-14-241940-3.

Skuse, C. J. *Pretty Bad Things*. Chicken House, 2011. 256p. $17.99. 978-0-545-28973-3.

Smith, Emily Wing. *Back When You Were Easier to Love*. Dutton, 2011. 224p. $17.99. 978-0-525-42199-3.

Violi, Jen. *Putting Makeup on Dead People*. Hyperion, 2012. 336p. $8.99. 978-1-4231-3485-5.

Williams, Carol Lynch. *Signed, Skye Harper*. Simon & Schuster, 2014. 352p. $17.99. 978-1-4814-0032-9.

Chapter 13

Relationships: Romantic, Platonic, and Those That Fall Between

I write contemporary YA because I have always looked for myself in books. Not that I can't find myself in another world or another time, but because in the novels I like best, the characters take center stage. That can happen in any type of work, of course, but in contemporaries, characters are given a little bit more of a chance to shine. There's (usually) no world-ending threat, no unfamiliar context that needs explaining. Just people living their lives and exploring the depths of who they are. It's those depths that interest me most: Why do people do what they do? Where are their hearts? How can we reach into a story and find the tiny details of humanity that produce spontaneous laughter and/or bring tears to each others' eyes? (Laughter through tears being the best mix, in my opinion.) – Melissa Walker, author of *Small Town Sinners* and *Unbreak My Heart*

The teen years are some of the most important and most challenging when it comes to understanding what goes into developing relationships, whether with a romantic other, friends and family, oneself, or those that pop up unexpectedly yet have a long-lasting and profound impact. Relationships are as much about learning and understanding self as they are connecting with others. They're about questioning sexuality, gender, and identity and about the roles each play in the grander scheme of life.

The following list explores relationships. There are romantic stories, as well as stories about the pursuit of developing an important relationship with oneself. Included are books about teen pregnancy, the search for sexual and gender identity, and relationships which aren't about romance or family or friendship at all.

Bigelow, Lisa Jenn. *Starting from Here*. Amazon, 2012. 288p. $16.99. 978-0-7614-6233-0.

Colby's girlfriend Rachel just broke up with her, and within days, Rachel's already got herself a boyfriend. Colby wants to avoid Rachel now, and she does this by spending as much time as she can with her best friend Van while ditching the meetings of the gay-straight alliance that all three are a part of. When she is out with Van, Colby finds a stray dog who is hit by a car. It's then Colby knows this dog belongs to her, even if it means telling a few lies to the people she loves, including her father. When Colby meets Amelia, a girl who at first comes on a little strong, Colby finds herself telling more than one or two little white lies about her sexuality, too. Can Colby's dad forgive her for those lies and accept her, her new pet, and her girlfriend?

Appeal Factors

- Family relationships
- Female main character
- Friendship
- Grief
- LGBTQ

- Road trip
- Romance
- Significant pets or animals
- Socioeconomic class

Read Alikes

- Even though a significant part of the story is about Colby and her relationships with Rachel (and the fallout therein), with Van (and how they have a safe and comfortable relationship with one another), with Amelia (and what it means to be open and honest about sexuality), and with her father (and what it means to connect with one another beyond shared grief), the relationship that resonates strongest is that between Colby and her new dog. It's a rare relationship in YA fiction, but it's one that's honest and searing. For readers taken with the way a person can relate to and love a four-legged pet, especially one that they didn't necessarily choose to have as a part of their life, an excellent pairing to this book would be Michael Northrop's *Rotten*. Both explore the depths to which a character can connect to a dog and use that bond to make tough choices and decisions in other relationships.

- Colby isn't struggling with her sexuality in Bigelow's book, but she does struggle to be open and honest about it, particularly when it comes to her father. Kirstin Cronn-Mills's *The Sky Always Hears Me: And the Hills Don't Mind* would make for a good read alike for the way families can impact one's acceptance of sexuality. Both stories have interesting threads within them regarding social class and friendship, too.

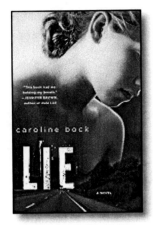

Bock, Caroline. *LIE*. St. Martin's Griffin, 2011. 224p. $9.99. Trade pb. 978-0-312-66832-7.

Skylar's boyfriend Jimmy has been accused of the unimaginable: brutally beating two Latino immigrants in a neighboring town. Now Skylar's being questioned about the incident since she was the only one there that night and the only witness. She doesn't want to say anything. She wants to protect her boyfriend as much as she can. But the more Skylar thinks about the events of that evening, the more she wonders if her choice to remain silent is just as much a crime as what she may or may not have witnessed. It's possible that Sean, one of Jimmy's best friends, may have had a hand in everything. Told through eight different perspectives, Bock's book explores hate crime through the eyes of not only the perpetrators and the victims, but also the families and adults in the lives of both those who attacked and those who were attacked.

Book Trailer

http://youtu.be/QZPmG1mrymk

Appeal Factors

- Abuse
- Female main characters
- Hate crime
- Immigrant families
- Intergenerational stories
- Male main characters
- Multiple points of view
- People of color
- Prejudice and race

Read Alikes

- Readers will find many similarities between LIE and Jennifer Brown's Hate List. In both stories, a character must deal with the fallout of having intimate knowledge of an individual who perpetuated a horrific and life-altering crime. There are many similarities in writing and execution of both books, as well. Likewise, though Jodi Picoult is an adult author, readers who want a similar story told through multiple points of view, including those of teens and adults, will find *Nineteen Minutes* a solid read alike.

Buzo, Laura. *Love and Other Perishable Items*. Alfred A. Knopf, 2012. 256p. $17.99. 978-0-375-87000-2. $8.99 Trade pb. 978-0-307-92974-7.

Fifteen-year-old Amelia just took her first job at the local grocery store, and it's here she meets twenty-one-year-old Chris. The two form a fast relationship. Even though Amelia finds herself crushing over Chris a little bit, he doesn't reciprocate with any physical advances nor does he lead her on. Instead, it's a strong friendship they develop, based on the values of trust and honesty. Amelia's struggling to find her place in the world and struggling to rectify her strong feminist ideals with the behaviors of her mother and her best female friend. Chris is working through the grief that accompanies a hard break up with a girl he thought was his forever love. Together, they are able to recenter one another and themselves through sharing, talking, and bonding in the way two like-minded and deeply-emotional individuals can. More than developing relationships with one another, Amelia and Chris are able to navigate relationships with the other important people in their lives.

Appeal Factors

- Alternative format
- Australia
- Dual points of view
- Family relationships
- Female main character

- Foreign setting
- Friendship
- Male main character
- Socioeconomic class

Read Alikes

- Readers who enjoy the style, pacing, and dynamics of Amelia and Chris's relationship, as well as both of their voices, will want to explore C. K. Kelly Martin's contemporary YA, especially her first novel, *I Know It's Over*. There are many parallels between Buzo's Chris and Nick in Martin's novel.

- The intelligent discussions of philosophy and feminism present in Buzo's novel would make Lia Hills's novel *The Beginner's Guide to Living* another strong read alike. Both novels also have an Australian flavor to them.

- Fans of Buzo's book will want to seek out the realistic novels of Melina Marchetta, who writes about relationships with similarly dynamic emotional tugs, and her novels also feature that Australian setting and styling.

Carter, Caela. *Me, Him, Them, and It*. Bloomsbury, 2013. 320p. $16.99. 978-1-59990-958-5.

Sixteen-year-old Evelyn can't stand her parents. They're distant, and they definitely don't care that she's got good grades or that she is well on her way to becoming class valedictorian. That's why Evelyn likes to act out. It gets their attention. But when she becomes pregnant with her not-boyfriend Todd, things get messy as her parents send her away to live with her aunt. Evelyn can't decide what it is she wants now. Does she keep the baby? Does she want Todd to be a father? Does she even like Todd? And does she want to continue going to high school in order to graduate at the top of her class and go on to college? Is that option even open to her anymore?

Appeal Factors

- Adoption
- Chicago
- Family relationships

- Female main character
- Moving
- Teen pregnancy

Read Alikes

- One of the biggest strengths in books that focus on teen pregnancy in today's contemporary YA is that nearly none of them are prescriptive. They aren't out to offer a story about what the right decision is in terms of keeping the baby or not. Often, readers interested in teen pregnancy stories aren't looking for answers or solutions to personal problems. Instead, it's a topic they simply enjoy reading about.

- Those who love Carter's novel will want to get their hands on a number of other strong teen pregnancy novels, including C. K. Kelly Martin's *I Know It's Over* (told from the point of view of the male, rather than the pregnant main character); Nina de Gramont's *Every Little Thing in the World* (which has further appeal to fans of Carter's novel due to the main character's desire to misbehave); Amy Efaw's *After* (which follows a girl who decides to give birth but hide the fetus post-birth); and Han Nolan's *Pregnant Pause* (which follows the girl and the baby's father as they're living together and figuring out the right choices for them and their child).

Cronn-Mills, Kristin. ***Beautiful Music for Ugly Children***. Flux, 2012. 262p. $9.99 Trade pb. 978-0-7387-3251-0.

Gabe was born Elizabeth. Up until a couple of months ago, he lived as Elizabeth, even though it meant fighting back everything he felt was true about himself. He's struggled for years with what it means to live his life as the person he doesn't feel like he is. When he finally accepts himself as Gabe, it's because of his gig as a DJ for the local community radio station. The anonymity offered in the role allows him to find his voice and his true "B-side." But what happens when Gabe's able to embrace himself and his friends and family – and those he knows from school and his community – aren't so willing to accept him yet?

Book Trailer

http://youtu.be/vmQOoXXkHCA

Appeal Factors

- Bullying
- Friendship
- Intergenerational stories
- LGBTQ

- Music
- Sexuality
- Small town setting
- Transgendered or transsexual characters

Read Alikes

- For those interested in the idea of traditional radio programming, Natalie Standiford's *How to Say Goodbye in Robot* should appeal for the way radio programming connects the main characters to one another and to themselves. Both books delve into the notions of identity and friendship.

- Although Gabe is trans and embraces that as his identity, this story is less about choosing an identity than it is accepting and acknowledging the wide varieties of sexualities that exist. For this reason, A.S. King's *Ask the Passengers*, which emphasizes the importance of loving and accepting one another as they are regardless of sexual identity, traverses similar territory.

- Readers who haven't read Cronn-Mills's first novel *The Sky Always Hears Me: And the Hills Don't Mind* will want to pick it up for the themes of sexuality, of not being straight in a small town in the midwestern United States, and for a strong and memorable teen voice.

- For another story about a trans individual, told through a grittier verse style, try Kristin Elizabeth Clark's *Freakboy*.

Griffin, Paul. *Stay With Me*. Speak, 2012. 320p. $8.99 Trade pb. 978-0-14-242172-7.

Mack is a high school dropout, and his best friend Tony – who is about to be deployed – has tasked him with taking care of his sister CeCe. Mack's a little worried about this request because he doesn't want to get too close with her, since she's a knockout dream girl type. Crossing any lines could ruin his friendship with Tony. Mack does get close with CeCe. It's not a bad thing, though. In fact, it's good for Mack. When he introduces her to his biggest passion, which is his ability to train dogs (specifically pits), she's scared because she'd once been a victim of a dog bite. Mack teaches her that even dogs with reputations can be loved, and she believes him enough that she finds herself wanting to adopt the rescue dog Mack's been working with. Unfortunately, Mack soon finds himself in prison, in solitary confinement, and now his talent of training dogs may be the only way to turn his life around. Will it be too late for him to reconnect with CeCe? Can he ever earn her or Tony's trust again?

Appeal Factors

- Fast pacing
- Friendship
- High school dropout
- Juvenile delinquency
- Male main character

- New York City
- People of color
- Romance
- Significant pets or animals

Read Alikes

- In terms of steamy romances, readers who enjoy Griffin's book will want to try Simone Elkeles's novels, particularly *Perfect Chemistry*, which features a "bad boy" and a good girl who find themselves falling in love despite the odds.

- Even though Michael Northrop's *Rotten* isn't as gritty, edgy, or mature as Griffin's novel, readers who are interested in the relationships that can develop between a teenager and an animal will see many similarities. Both explore how an animal can change the life of a teenager and rescue him from continuing to make poor decisions.

Halbrook, Kristin. *Nobody but Us*. Harper Teen, 2013. 304p. $8.99 Trade pb. 978-0-06-212126-4.

Will rescues Zoe from her home and the two of them set off toward Vegas. She's escaping an abusive and destructive father, and he's hoping to escape the stigma and history he's had as a kid lost to "the system." They're going to start fresh in a new place, living a life together that's loving and caring toward one another. They want to shed their broken pasts as best they can. Of course, it won't be and can't be that easy, as the past isn't just something they can easily forget. It's part of who they are, and it impacts the decisions they make. But, as one character sees the past as their definition, the other character chooses instead to use it as guidance to make hard choices. It's because Will and Zoe cannot see eye to eye that their new and perfect start in Vegas isn't what they imagined it to be. They're on the run, but it might not be the best decision Zoe and Will have ever made. It might be making their lives even harder than they already were.

Appeal Factors

- Abuse
- Dual points of view
- Family relationships
- Female main character
- Gritty
- Male main character
- Road trip
- Romance

Read Alikes

- Fans of this book will want to check out Heidi Ayarbe's *Wanted* for the grittiness, the unforgiving and harsh Nevada setting, as well as the way that a male and female character who feel trapped by their own histories work toward breaking free of them in order to redefine themselves.

- Halbrook's writing is reminiscent of Kody Keplinger's in terms of style and frankness to subject. Readers will be well-served reading any of Keplinger's YA novels, especially *A Midsummer's Nightmare*.

Klise, James. *Love Drugged*. Flux, 2010. 312p. $9.95 Trade pb. 978-0-7387-2175-0.

Fifteen-year-old Jamie shares a condo with his grandparents and his parents, and he cannot wait to get through high school and get on with his life. It's rough in his school, but he knows he's lucky that his peers don't know his biggest secret: he's gay. They don't know because he's best friends with Celia, one of the hottest girls in school. People assume they're an item, and sometimes even they think they're an item, but at the end of the day, they're really just close friends. Celia's father is a druggist who creates pharmaceutical drugs to help sick people with their ailments, and his latest creation is an experimental pill that helps gay people rid themselves of their homosexuality. It alters their brain chemistry. Because Jamie doesn't want people to know he's gay and because he himself isn't sure whether he wants to be or not, he steals a supply of pills from Celia's house, unaware of what the side effects may be. All he knows is that this could be his ticket out of a life he's not sure he wants to have.

Appeal Factors

- Chicago
- Drug abuse
- Family relationships
- Friendship

- Male main character
- LGBTQ
- Romance
- Sexuality

Read Alikes

- Although Kirstin Cronn-Mills's *Beautiful Music for Ugly Children* follows the story of a transsexual main character, there are many elements about the questioning of sexuality and the questioning and acceptance of self that make it an excellent read alike to Klise's novel. Both explore what it means to be one's self and whether or not that is something that is fluid or static. Both push the main characters to think about the consequences of their choices on those around them – not because they should worry about what other people think of them but because other people's reactions may not be quite what they hoped for.

Madigan, L. K. *Flash Burnout*. Graphia, 2010. 336p. $7.99 Trade pb. 978-0-547-40493-6.

Blake has a girlfriend named Shannon and a good friend named Marissa who just happens to be a girl. It's when he is working on an assignment for school and takes a picture of a person he saw on the street that a series of questions emerge. The photo he took was of Marissa's mom, who disappeared years ago and found herself on the streets and addicted to meth. Now, he's questioning what his role is as a boyfriend and as a boy friend, as he spends more and more time with Marissa, helping her piece together her family, and less and less time with Shannon. Blake's beginning to learn that it's not always easy to figure out what love is and that love comes in many shades.

Appeal Factors

- Drug abuse
- Family relationships
- Friendship
- Grief
- Male main character

- Methamphetamine
- Photography
- Romance
- Significant pets or animals

Read Alikes

- Blake's voice in this book is strong and makes for an excellent read alike to any of John Green's male-led stories, particularly *Looking for Alaska* or *Paper Towns*. Readers who want a smart, funny, and romantic lead character who wants to do the right thing will find many similarities.

McCahan, Erin. *I Now Pronounce You Someone Else*. Arthur A. Levine, 2010. 272p. $16.99. 978-0-545-08818-3.

Eighteen-year-old Bronwen Oliver has never felt like she fit in her family. She's not the perky cheerleader type of daughter her mom wants her to be. Bronwen's even gone as far as creating a fake persona and family, and she lives as Phoebe Lilywhite in her head. But when Bronwen starts hanging out with Jared, a college guy and former friend of her brother, she learns that maybe being herself isn't too bad. He's a good guy and their relationship is strong and solid. He respects her decision to want to remain a virgin until marriage. As their relationship continues to work, Jared proposes marriage, and they plan on it happening once she graduates high school. Is it possible for Bronwen to be creating the family she always wanted now with Jared by her side?

Appeal Factors

- "Clean" read
- Family relationships
- Female main character
- Romance
- Teen marriage

Read Alikes

- One of the discussions in the book is about virginity and remaining pure until marriage. This discussion is very character-centric in that it's not meant to have a definitive message for readers to walk away with. Readers who are interested in similar stories with girls who consider the value of virginity and the way it relates to marriage and romantic relationships will want to read Tera Elan McVoy's *Pure* and Jackson Pearce's *Purity*, both of which develop full characters who consider this decision. It's not their entire lives, but an important and valued part of them.

- The character-driven narrative, with a focus on growing up, on family, and on relationships, makes this book is a great pick for readers who enjoy Sarah Dessen. Readers who pick up McCahan's novel and haven't experienced Dessen's work would do well trying *What Happened to Goodbye* or *The Truth about Forever*, in particular.

- Readers eager to read another story where a teen character considers – and plans for – a marriage immediately after high school will want to read Jenny Han's *The Summer I Turned Pretty* series. The final book is about the main character coming to terms with her love for one of the males in her life and choosing to pursue a more permanent relationship.

Nolan, Han. *Pregnant Pause*. Grafia, 2012. 352p. $9.99 Trade pb. 978-0-547-85414-4.

Eleanor is sixteen and she's pregnant. She's more than a little bit stuck, too – she wants to have the baby, but she doesn't have an easy or safe place to be at the moment. Her parents are missionaries, and they're going to be spending time in Kenya. The baby's father, who may or may not be there for her as a boyfriend, is spending the summer working at his family's summer camp. It's not an ordinary camp though; it's one for fat kids who need to lose weight. Ellie chooses her fate, rolls up her sleeves, and knows she's going to be working harder than she'd ever want to while pregnant by choosing to live with her boyfriend at the camp. Even though she starts out with a crummy attitude about it, Ellie comes to love her job. She loves it so much that when one of her campers experiences a traumatic event on the day of her baby's birth, Ellie's mind is less about what's going on with her own body but instead, what's going to happen to her new friend. When the baby arrives, Ellie finds herself having to make an even tougher choice than she did at the start of summer.

Appeal Factors

- Adoption
- Female main character
- Romance
- Summer setting
- Teen pregnancy

Read Alikes

- This is a strong read alike to Caela Carter's *Me, Him, Them, and It*. Both are stories of teen pregnancy and both feature teens who ultimately struggle with the choice of whether to keep their child or give it up for adoption. Both also feature an array of interesting characters who surround the pregnant teen. In Nolan's book, the bulk of those in her life, including the baby's father, are standoffish or downright jerks to Ellie, and in the Carter's book, those in Evelyn's life are more interested in getting rid of her and shying away from her problems than working through them with her.

Northrop, Michael. **Rotten**. Scholastic, 2013. 256p. $17.99. 978-0-545-49587-5.

Jimmer Dobbs – JD for short – just returned from a summer in upstate New York. He tells his friends he spent the season "with his aunt," but no one believes that story for a second. When JD arrives home, he's greeted not only by his mother, but also a new roommate: a giant Rottweiler. The dog has no name. JD's mom informs him that the dog had been a rescue from an abusive home and she asks JD to name him. It's when he chooses to call the dog Johnny Rotten – JR for short – that the two of them establish their first bond. When one of JD's friends claims that JR bit him and legal consequences, including euthanasia, are on the table, JD's true bond and love for JR comes through. The two of them have reputations to overcome. Can they do it together?

Appeal Factors

- Family relationships
- Friendship
- Humor
- Male main character
- Peer relationships
- Significant pets or animals
- Socioeconomic class

Read Alikes

- Although Northrop's book features no romantic storyline, the bonds that form between the main character and his new dog make this a strong pairing with Lisa Jenn Bigelow's *Starting from Here*.

- Readers who are ready for a more mature story of teen-animal bonding will want to check out Paul Griffin's grittier, edgier title, *Stay with Me*.

- Northrop's book has a lot of humor to it because JD isn't necessarily the most mature or philosophical teen male character. For those who like this tone, check out Northrop's earlier adventure-survival novel *Trapped*.

Scheidt, Erica Lorraine. *Uses for Boys*. St. Martin's Griffin, 2013. 240p. $9.99 Trade pb. 978-1-250-00711-7.

When Anna's mom starts dating again, Anna moves from being the center of her mother's world to the sometimes-very-last-thing her mother thinks about. It's a vicious cycle in her home, of her mother finding a boyfriend, marrying him, and then divorcing him. It's her mom's way of survival and of finding them money and a safe place to live. Now that she's a teenager, Anna follows in her mother's footsteps, seeking out boy after boy, hoping that the next one will be the one who will not only give her a safe place to be, but who will love her for who she is. But each boy brings disappointment and slowly tears away at who Anna is deep inside. When Anna finally meets a girl she can call a friend, she feels like maybe things could settle for her. It turns out that friend, though, may be more imaginary than she is real. Can Anna ever find someone who will love and comfort her in the way she needs? Does she even need anyone at all?

Appeal Factors

- Family relationships
- Female main character
- Gritty
- High school dropout
- Romance
- Sexuality
- Sparse writing
- Teen pregnancy

Read Alikes

- At heart, this isn't at all a story about romance or about relationships Anna has with boys. It's a story about Anna coming into her own and figuring out the things which matter to her. Does she need anyone else to define her or can she do so herself? These questions, which hang just below the surface of Anna's actions, mirror what happens in Amy Reed's *Beautiful*. Both feature very lost girls who find themselves doing "bad" things to themselves as a means of figuring out who it is they are now and who it is they wish to be.

- The brutal honesty, the grittiness, and the unflinching but sparse prose in this novel make it an excellent read alike to Ellen Hopkins in terms of style and execution. Scheidt's writing is short and staccato, which while not verse, is readable in a similar manner.

Schmidt, Tiffany. *Bright before Sunrise*. Walker, 2014. 288p. $17.99. 978-0-8027-3500-3.

Even though Jonah didn't move far from his old home, moving still meant giving up all of the things he once had: his friends, baseball, a girlfriend, and his dad. Everything in Cross Pointe just feels different. Brighton, a popular, good-looking, and downright nice girl likes to spend her time and energy helping others as a means of forgetting what it is that's weighing her down following her father's death. But Jonah knows immediately he doesn't like Brighton and Brighton doesn't know why but she's bound and determined to find out. Over the course of one night, the two forge a relationship of trust, honesty, self-discovery, and maybe even something more. What they have in common may be more than what either could imagine.

Appeal Factors

- Dual points of view
- Family relationships
- Female main character
- Friendship
- Grief

- Humor
- Making new friends
- Male main character
- Moving

Read Alikes

- Readers who want a story similarly structured, with dual points of view told over the course of a single night will want to check out Cath Crowley's *Graffiti Moon*. Both Crowley and Schmidt show their stories through a male and female point of view.

- *Love and Other Perishable Items* by Laura Buzo is another potential read alike for Schmidt's novel. It, too, is told through two points of view, and it's a story about a relationship between an older male and younger female that's less about romance and more about self-discovery for each of the characters.

Schroeder, Lisa. *The Day Before*. Simon Pulse, 2011. 320p. $16.99. 978-1-4424-1743-4. $9.99 Trade pb. 978-1-4424-1744-1.

Amber needs to spend the day before – the day before she's about to have one of the biggest, most alarming changes in her life – alone. She grabs her iPod and heads to the beach. When she's there, she meets Cade: a boy who also needs to spend this day alone. He knows he can't escape the dark things in his life, but just getting away is what he needs for a temporary reprieve. It's instant attraction for Amber and Cade, and they choose to make this not a day alone, but a day together where they're unafraid to share their thoughts and feelings with each other. It's a day where they permit themselves to maybe even fall in love. But can this one day change the futures at all, as they both prepare for the realities lying before them? It's possible that this one day of love and of possibility is at least enough to send them into the unknown with a little bit more hope.

Appeal Factors

- Family relationships
- Fast pacing
- Female main character
- Health and well-being
- Romance
- Verse novel

Read Alikes

- This emotionally-driven novel has appeal for fans of Gayle Forman's *If I Stay*. Both novels tease out the value of a romantic relationship and the challenge of staying or leaving, albeit in very different ways.

- Because of the styling of the story – the one day to experience it all when it comes to fun and romance – this is a potential read alike to David Levithan and Rachel Cohn's *Nick and Norah's Infinite Playlist*.

- Readers who are looking for visual "read alikes" would do well watching the film *Before Sunrise* for the "chance-encounter" element present in Schroeder's book, and they would do well with the show *Switched at Birth*, since that is at the heart of Amber's back story.

◼ More Books Tackling Relationships to Self and Others

Beam, Cris. *I Am J*. Little, Brown, 2011. 352p. $8.99 Trade pb. 978-0-316-05360-0.

Brezenoff, Steve. *Guy In Real Life*. Balzer & Bray, 2014. 400p. $17.99. 978-0-0622-6683-5.

Brezenoff, Steve. *The Absolute Value of -1*. Carolrhoda, 2010. 290p. $16.95. 978-0-7613-8130-3.

Clark, Kristin Elizabeth. *Freakboy*. Farrar, Straus and Giroux, 2013. 448p. $18.99. 978-0-3743-2472-7.

Crowley, Cath. *Graffiti Moon*. Alfred A. Knopf, 2012. 272p. $16.99. 978-0-375-86953-2.

de Gramont, Nina. *Every Little Thing in the World*. Atheneum, 2011. 288p. $8.99 Trade pb. 978-1-4169-8015-5.

Eulberg, Elizabeth. *Better Off Friends*. Point, 2014. 288p. $17.99. 978-0-5455-5145-8.

Freitas, Donna. *This Gorgeous Game*. Square Fish, 2011. 240p. $9.99 Trade pb. 978-0-312-67440-3.

Greenman, Catherine. *Hooked*. Ember, 2012. 288p. $9.99 Trade pb. 978-0-385-74009-8.

Han, Jenny. *To All The Boys I've Loved Before*. Simon & Schuster, 2014. 368p. $17.99. 978-1-4442-2670-2.

Hoole, Elissa. *Kiss the Morning Star*. Amazon, 2012. 240p. $17.99. 978-0-7614-6269-9.

Hopkins, Ellen. *Tilt*. Margaret K. McElderry, 2012. 608p. $18.99. 978-1-4169-8330-9.

King, A. S. *Ask the Passengers*. Little, Brown, 2012. 296p. $17.99. 978-0-316-19468-6.

Knowles, Jo. *Jumping Off Swings*. Candlewick, 2011. 240p. $7.99 Trade pb. 978-0-7636-5296-8.

Levithan, David. *Two Boys Kissing*. Knopf, 2013. 208p. $17.99. 978-0-307-93190-0.

Littman, Sarah Darer. *Want to Go Private?* Scholastic, 2011. 336p. $17.99. 978-0-545-15146-7.

Lord, Emery. *Open Road Summer*. Walker, 2014. 336p. $17.99. 978-0-8027-3610-9.

Martin, C. K. Kelly. *The Lighter Side of Life and Death*. Random House, 2011. 256p. $9.99 Trade pb. 978-0-375-84589-5.

Mesrobian, Carrie. *Sex & Violence*. Carolrhoda, 2014. 304p. $17.99. 978-1-4677-0597-4.

Rowell, Rainbow. *Fangirl*. St. Martin's Griffin, 2013. 448p. $18.99. 978-1-2500-2095-5.

Sanchez, Alex. *Boyfriends with Girlfriends*. Simon & Schuster, 2012. 224p. $8.99 Trade pb. 978-1-4169-3775-3.

Schroeder, Lisa. *Falling for You*. Simon Pulse, 2013. 368p. $16.99. 978-1-4424-4399-0.

Siegel, Philip. *The Break-up Artist*. Harlequin Teen, 2014. 304p. $17.99. 978-0-3732-1115-9.

Smith, Jennifer E. *The Geography of Me and You*. Poppy, 2014. 352p. $18.00. 978-0-3162-5477-9.

Smith, Jennifer E. *The Statistical Probability of Love at First Sight*. Poppy, 2013. 272p. $9.99. Trade pb. 978-0-316-12239-9.

Sones, Sonya. *To Be Perfectly Honest*. Simon and Schuster, 2013. 496p. $17.99. 978-0-689-87604-2.

Tibensky, Arlaina. *And Then Things Fall Apart*. Simon Pulse, 2011. 272p. $9.99 Trade pb. 978-1-4424-1323-8.

Walker, Melissa. *Unbreak My Heart*. Bloomsbury, 2012. 256p. $16.99. 978-1-59990-528-0.

Chapter 14

On the Field and Off: Sports and Athletes

Looking for Alaska by John Green forever changed my approach to young adult fiction. I found the characters, dialogue, and emotion in that book to be so real and affecting that I was able to stop questioning what I might be "allowed" to include in my own work. Instead, I now try to focus on always writing what's genuine. – Mindi Scott, author of *Freefall* and *Live through This*

Sports books may be among some of the strongest in contemporary YA fiction, and all these stories go well beyond a teen passionate about the game he or she is playing. These are stories where sports play a significant role, but they are woven into the development of character and can be used as the impetus for discovery, for relationship-building, and for life-altering decisions and changes. Contemporary sports books feature characters who represent a host of sexualities, races, ethnicities, and backgrounds. Some were born to play the game and others stumbled upon their athletic talents by chance.

Chris Crutcher, Carl Deuker, John Feinstein, Tim Green, Walter Dean Myers, and Paul Volponi are well-known authors who have published numerous books in the last decade (or longer) tackling teens and sports. Some of their titles are included in the list below, though it's worth exploring their back lists for more. Not included here are books published through Orca Book Publishers, though it's worth checking out their series of short, high interest books, Orca Sports, aimed at more reluctant readers or those who struggle to read at grade/age level. Another worthwhile series to explore is from Canada's Lorimer Publishing, titled the Podium Sports Academy. These should help fill out the gaps for fast-paced, gripping sports stories in any collection where there is a need.

Ayarbe, Heidi. **Compulsion**. Balzar & Bray/HarperTeen, 2011. 304p. $17.99. 978-0-06-199386-2.

Jake Martin's been to the state soccer championship two times before, and this Saturday will be his third. He's confident because three is a prime number, which means it has to be good luck. There's no way the rival team can win with that sort of power on his team's side. More than that, though, if his team does win on Saturday, Jake will no longer need to make excuses for his behavior, his fixation on certain numbers and patterns, or why he can't make friends like other people can. It might be the thing he needs to prove to his dad that he's worth something, too. For a boy who has suffered with obsessive compulsive disorder growing up in a household where his own parents don't care about him, this is not only a chance to win the championship, but a way to finally make it clear he is serious about his condition.

Book Trailer

http://youtu.be/pGbA_LGu-wQ

Appeal Factors

- Abuse
- Family relationships
- Male main character
- Mental illness
- Obsessive compulsive disorder
- Siblings
- Soccer

Read Alikes

- For the exploration of obsessive compulsive disorder, but from the compulsive lens rather than the obsessive lens, readers will want to try Janet Ruth Young's *The Babysitter Murders* (in paperback titled *Things I Shouldn't Think*).

- The challenging and problematic family relationship in this novel is written in a raw, honest manner. Readers who appreciate the way that Ellen Hopkins allows her characters to speak and think through the tough issues in their lives will find Ayarbe a great next read, and vice versa.

Cohen, Joshua. *Leverage*. Speak, 2012. 432p. $9.99. Trade pb. 978-0-14-242086-7.

Kurt Brodsky is the new kid at school. Even though he's a hulking football player, he isn't the sort of intimidating presence the other players on the team are. In fact, he has a pretty big weakness he can't hide forever. Danny Meehan is a member of the school's gymnastics team, which faces daily teasing in the locker rooms. Gymnasts aren't real athletes, or at least that's what the football players think. One day, the teasing in the locker room goes a little further than teasing, and both Danny and Kurt witness one of the most senseless and brutal acts of bullying imaginable. Left to figure out how to speak up without finding themselves at risk for the same sort of attack, Danny and Kurt befriend one another in order to seek justice for the bullied. Amid the bullying storyline are the competitive aspects of football and gymnastics, as well as the pressures both types of athletes face in their respective games.

Appeal Factors

- Bullying
- Drug abuse
- Dual points of view
- Football
- Gymnastics
- Male main characters
- Performance enhancing drugs

Read Alikes

- For the brutal, painful, and honest portrayal of bullying in high schools, readers will want to read Courtney Summers's *Some Girls Are*. Though its focus is on female bullying, there is much similar territory explored, and there is much to consider in terms of the forms and methods of bullying and how they may or may not differ among male and female characters.

- While football plays a role in the story, the biggest aspect of the football backdrop has to do with pressure to take performance-enhancing drugs in order to become a stronger athlete. Readers will find Carl Deuker's *Gym Candy* a great read alike for this particular element.

- The story's intensity and brutality will appeal to fans of Ellen Hopkins or Heidi Ayarbe, particularly her above-discussed *Compulsion*.

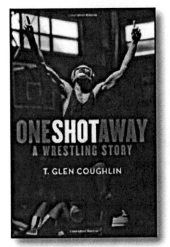

Coughlin, T. Glen. *One Shot Away*. HarperTeen, 2012. 336p. $17.99. 978-0-06-208323-4.

Diggy, Jimmy, and Trevor are all seniors, and it's their last season wrestling for high school. All three are dying for the chance to win now, except it won't be easy. Diggy's fighting to stand out against the legacy his brother left before him and the fact he could lose his spot on the team to Trevor, the new kid. Jimmy's girlfriend's not doing him any favors and he finds himself in a little bit of trouble with the law. With pressure mounting and the need to make a lasting impression during this final season, Diggy betrays a member of the team. Can he ever expect forgiveness for what he's done?

Appeal Factors

- Abuse
- Accidents
- Family relationships
- Grief
- Juvenile delinquency
- Male main characters
- Multiple points of view
- Socioeconomic class
- Wrestling

Read Alikes

- Readers who enjoy the wrestling aspect of this novel will want to pick up one of the few YA novels tackling the sport in Alfred Martino's *Pinned*.

Fjelland Davis, Rebecca. ***Chasing Alliecat***. Flux, 2011. 288p. $9.95 Trade pb. 978-0-7387-2130-9.

Sadie's spending the summer with her family in small town Minnesota after her parents decided to go to Egypt. For Sadie, this sounds like the worst punishment possible. But it's during that summer with her cousin she discovers her passion and her skill for mountain biking. It's become her way to get through the summer. And while all seems to be finally going well, Sadie's new friend Allie finds a dead body not far from where Sadie likes to bike. It doesn't take long before they realize there is something much darker and sinister going on.

Book Trailer

http://youtu.be/IXxnSf1EugQ

Appeal Factors

- Family relationships
- Female main character
- Friendship
- Mountain biking

- Mystery
- Small town setting
- Summer story

Read Alikes

- This book is included here because of the focus and fascination with mountain biking. The execution of the mystery and the means by which the characters make their way from point A to point B is reminiscent of Mary Jane Beaufrand's *The River* (in paperback retitled *Dark River*). In both, the story is less focused on the whodunit and more involved with character and story development. There just happens to be a mystery to untangle, too.

Herbach, Geoff. ***Stupid Fast***. Sourcebooks Fire, 2011. 311p. $9.99 Trade pb. 978-1-4022-5630-1.

Felton Reinstein's had an incredible and unexpected growth spurt, and he's gone from the runner known as "Squirrel Nuts" to one of the most valuable members of his high school's football team. Even though Felton's best friend Greg isn't around this summer, he's not entirely lonely. The family renting Greg's house happens to have a girl Felton's age living there – and he may be falling for her. But this isn't simply a story about football and romance. Felton's mom is having trouble functioning now that her son's had this growth spurt and he can't figure out what's causing her to go more crazy than she already is. Felton wants to know what he can do to make his mom feel better, if anything.

Appeal Factors

- Family relationships
- Football
- Humor
- Interracial relationship
- Male main character

- People of color
- Romance
- Running
- Summer story

Read Alikes

- Because of the setting in small-town Wisconsin, along with the focus on family and interest in football shared with both main characters, this book is a strong read alike to Catherine Gilbert Murdock's *The Dairy Queen* series.

- Felton's self-deprecating and self-aware humor make books by Josh Berk and Allen Zadoff great read alike options.

Series Alert

Nothing Special. Sourcebooks Fire, 2012. 290p. $9.99 Trade pb. 978-1-4022-6507-5.

I'm With Stupid. Sourcebooks Fire, 2013. 320p. $9.99 Trade pb. 978-1-4022-7791-7.

Kenneally, Miranda. *Catching Jordan*. Sourcebooks Fire, 2011. 281p. $8.99. Trade pb. 978-1-4022-6227-2.

Jordan Woods is the quarterback and captain of her high school football team, and she knows what it's like to be surrounded by the kinds of guys any girl would kill to be around. Except, Jordan's so used to them she doesn't even think about it. She's focused on playing the game so she can get a scholarship and attend a good college. Things change when Ty Green comes to town. He's a great quarterback himself, and, well, he's not hard on the eyes, either. For the first time, Jordan might be fumbling. Can she focus on football and her dreams of an athletic scholarship or will she pursue Ty instead? Can she do both?

Appeal Factors

- Family relationships
- Female main character
- Football

- Friendship
- Romance
- Siblings

Read Alikes

- *Catching Jordan* is Kenneally's first novel, and it's the first in her *Hundred Oaks* series. Readers who enjoy the female athletic story converging with romance will want to check out the other books in the series, particularly *Stealing Parker*.

- For the female athletic story, especially as it relates to family relationships and romance, Liz Fichera's *Hooked* (which is the first in a proposed trilogy) will appeal to fans of Kenneally's book.

Series Alert

Stealing Parker. Sourcebooks Fire, 2012. 242p. $9.99 Trade pb. 978-1-4022-7187-8.

Things I Can't Forget. Sourcebooks Fire, 2013. 320p. $9.99 Trade pb. 978-1-4022-7190-8.

Racing Savannah. Sourcebooks Fire, 2013. 304p. $9.99 Trade pb. 978-1-4022-8476-2.

Klass, David, and Perri Klass. ***Second Impact.*** Farrar Strauss and Giroux, 2013. 288p. $16.99. 978-0-374-37996-4.

Jerry Downing has a second chance to play for his high school football team following a series of bad decisions that led to a drinking and driving accident last year. To say he let his ego get to him would be an understatement. To redeem himself, he's taken on a position as a blogger for the school's newspaper in order to talk about the game and help ramp up excitement and school spirit. Carla Jenson, former soccer player who injured her knee, blogs alongside Jerry for the paper. Together, the two of them learn what it means to not only work through the toughest challenges of sports – redemption, team spirit, injuries – but also the challenges of journalism, of reporting, and maybe most importantly, trust, honor, and reputation. Neither Jerry nor Carla is perfect, but together, they're able to highlight the best of sports reporting and of playing the game itself.

Appeal Factors

- Accidents
- Dual points of view
- Female main character
- Football
- Male main character
- Peer relationships
- Soccer
- Sports injuries
- Writing

Read Alikes

- Readers who are interested in the impact of sports injuries, as well as the value of sports as seen through the eyes of student reporters, will want to try Jordan Sonnenblick's *Curveball*. Though written at a slightly lower level, the challenges of overcoming athletic injuries, as well as the lingering feelings related to team members who can continue to play, will resonate. Where Klass and Klass showcase the use of blogging as a way to capture a school's athletic endeavors, Sonnenblick's book uses photography.

- For fans of the journalism angle in particular, as well as the controversies and challenges of being a member of the press when covering sports, Bill Konigsberg's *Out of the Pocket* is a strong next read.

Koertge, Ron. *Shakespeare Makes the Playoffs*. Candlewick, 2012. 176p. $5.99 Trade pb. 978-0-7636-5852-6.

Kevin's baseball team has made the playoffs this year. While he's excited about it, he's still not completely over his mom's recent death and it weighs on his mind. As a means of working through the grief, Kevin's father – who is a writer – gifts him a blank notebook and directs Kevin to write through it. What emerges is poetry that he feels pretty okay about. As okay as a fourteen-year-old baseball-loving boy would feel about poetry, that is. But when he performs one of his pieces at an open mic night, Kevin could have never guessed that it would lead him to Amy. Even though he kind of has a girlfriend already, Amy might be the girl he needs, not just because he likes her a lot, but because she might be able to help him work through the grief in the way he needs to.

Appeal Factors

- Baseball
- Fast pacing
- Grief
- Male main character
- Romance
- Verse novel
- Writing

Read Alikes

- Because of the younger voice, this should appeal to fans of Gordon Korman's writing, particularly novels like *Pop*, which are aimed at the readership just outside middle grade books. There are no issues to worry about in terms of content in either Korman or Koertge's novels.

- Readers looking for a challenge after finishing this book and are fascinated with the use of writing to overcome grief will want to check out Conrad Wesselhoeft's *Adios, Nirvana*.

Series Alert

Shakespeare Bats Clean-Up. Candlewick, 2006. 128p. $5.99 Trade pb. 978-0-7636-2939-7.

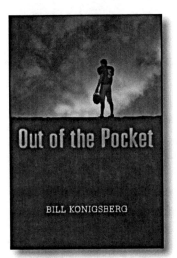

Konigsberg, Bill. *Out of the Pocket*. Dutton, 2008. 272p. $16.99. 978-0-525-47996-3.

Not only is Bobby Framingham the star quarterback of his school's football team, he's also one of the most well-respected and most-talented players in the entire state. The thing is, Bobby's different from almost everyone else on the field around him. He's gay. Even though Bobby would want his teammates to know this, he wants to be the one to deliver the news on his own terms. Unfortunately, he doesn't get the chance when a school reporter outs him publicly. And while the consequences aren't as ugly as he'd expected, Bobby still has to work to earn the trust and confidence of his teammates again – they're disappointed he didn't tell them, not that he is who he is.

Appeal Factors

- Family relationships
- Football
- Health and well-being
- LGBTQ

- Male main character
- Peer relationships
- Sexuality

Read Alikes

- Issues of sexuality seem to be emerging more frequently in sports novels, and one of the stronger explorations of this theme is in Paul Volponi's *Crossing Lines*. Readers invested in Konigsberg's book will want to try Volponi's for an entirely different story about sexuality, bullying, and the challenges of maintaining status as an athlete.

- David and Perry Klass's *Second Impact* is a sports story told through the eyes of former athletes turned journalists.

Schindler, Holly. *Playing Hurt*. Flux, 2011. 312p. $9.95 Trade pb. 978-0-7387-2287-0.

Chelsea always saw herself playing basketball in college. It would be her ticket to affording school, and she loved the game. That dream comes crashing down after a devastating injury on the court. She knows she's out for good. Clint is a former hockey star who also saw himself with a future playing in the big leagues. But something bad happened in his past that forced him to give up his own athletic pursuits. When Chelsea and Clint meet at a summer camp – she's there with her family and he works as a guide there – they find comfort and solace in one another's company. Their shared feelings about losing everything they'd worked hard for might not manifest itself in grief though. It may lead them to something more romantic.

Appeal Factors

- Accidents
- Basketball
- Dual points of view
- Family relationships
- Female main character

- Grief
- Hockey
- Male main character
- Romance
- Summer story

Read Alikes

- There are interesting similarities between Clint's hockey back story and the back story of Will in Donna Freitas's *The Survival Kit*. Both books explore grief and loss in similar fashion and weave romance into the grieving process.

- Readers who enjoy the family relationships and friendships explored in Schindler's book, as well as the use of sports to bring people together (and tear them apart), will find much to enjoy in Catherine Gilbert Murdock's *The Dairy Queen* series.

- For exploration of life after an injury sidelines a teen athlete, a good read alike would be Wendelin Van Draanen's *The Running Dream*.

Skilton, Sarah. *Bruised*. Amulet, 2013. 288p. $16.96. 978-1-4197-0387-4.

Imogen is a sixteen-year-old Tae Kwon Do black belt, a rare honor for someone her age. She earned it through hard work and dedication to the sport. At least that's what she thought before the night when everything changed. The night when she was at the local diner when there was a hold up, a gun, and a dead body. Instead of stepping forward and trying to stop the situation, Imogen hid beneath one of the diner's tables, too afraid to get involved. Now, she can't shake the memory and she finds herself acting out in ways that aren't congruent with the Tae Kwon Do mentality. Her behavior has gone so off track that she's asked to take a leave from the sport. With memories of that night fresh in her mind and her inability to "get over it," is it possible for Imogen to ever feel normal again? Will she ever find the love for the sport she once had?

Appeal Factors

- Disabilities
- Family relationships
- Female main character
- Health and well-being
- Mental illness

- Peer relationships
- Post-traumatic stress disorder
- Romance
- Tae Kwon Do

Read Alikes

- Imogen's voice has undertones of humor, despite the situations she finds herself in being anything but funny. This humor is reminiscent of Devan's in Amy Spalding's *The Reece Malcolm List* and readers will enjoy the way these characters tell their stories without becoming too sad or angsty.

- For readers interested in the ways post-traumatic stress disorder play out in different individuals, Trish Doller's *Something Like Normal* and Anna Jarzab's *The Opposite of Hallelujah* showcase two very different experiences of PTSD.

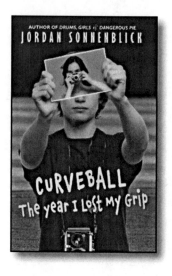

Sonnenblick, Jordan. *Curveball: The Year I Lost My Grip*. Scholastic, 2012. 304p. $17.99. 978-0-545-32069-6.

Peter loves baseball. He eats, sleeps, and breathes it, just like his best friend AJ. But when Peter's arm injury goes from bad to worse and he's told he no longer has a future in the game, he knows he has to come up with something to fill the void in his life. Enter photography. Peter's always been a fan of his grandpa's work and had recently been given his grandpa's equipment. That's part of the problem, though: in addition to losing the ability to play baseball, Peter's preoccupied with the way his grandfather's been acting lately. He's been giving away his favorite items and he's had periods of forgetting important things in his life, including the name of his own wife. When Peter earns a reputation as a strong sports photographer, he feels like he's figured out his passion. But can he do that without sacrificing his friendship with AJ, who he hasn't fessed up to yet about the severity of his injury? And what happens when Peter's grandfather takes a turn for the worse? Peter's first year of high school is nothing like he imagined.

Appeal Factors

- Alzheimer's disease
- Baseball
- Family relationships
- Friendship
- Health and well-being
- Intergenerational stories
- Male main character
- Photography
- Sports injuries

Read Alikes

- This book is an excellent read alike to Gordon Korman's *Pop*. Both stories are told through the voices of younger teen protagonists. Where Sonnenblick's story is about a teen's ongoing relationship with an older male, Korman's story is about a teen who forges a new relationship with an older male through playing football. Both confront what happens when that older friend is impacted by his own illness and physical limitation. But neither story is only about that. They're about the value of those friendships and relationships and about how sports, even if they aren't front and center in the lives of these teens, still help them find a way through adversity.

Van Draanen, Wendelin. *The Running Dream*. Knopf, 2011. 352p. $17.99. 978-0-375-86667-8. $9.99 Trade pb. 978-0-375-86628-9.

A horrible bus accident turns Jessica's life upside down in more ways than she can imagine. She loses her leg and is now bound to life with a prosthetic. For someone who was a runner, the sting is extra sharp. Aside from the obvious reasons why it's a tough adjustment, Jessica finds that life has changed because she's now seen by some as the girl who lost her leg and she's not even seen at all by others, for the same reason. She's the center of attention and completely invisible at the same time. But when Jessica befriends Rose, a girl suffering from cerebral palsy and who has always been in the position Jessica now finds herself socially, Jessica realizes things aren't over for her. Slowly but surely, she discovers that she not only still possesses her athletic abilities, but Jessica discovers that quality relationships – both with friends and family – are the kind you have to work at hard in order to make them successful.

Appeal Factors

- Accidents
- "Clean" read
- Disabilities
- Female main character
- Friendship
- Health and well-being
- Running

Read Alikes

- Though a much different issue and more mature in content than Van Draanen's book, Amy Efaw's *After* may make a solid read alike. In Efaw's novel, Devan is forced to give up her sport when she discovers she's pregnant. Maybe it's less because she's pregnant as the reason she's giving up her sport and more because of what she does when she discovers she's pregnant. While Van Drannen's novel explores what happens when an outside event knocks a character's life out of line and Efaw's explores what happens when a deliberate (though desperate) choice by the main character challenges her way of life, they each explore the "after."

- The writing style in Van Draanen's novel is similar to more classic YA authors such as Phyllis Reynolds Naylor and Cynthia Voigt, as well as similar to Sarah Dessen in terms of character relationships and development.

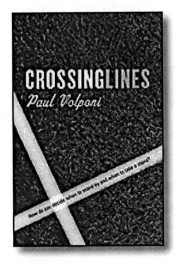

Volponi, Paul. *Crossing Lines*. Viking, 2011. $16.99. 978-0-670-01214-5.

Adonis has it all: he's on the football team, he's got the jock reputation preceding him, and he's dating one of the finest girls around. When new kid in school, Alan, shows up wearing lipstick and eagerly joins the fashion club, he becomes the center of peer teasing. But it's more than teasing – the football team is actually out to get him. While Adonis plays along with his teammates, when they decide to do something that would humiliate Alan in the worst possible way, Adonis can't commit. He's torn between the choices of going along with his teammates to maintain his cool or not going along and instead protecting the new kid. Adonis must decide just how much his own reputation is worth.

Appeal Factors

- Bullying
- Football
- LGBTQ
- Male main character
- Peer relationships
- People of color
- Sexuality

Read Alikes

- For an intense exploration of bullying and athletes, Joshua Cohen's *Leverage* makes for an excellent read alike. Both stories include an element of football and the culture of team mentality both on the field and off.

- Readers wanting another story where sexuality is the cause for bullying in high school athletic culture, Bill Konigsberg's *Out of the Pocket* is a strong choice.

Zadoff, Allen. *Food, Girls, and Other Things I Can't Have*. EgmontUSA, 2011. 320p. $8.99 Trade pb. 978-1-60684-151-8.

Andrew was always the geeky kid. He'd skip out on gym class, eat to his heart's content, and loved hanging out and participating with the Model UN guys. But now that he's hit the middle of high school, things aren't working out so well for him anymore. He's having trouble fitting in at home, in his clothes, and worse, in his own high school, where athletes reign supreme. Then there's April, the new girl. Andy wants to be her boyfriend so bad, and he's willing to go the extra mile to do that. It's when he's rescued by the high school quarterback just as he's about to get beat up by the school bully that Andy realizes maybe it's time to see if he can get in with the football team. It might be the key to solving all of his personal and romantic problems.

Appeal Factors

- Body image
- Bullying
- Family relationships
- Football
- Friendship

- Humor
- Male main character
- Obesity
- Peer relationships
- Romance

Read Alikes

- Zadoff's book is bursting with humor. Readers who enjoy this book for that element would do well trying the *Carter Finally Gets It* series by Brent Crawford. Readers will also want to try out Don Calame's *Swim the Fly* series. Both Crawford and Calame's books take readers into the minds of young high school boys in authentic and funny ways.

- Readers who haven't tried Zadoff's other contemporary titles, *My Life, The Theater, and Other Tragedies* and *Since You Left Me* will want to for their strong voices.

■ MoreTitles Exploring Sports and Athletic Culture

Aronson, Marc, ed. *Pick-up Game: A Full Day of Full Court*. Candlewick, 2012. 176p. $6.99. 978-0-7636-6068-0.

Avery, Lara. *Anything But Ordinary*. Hyperion, 2012. 336p. $16.99. 978-1-4231-6386-2.

Carbone, Elisa. *Jump*. Speak, 2011. 288p. $8.99 Trade pb. 978-0-14-241913-7.

Chen, Justina. *Girl Overboard*. Little, Brown, 2009. 339p. $7.99 Trade pb. 978-0-316-01129-7.

Cumyn, Alan. *Tilt*. Groundwood, 2011. 288p. $16.95. 978-1-55498-119-9.

De La Pena, Matt. *Mexican Whiteboy*. Delacorte, 2010. 256p. $8.99 Trade pb. 978-0-440-23938-3.

Deuker, Carl. *Payback Time*. Graphia, 2012. 304p. $8.99 Trade pb. 978-0-547-57733-3.

_____. *Swagger*. Houghton Miffling, 2013. $17.99. 978-0-547-97459-0.

Feinstein, John. *Foul Trouble*. Knopf, 2013. 400p. $17.99. 978-0-375-86964-8.

Halpin, Brendan. *Shutout*. Farrar Straus Giroux, 2010. 192p. $16.99. 978-0-374-36899-9.

Kenneally, Miranda. *Breathe, Annie, Breathe*. Sourcebooks, 2014. 304p. $16.99. 978-1-4022-8479-3.

Korman, Gordon. *Pop*. Balzar + Bray/HarperTeen, 2011. 272p. $8.99 Trade pb. 978-0-06-174261-3.

Lipsyte, Robert. *Center Field*. HarperTeen, 2010. 288p. $16.99. 978-0-06-055704-1.

Lupica, Mike. *QB1*. Philomel, 2013. 272p. $17.99. 978-0-399-25228-0.

_____. *True Legend*. Philomel Books, 2012. 240p. $17.99. 978-0-399-25227-3.

Lynch, Chris. *The Big Game of Everything*. HarperTeen, 2010. 288p. $8.99 Trade pb. 978-0-06-074036-8.

Mackel, Kathy. *Boost*. Speak, 2010. 256p. $7.99 Trade pb. 978-0-14-241539-9.

McKissack, Fredrick. *Shooting Star*. Atheneum, 2010. 288p. $9.99 Trade pb. 978-1-4169-9774-0.

Meyerhoff, Jenny. *Queen of Secrets*. Farrar Straus Giroux, 2010. 240p. $16.99. 978-0-374-32628-9.

Mikulski, Keri. *Head Games*. Razorbill, 2011. 272p. $9.99 Trade pb. 978-1-59514-387-7.

Norris, Shana. *Troy High*. Amulet Books, 2010. 272p. $6.99 Trade pb. 978-0-8109-9665-6.

Padian, Maria. *Jersey Tomatoes Are the Best*. Ember, 2012. 352p. $9.99 Trade pb. 978-0-375-86563-3.

Pyron, Bobbie. *The Ring*. Westside, 2011. 253p. $9.95 Trade pb. 978-1-934813-60-7.

Quick, Matthew. *Boy21*. Little, Brown, 2012. 250p. $17.99. 978-0-316-12797-4.

Smith, Jennifer E. *The Comeback Season*. Simon & Schuster, 2010. 256p. $8.99 Trade pb. 978-1-4169-9606-4.

Spring, Melanie. *Game On*. Poppy, 2013. 272p. $10 Trade pb. 978-0-316-22727-8. (First in the *Game On* series).

Toor, Rachel. *On The Road To Find Out*. Farrar, Straus and Giroux, 2014. 320p. $17.99. 978-0-3743-0014-2.

Volponi, Paul. *The Final Four*. Speak, 2013. 272p. $9.99 Trade pb. 978-0-14-242385-1.

Chapter 15

The Survival Instinct: Getting Through it All

The contemporary book that has influenced me the most is The Chocolate War *by Robert Cormier. I first read it as I was edging out of my teens and wanted so badly to invent a time machine and hand it to my younger self. I didn't share Jerry Renault's exact experiences growing up, but that there was an author out there who wasn't afraid to write about how tough it is to exist in a world that doesn't always play fair--no matter how good a person you are--made me feel less alone. It made me resolve to be as honest as possible in my own work and to never shy away from the harder truths.* – Courtney Summers, author of *Some Girls Are* and *Fall for Anything*

Survival encapsulates a wide range of contemporary stories, from those about battles against nature to those stories about abuse, brutal home situations, bullying, cults, and more. And while it may seem that weathering a massive snowstorm has nothing to do with living through and thriving after sexual assault, the theme is universal: It's part determination and part doing, acting, and hoping that things can and will change. Survival is about balancing the act of holding out with the act of pushing forward enough to get through it. What is adolescence if not an exercise in survival?

The following titles tackle survival at all extremes – from the physical to the emotional. Many of these stories delve unflinchingly into the dark and gritty corners of adolescence.

Anthony, Joelle. **The Right and the Real**. Putnam, 2012. 288p. $17.99. 978-0-399-25525-0.

When Jamie's father marries Mira, he signs himself over to a church called the Right and the Real. But now that Jamie has reached the point of being able to sign herself over to the church as well, she's not sure she can do it. In fact, she knows she can't. Even though joining the church was originally her idea, Jamie's not ready to make the commitment, and in abandoning her devotion, her father and Mira kick her out of her home. Not only that, Jamie's boyfriend Josh also dumps her. Now she is faced with figuring out how to grow up and live on her own, as well as how to make friends and develop relationships, since so many of the ones she had were tied to the Right and the Real. Jamie also needs to figure out how to save her father from the church's indoctrination before she loses her family completely.

Appeal Factors

- Cults
- Family relationships
- Female main character
- Friendship
- Homelessness
- Non-traditional families
- Romance
- Spirituality and religion

Read Alikes

- Holly Cupala's *Don't Breathe a Word* would make for a strong read alike because in both stories, the female lead struggles to live her life without a home. Each character must figure out how to force an existence when the family home isn't a choice and in both cases, it's through forging relationships outside the home that helps them through their struggles.

- Readers who are taken with the cult aspect of Anthony's novel will want to read Carol Lynch Williams's *The Chosen One* and Michele Green's *Keep Sweet*. Both Williams and Green explore life within a cult, which makes for an interesting contrast to Anthony's story, which focuses on what life is when someone is outside the cult.

Avasthi, Swati. **Split**. Alfred A. Knopf, 2010. 288p. $16.99. 978-0-375-86340-0. $9.99 Trade pb. 978-0-375-86341-7.

With only $3.84 in his pocket, sixteen-year-old Jace shows up at his brother Christian's house thousands of miles away from his own home. Jace isn't only money-broke. He's spirit-broke, too, and it shows all over his bruised and beaten face (courtesy of his father). Christian takes him in, but adjusting to a new life isn't easy. Jace can take a new job, start at a new school and do well, and make new friends, but it doesn't make what happened in his past easy to accept. Especially since he knows that he's escaped and his mother hasn't. It's not just the abusive situation that keeps Jace wanting to go back home and protect his mom. He has a secret, and he doesn't know if he can live with himself until he goes back to the place where he endured the brutality.

Book Trailer

http://youtu.be/htjU0LccQ6E

Appeal Factors

- Abuse
- Family relationships
- Gritty
- Making new friends

- Male main character
- Moving
- Siblings

Read Alikes

- Stephanie Kuehn's *Charm and Strange* has a number of fascinating parallels to Avasthi's book, in that both stories feature a male main character coming to terms with a history of family abuse. More than that, Kuehn's book is the further internalization of what happens when the abused fears he may become an abuser himself, and as we learn in Avasthi's book, this is what torments Jace.

- Readers who want to read further tales of domestic abuse will want to read Nancy Werlin's *The Rules of Survival*. Likewise, those readers seeking more stories about relationship abuse will want to pick up Jennifer Brown's *Bitter End*.

Baer, Marianna. *Frost*. Balzar + Bray, 2011. 400p. $17.99. 978-0-06-179949-5.

Leena's a senior at her boarding school, and she's convinced the Dean to allow her and three of her friends to live in the Frost House, which lays slightly off-campus. The old Victorian home had been a boys' dorm for years. When she arrives for senior year, Leena isn't surprised to see only two of her three roommates are there – Kate, who was supposed to share a room with her, wasn't there yet since she was studying abroad. But Leena is surprised to learn she's getting a semester-long roommate named Celeste. She's not happy because Celeste has never been friendly with her, but Leena is going to make the best of the arrangement anyway. It's only for a semester. Except things start getting weird immediately. Celeste acts irrationally, covering Leena's bed in dead insects in one instance, though that's far from the only bizarre thing she does. Frost House itself seems haunted. Picture frames fall off the walls without warning, furniture shifts and adjusts, and doors seem to lock by themselves. Leena finds herself needing to resort to anti-anxiety medication to calm down. And it goes from bad to worse as both girls exhibit mental instability and physical scars that prove something absurd is happening in their room. Will they even make it out of Frost House alive?

Appeal Factors

- Fast pacing
- Female main character
- Mental illness

- Mystery
- Peer relationships
- Private/boarding school

Read Alikes

- Even though it sounds like a ghost story, Baer's book is wholly contemporary, using elements of gothic, horror, and thriller storytelling to propel the plot forward and force the reader to question whether what's going on is actually happening or if it's entirely in Leena's head. Because of that, this book would make an excellent read alike for Adele Griffin's *Tighter* or Francine Prose's *The Turning*. Both Griffin and Prose walk a fine line, like Baer, in forcing the reader to wonder whether their stories are happening or are the work of specters. Readers who want their stories to keep them on their toes and make them question what's real and what is not will be satisfied.

- Though Nova Ren Suma's *17 & Gone* toes the line of realistic and thriller/supernatural, it would be a good follow up to Baer's book because of the storytelling, compulsively readable and fluid prose, the tension-building, and ultimately, the way readers wonder whether what's going on is really happening, if it's in the narrator's head, or if it is the work of some type of "other." Both Baer and Suma force readers to consider mental illness as a cause for their character's behavior without ever laying out specifically whether it is the explanation.

Brown, Jennifer. ***Bitter End***. Little, Brown, 2012. 384p. $8.99. Trade pb. 978-0-316-08696-7.

As soon as Alex meets Cole, she falls head over heels in love with him. He's been assigned to her as a tutee, since he's a little bit behind in classwork, having just transferred from a new school. Cole also happens to be a football star and everything about him says this is the kind of guy Alex wants to be with romantically. But when they begin dating, Alex's best friend Zack becomes a problem for Cole. He has some jealousy issues, and he doesn't want Alex to spend any time with Zack because it would take time away from him. When Cole walks in on Zack and Alex goofing off, that's the tipping point, and from there on, Cole can't keep his hands off Alex – and not in a good way. She writes off the incidents as accidents, but they're anything but accidental. Cole's controlling nature manifests not only in those bruises, but also in the way he stalks and watches Alex like a hawk. Anything he sees that doesn't make him happy, he takes out on her. But Alex loves Cole. Can she possibly admit to what it is he is doing to her and get out before it's too late?

Appeal Factors

- Abuse
- Female main character
- Friendship
- Peer relationships

Read Alikes

- Brown's story starts at the beginning – readers experience the abuse right along with Alex and do so having insight into her mind as she's being victimized. Deb Caletti's *Stay* makes for a strong read alike, though the story isn't told through the eyes of the victim as she's experiencing abuse at the hand of her boyfriend; the story is instead told once she realized she was victimized and thus needs to get away.

- Another read alike is Amanda Grace's *But I Love Him*, which tells the abusive story backwards, from the point of getting out of the relationship through to what made the main character want to get involved with her boyfriend in the first place.

Christopher, Lucy. *Stolen*. Chicken House, 2012. 320p. $9.99 Trade pb. 978-0-545-17094-9.

When Gemma wakes up, she's no longer in the airport with her parents. She's in a strange house in what appears to be a never-ending desert with a guy she doesn't know. When she comes to a little more, Gemma realizes she does know this guy – he's the one who wanted to buy her a drink at the airport in Bangkok. And that's the last thing she remembers about Ty. Ty has her trapped in this place with no way out, and even if there was a way out, Gemma isn't entirely sure she wants out. Is it possible that now Ty has her all alone and promises to take care of her and love her without end that she's starting to sympathize with him? Worse, is she falling for him? Gemma doesn't know if it's better to stay and allow Ty to prove his devotion or if she needs to get out and save herself before it's too late and he doesn't take care of her the way he promises he will.

Appeal Factors

- Abuse
- Australia
- Female main character
- Foreign setting
- Kidnapping
- Mental illness
- Stockholm syndrome

Read Alikes

- A recent title tackling abduction, returning to the "normal" world, and the adjustment period therein is Liz Coley's *Pretty Girl-13*. Readers who haven't yet discovered Elizabeth Scott's *Living Dead Girl* will want to try it, since it was among the first exploring the disappearance of girls and the exploitation that can happen in those situations.

- Although neither *Forbidden* by Tabitha Suzuma nor *The Babysitter Murders* (in paperback as *Things I Shouldn't Think*) by Janet Ruth Young tackle Stockholm Syndrome nor do they explore kidnapping, both stories would make interesting read alikes to Christopher's title because they take on subjects that are less-explored and do so while forcing the reader to consider the sympathetic nature of the main characters. Suzuma's story is about incest – a very taboo topic – but it forces the reader to think about the characters and why they're going to that place, much as readers are forced through seeing what it was that Gemma found attractive and appealing about Ty, despite what it was he did to her. In Young's book, readers are forced to understand why it is the main character feels compulsions toward violence and murder, and they're forced to do so while also sympathizing with this tough mental illness.

Cupala, Holly. ***Don't Breathe a Word***. Harper Teen, 2012. $8.99. Trade pb. 978-0-06-176669-5.

Joy has asthma, but that's not what causes her to feel like she's suffocating all the time. The credit for that goes to her boyfriend Asher. He's abusive and controlling, and he masks it as wanting to protect her now that her older brother has gone away to college and can't do it anymore. Joy's parents are no award-winners, either. The only thing she can think to do is get out and get out fast. She cuts off her hair, packs some cash and granola bars, hops a bus out of her suburban home, and gets off at the Capitol Hill neighborhood in Seattle. She met a boy there not too long ago, and she hopes she can run into him again. He might be the exact answer she needs to solve her problems. Except as it turns out, life on the street isn't easy and Joy's not prepared for the hardship, for the ways of interaction, and for the gritty, raw reality of being homeless. Even when she is able to reconnect with Creed, he might not offer the answers she hopes exist. It's possible she's made the wrong choice entirely and has suffocated herself. Stuck between wanting to figure it out and go back home and face the music, Joy doesn't know which choice is the best one for true survival.

Appeal Factors

- Abuse
- Family relationships
- Female main character
- Homelessness
- Runaways
- Seattle
- Street culture

Read Alikes

- On a content and style level, Cupala's books are the prose-equivalent of Ellen Hopkins's novels. Where Hopkins writes dark, sharp novels about teens feeling stuck between tough spots, Cupala does just that in *Don't Breathe a Word*. Readers who want to stick with prose, rather than explore the verse novels of Hopkins, will find similarities between Cupala's writing style and that of Courtney Summers.

- Readers interested in the abuse storyline and the way it plays out will find many similarities between this title and Swati Avasthi's *Split*.

- Cupala's book makes for an interesting and worthwhile read alike to Joelle Anthony's *The Right and The Real*, as both Joy and Jamie are homeless and must figure out how to seek shelter, how to find a job, and how to make the sorts of connections they need to make without an adult to guide them through the process. While Joy's homelessness comes of choice and Jamie's is forced, the struggles they endure are similar.

King, A. S. *Everybody Sees the Ants*. Little, Brown, 2011. 279p. $17.99. 978-0-316-12928-2. $9.99. Trade pb. 978-0-316-12927-5.

Things suck for Lucky Linderman. He's constantly bullied by Nader McMillan and recently, Nader's been more abusive than usual. Even though Lucky's parents know what's going on, they've decided that staying out of it is the best way to handle the problem. Lucky's dad is obsessed with his own father who went MIA in Vietnam – and it's this same grandfather who Lucky visits in the trenches of war within in his own vivid dreams. The dreams Lucky has are so strong that he sometimes wakes up holding the very items his grandfather had been referencing in the dreams. After an argument between his parents, Lucky's mom takes them to Arizona to live with her sister for a while as a way to get some distance. It's here when things go to a whole new level with his dreams and with the mysterious ants that keep invading Lucky's mind and vision. What do those ants have to do with his grandfather and with the bullying he's experienced at school? Are they real?

Book Trailer

http://youtu.be/5juiTIH2qTI

Appeal Factors

- Abuse
- Bullying
- Family relationships
- Intergenerational stories
- Male main character
- Peer relationships
- Romance

Read Alikes

- King's books are in a bit of a class by themselves, as her writing blurs the line between what is realistic and what is surreal or potentially supernatural. While it's a matter of reader interpretation, the basis of those moments that feel unreal tend to be cerebral, rather than the work of some element beyond the character or real world story setting. Readers who like *Everybody Sees the Ants* will want to check out King's other titles, including *Please Ignore Vera Dietz* and *Ask the Passengers* because the style in each maintains that surrealistic quality while taking on big issues (grief and sexuality, respectively).

- Topically – particularly where it comes to Lucky's mental health and well-being – and in terms of the lines being blurred between reality and fantasy, readers may find Han Nolan's *Crazy* a worthwhile next read.

Lange, Erin Jade. **Butter**. Bloomsbury, 2012. 320p. $17.99. 978-1-59990-780-2. $9.99. Trade pb. 978-1-61963-121-2.

No one would deny that Butter is fat. He wouldn't deny it himself, either. It's part of why he's such an outcast at school, why he knows he'll never fit in, and why he knows he'll continue to be socially invisible, even though his size makes him hard to ignore. Butter's developed a relationship with a girl at school named Anna, one of the popular kids. Except, she has no idea that the person she's been talking with online is Butter – she thinks it's someone else entirely. When Butter finally opens up to her, not only is she shocked and unwilling to accept it, it sets off a spiral of bullying aimed at him. He knows things have to change and he knows how he'll make it happen: he's going to kill himself. And he's going to do it by eating himself to death online so everyone can watch it happen. But how far is too far to go? Will the bullies learn their lesson if their target kills himself for their own entertainment?

Book Trailer

http://youtu.be/ta-a06kH3Vw

Appeal Factors

- Abuse
- Body image
- Bullying
- Fast pacing

- Humor
- Male main character
- Obesity
- Suicide

Read Alikes

- Even though their books tackle entirely different aspects of abuse, Jace in Swati Avasthi's *Split* has a very similar voice to Butter's. Readers who want that sort of male voice would find these excellent read alikes. Both also offer strong narrative tension to keep the reader pushing through to the end.

- K. M. Walton's *Cracked* tackles bullying head-on, wherein the bully and the bullied find themselves face to face after near-death experiences. The tension and stakes in Walton's story, as well as the voice of the bullied, will resonate.

McDowell, Beck. **This Is Not a Drill**. Nancy Paulsen, 2012. 224p. $17.99. 978-0-399-25794-0.

Brian Strutts walks into the first grade classroom where high schoolers Emery and Jake are tutoring the students. Brian demands to take his son Patrick home. But when the teacher says he has to go through the front office, Patrick takes everyone hostage. He doesn't want to go through the office to get his son. He believes he should just be able to take Patrick home. Now that the classroom has been held hostage, the chances of people dying isn't just a possibility; it's a reality. What's wrong with Strutts isn't entirely clear, though. This situation isn't about taking his son home: it's his post-traumatic stress disorder reaction. It's up to Emery and Jake to not only protect the first graders, but themselves and – if they can – Strutts, too.

Appeal Factors

- Dual points of view
- Fast pacing
- Female main character
- Male main character

- Mental illness
- Post-traumatic stress disorder
- School hostage situation

Read Alikes

- McDowell's title has appeal to more reluctant readers because it is fast paced and takes place over the course of a single day. Readers who like the premise and are willing to challenge themselves would find much to appreciate in Michael Hassan's *Crash and Burn*. Both stories follow mentally-ill characters holding a classroom hostage.

- Readers who want a story about the effects of war on individuals – the root cause of Strutt's behavior in this book – will want to read Dana Reinhardt's *The Things a Brother Knows*, as well as E. M. Kokie's *Personal Effects*. For the added element of PTSD on returning vets, Trish Doller's *Something Like Normal* explores similar territory, though the outcomes for Strutts and Doller's main characters are much different.

Michaelis, Antonia. *The Storyteller*. Amulet, 2012. 416p. $18.95. 978-1-4197-0047-7.

Anna lives a charmed life. It's no secret nothing in her life has been hard. But when she discovers a lost doll that belongs to Abel – or rather, his little sister – Anna cannot help wondering about this weird boy who everyone calls the Polish peddler. She's drawn to him not just because she knows his life is so much different than hers, but she's curious about this fairy tale she's overheard him telling his little sister. One that Anna herself wants to know the end. Through the course of getting to know Abel and Micah, Anna discovers the dark and tortured world to which they belong, one riddled with absent parents, physical and mental abuse, drugs, and death of the most heinous kind. As it turns out, the fairy tale Abel spins for his sister may be something much bigger than a story. Anna hopes the ending is one of happily ever after.

Appeal Factors

- Abuse
- Drug abuse
- Family relationships
- Female main character

- Grief
- Peer relationships
- Sexuality
- Siblings

Read Alikes

- It's hard to place strong read alikes to this title because it's less about the plot elements that make it a worthwhile read (though those are certainly standout). It's more about the method through which the story is told. It's dark and disturbing. Readers who appreciate Michaelis's novel for its bleak philosophical, and metaphoric underpinnings will see similarities with Janne Teller's *Nothing* and with Blythe Woolston's books, particularly *Black Helicopters*. This book is a translation, which further gives it an interesting comparative element to Teller's novel, which is also a translation.

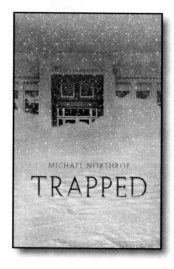

Northrop, Michael. *Trapped*. Scholastic, 2012. 240p. $9.99 Trade pb. 978-0-545-21013-3.

Everyone went to school the day of the big snowstorm. It didn't seem like much at first, but things picked up quickly. As the snow began to fall hard and the wind began to whip, the school closed early and students and staff made their way home. But not everyone got the message. Scotty and his friends Pete and Jason took this as an opportunity to sneak into the shop room to work on Jason's flammenwerfer. Without teachers around to stop or question them, it was the perfect opportunity to work without getting into trouble – that is, until they realized the storm outside was much worse than they thought. Now they're stuck with no adults, no power, no phones or computers and no idea how to get into the cafeteria to eat. Not to mention the bathroom situation. Is it possible for this crew of teens trapped in their high school to ever get home again?

Appeal Factors

- Adventure
- Fast pacing
- Humor

- Male main character
- Peer relationships
- Winter story

Read Alikes

- Northrop writes teen boys who are funny, and readers who love Scotty's voice in this novel will want to check out this author's other titles, including *Gentlemen* and *Rotten*. All three feature that hero who thinks and says the right line at the right time without trying hard to be funny.

- Readers who enjoy the survival aspect as it relates to nature will want to check out Roland Smith's title, *Peak*.

Scott, Mindi. *Live through This*. Simon Pulse, 2012. 304p. $9.99 Trade pb. 978-1-4424-4060-9.

Coley's not looking forward to her family's trip to Canada, despite the fact her boyfriend Reece will be able to join them. She's worried she'll endure sexual abuse in the way she has been for years from her brother. Coley loves her brother fiercely, as does anyone who has met him, and she wrestles with how best to end his treatment of her. How does she get out of the situation without making it worse for herself? When it turns out the girl she's never gotten along with at school may be the person she needs to turn to, Coley wonders if she can possibly feel good after sharing the truth. How can she save herself without ruining the life of someone she loves?

Book Trailer

http://youtu.be/zNHG2UHvmyo

Appeal Factors

- Abuse
- Family relationships
- Female main character
- Non-traditional families
- Quieter read
- Sexual violence
- Siblings

Read Alikes

- Colleen Clayton's novel *What Happens Next* is an exploration of sexual assault and would make a solid read alike. Both novels are internally-driven and feature a main character who struggles with whether or not to open up about the experience.

- Readers who want to read a story about sexual assault wherein the victim turns to vigilante justice for those who have experienced similar situations and felt they had no adult to turn to for help should pick up Daisy Whitney's *The Mockingbirds*.

- Those who have yet to read Laurie Halse Anderson's classic *Speak* will find this book follows similar themes.

Summers, Courtney. *Some Girls Are*. St. Martin's Griffin, 2010. 256p. $9.99 Trade pb. 978-0-312-57380-5.

After Regina is falsely accused of sleeping with best friend Anna's boyfriend, she's frozen out of her clique of popular girls. But she's not just frozen out – she's the subject of unrelenting bullying and torment. None of the girls know the truth, which is that Anna's boyfriend made an unwelcomed advance on her, not the other way around. Regina reaches out to Michael, a boy she once tormented herself, in hopes of making a friend. But sometimes, those fences aren't so easy to mend. Can Regina make friends again? Or is she stuck in a never-ending spiral of abuse at the hands of her former friends?

Book Trailer

http://youtu.be/tQReTV_Pxno

Appeal Factors

- Abuse
- Bullying
- Fast pacing
- Female main character
- Peer relationships
- Sexual violence

Read Alikes

- Hannah Harrington's *Speechless*, which features similarly tight, quick-paced writing and plotting, follows a girl who becomes bullied after spilling the secret she discovers about classmates. Like Regina in Summers's title, Harrington's character goes from top of the social order to becoming victim of her former friends' torment and ridicule.

- This book, like Scott's title above, features many of the elements of Laurie Halse Anderson's *Speak*, and readers will see many of the elements of silencing, of social shaming, and of victimizing in each.

Walton, K. M. *Cracked*. Simon Pulse, 2012. 336p. $16.99. 978-1-4424-2916-1. $9.99 Trade pb. 978-1-4424-2917-8.

Bull never lets up on Victor, bullying him endlessly. Victor doesn't fight back; he lets Bull have at him. But this isn't as simple as who is the bully and who is the bullied. Bull comes from a home where his parents hardly make enough money to stay afloat, and they are vicious toward Bull. Victor is the complete opposite – he comes from what looks like a stable home, one where money is never a problem or an issue. Except, it's not that simple. Victor's parents are never home since they're always out chasing more money and working more hours. They find their son to be a burden. Being the bullied, even as awful as it is, may be the only reason Victor gets attention from anyone at all. What happens when both boys wake up in a shared hospital room and have to face not only their own demons, but each other?

Book Trailer

http://youtu.be/8JulvfjJIxc

Appeal Factors

- Abuse
- Bullying
- Dual points of view
- Family relationships
- Male main characters
- Significant pets or animals
- Socioeconomic class
- Suicide

Read Alikes

- Readers who like the dual points of view offered in this story – especially as it relates to two male characters who come from significantly different backgrounds – and those who are drawn in with the bullying storyline, will want to read Joshua Cohen's *Leverage*. Even though Walton's story delves into the notion of what it means to be a bully or to be bullied, at the heart it is a story about what bullying is and where it comes from, as well as what the consequences of bullying are through a broader perspective. Cohen's novel explores these similar ramifications.

- Erin Jade Lange's *Butter* is another strong read alike to this title, especially as it relates to bullying and a strong male voice. Like Walton's story, there is high tension and quick pacing.

- Because Walton's book explores the personal backgrounds of abuse both Bull and Victor experience at home and the ways those backgrounds play into how they find their roles as bully and victim, there are many parallels to Swati Avasthi's *Split*, as well as Steph Kuehn's *Charm and Strange*.

Woolston, Blythe. ***Black Helicopters***. Candlewick, 2013. 176p. $12.99. 978-0-7636-6146-5.

When fifteen-year-old Val was younger, her mother was killed by the black helicopters. Since then, her father has used Val as his tool to fight. She and her brother are kept hidden away, told they should be paranoid, and Val, in particular, has been educated to resist, to hide, and to know that her mission in life is to destroy when the time is right. She has almost no privileges until that time comes. She needs to save herself for it. When her house burns down and her father dies, she and her brother now have to figure out where to live. They find shelter through father's friend, but what Val also finds is that there were many secrets in her father's life. The paranoia he had and used as a guide to raise Val meant Val never got to figure things out on her own. Now that she's armed with this knowledge, she can be a real weapon.

Appeal Factors

- Abuse
- Family relationships
- Female main character
- Homelessness
- Rural setting

- Sexual violence
- Siblings
- Socioeconomic class
- Trafficking

Read Alikes

- Stylistically and thematically, readers who enjoy Woolston's writing style and storytelling will want to seek out Adam Rapp's books. For this story in particular, readers may want to check out *The Children and the Wolves*. Both Woolston and Rapp force readers to consider the story at the story level, as well as the stories that play out on a grander, more literary level. The parallels between Woolston's novel and Rapp's don't end at their style and storytelling; both contain fascinating threads about the roles of adults in a teen's development and search for independence.

■ More Books Featuring Stories of Survival

Ayarbe, Heidi. *Wanted.* Balzar + Bray, 2012. 400p. $17.99. 978-0-06-199388-6.

Bock, Caroline. *LIE.* St. Martin's Griffin, 2011. 224p. $9.99. 978-0-312-66832-7.

Caletti, Deb. *Stay.* Simon Pulse, 2012. 336p. $9.99 Trade pb. 978-1-4424-0374-1.

Cent, 50. *Playground.* Razorbill, 2011. 320p. $17.99. 978-1-59514-434-8.

Chayil, Eishes. *Hush.* Walker, 2012. 386p. $9.99 Trade pb. 978-0-8027-2332-1.

Clayton, Colleen. *Happens Next.* Poppy, 2012. 320p. $17.99. 978-0-316-19868-4.

Cohen, Joshua. *Leverage What.* Speak, 2012. 432p. $8.99 Trade pb. 978-0-14-242086-7.

Colasanti, Susane. *Keep Holding On.* Viking, 2012. 240p. $17.99. 978-0-670-01225-1.

Coley, Liz. *Pretty Girl-13.* Katherine Tegen, 2013. 352p. $17.99. 978-0-06-212737-2.

Cummings, Priscilla. *The Journey Back.* Dutton, 2012. 224p. $16.99. 978-0-525-42362-1.

Draper, Sharon M. *Panic.* Atheneum, 2013. 272p. $17.99. 978-1-4424-0896-8.

Grace, Amanda. *But I Love Him.* Flux, 2011. 245p. $9.95 Trade pb. 978-0-7387-2594-9.

Harrington, Hannah. *Speechless.* Harlequin Teen, 2012. 288p. $9.99 Trade pb. 978-0-373-21052-7.

Hassan, Michael. *Crash and Burn.* Balzar + Bray, 2013. 544p. $18.99. 978-0-06-211290-3.

Kelley, Ann. *Lost Girls.* Little, Brown, 2012. 336p. $17.99. 978-0-316-09062-9.

Morel, Alex. *Survive.* Razorbill, 2012. 259p. $17.99. 978-1-59514-510-9.

Murdoch, Emily. *If You Find Me.* St. Martin's Griffin, 2013. 256p. $17.99. 978-1-250-02152-6.

Myracle, Lauren. *Shine.* Abrams, 2012. 376p. $7.99 Trade pb. 978-1-4197-0184-9.

Purcell, Kim. *Trafficked.* Viking Children's, 2012. 400p. $17.99. 978-0-670-01280-0.

Quick, Matthew. *Sorta Like a Rock Star.* Little, Brown, 2011. 384p. 978-0-316-04353-3.

Rapp, Adam. *The Children and the Wolves.* Candlewick, 2012. 160p. $16.99. 978-0-7636-5337-8.

Whitney, Daisy. *The Mockingbirds.* Little, Brown, 2010. 352p. $16.99. 978-0-316-09053-7.

Part 3

Real Talk

While books are often read in isolation, achieving a deeper connection with and an appreciation for material can happen through dialog. A great way to encourage book discussion is through conversation starters.

Conversation starters are a way to talk about books that share common themes and topics present in today's world and zeitgeist. These aren't just themes that emerge through the books; they're themes that will follow readers through their teen years and through the rest of their adult lives. The topics explored here should get conversation flowing about the books included in the selection and elicit dialog more broadly about reading and analyzing texts.

Included here are five conversation starters, each containing between four and seven titles, on the following topics:

- Bullying

- Sex, sexual assault, and rape

- Teens and technology

- Unlikable female characters

- Young people and war

There are additional suggestions for conversation topics, meant to provide further means of thinking about contemporary YA fiction and methods through which to talk about these books with readers.

Also included in this section are a toolkit to help with advocating for contemporary YA fiction and an annotated list of further resources.

Chapter 16

Conversation Starter: Bullying

When it comes to books about bullying, what I typically see people talking about them in terms of the bully and the bullied -- and, truth be told, those are usually the two main protagonists in such books. But I think that who these books are for are not those teens. The bully won't recognize him or herself; the bullied may not be in a place where they can read about an experience as bad as, or worse than, what they are living every day. Who benefits? The bystanders. The teens standing on the edges of the bullying going on around them, who may not even have realized that what is happening at the table next to them is something more than "teasing" or "kidding." I believe that these books will help those bystanders recognize what is going on around them, and give them the tools to stand up, to become a friend, become an ally, and if not stop the bullying -- make it better by becoming a friend. -- Elizabeth Burns, librarian

Bullying has been around forever, but over the course of the last decade, our awareness of bullying and the ill effects of relentless teasing and physical intimidation has made it an issue worth talking about. Because teens deal with bullying on a daily basis – either because they're a victim themselves or they know someone who is – it's something that teens can make a real difference in changing. The more teens are empowered with the ability to identify acts of bullying when they see or experience them, the more they can then be empowered to speak up and out about what's happening and prevent it from continuing.

Bullying is not always in the form of physical brutality. Sometimes, it comes through the silent treatment (the freeze-out), through small acts of passive aggressiveness, or through relentless verbal teasing. Likewise, there is much to consider in what events lead up to bullying and what those events might say about such things as gender stereotypes, about respect for choice, and in the way aggression may or may not differ when it's perpetuated between a group of boys or a group of girls. These books give a glimpse inside the psychology of bullying at the ground level. Many of these books may cause visceral reactions from readers because of how unflinching they are in exploring the brutality of physical, mental, and emotional torment.

A number of strong non-fiction titles addressing bullying are worth mentioning here, not only as important reading for adults who work with teens, but many of these are books that appeal to teen readers with an interest in the subject.

Though most teens' first exposure to bullying in media may be through the film Mean Girls, the screenplay was adapted from Rosalind Wiseman's *Queen Bees* and *Wannabes: Helping Your Daughter Survive Cliques, Gossip, Boyfriends, and Other Realities of Adolescence*. Rachel Simmons explored girl-on-girl bullying in her book *Odd Girl Out: The Hidden Culture of Aggression in Girls* and more recently, Emily Bazelon tackles bullying in her *Sticks and Stones: Defeating the Culture of Bullying and Rediscovering the Power of Character and Empathy*. Also worthwhile is Dave Cullen's *Columbine*, which looks at the psychology of the perpetrators behind the Columbine High School shooting.

In conjunction, the titles presented and discussed below could be paired well with any of the non-fiction titles listed here to offer both a wide and deep exploration of bullying through a number of different channels.

Cohen, Joshua. *Leverage*. Speak, 2012. 432p. $8.99 Trade pb. 978-0-14-242086-7.

Danny is a gymnast and he and the rest of his teammates are used to abuse in the locker room by the football players for being little. When Kurt moves to town – a hulking new addition to the football team – Danny certainly never thinks the two of them will be friends. But when both of them are witnesses to a brutal incident of bullying toward another member of the gymnastics team, they have shared the sort of bond that they cannot separate themselves from easily. Worse, when the bullied player dies, the two of them know they have to confront what it is they saw and make sure that sort of behavior never happens again.

• This brutal, unrelenting story is honest in its portrayal of male aggression and bullying, and it's fueled in part by performance-enhancing drugs. Cohen's dual-voiced novel brings up questions about what it is that causes someone to want to partake in bullying: Is it something individuals are inclined to instinctively or does something need to provoke them? Is aggression amplified when their minds and bodies are impacted by drugs? Could these violent tendencies have anything to do with honor and masculinity and if so, at what lengths will someone go to remain alpha male?

• There are questions to consider in regards to what happens to the person being bullied. In this story, the bullied cannot live with what happened and chooses to commit suicide. The consequences of bullying impact not only him, but also his family, friends, peers, and teammates. What punishments for the bully are justified? Can those who witnessed the incident stand up for the victim? What can they do or say that might change the course of actions in the future?

- Cohen offers much to dissect in terms of sports culture and what can make one athletic team feel more privileged than another. Contrast the ways bullying plays out in Cohen's novel with *Some Girls Are* below, in terms of the methods that a male may implement in order to intimidate another male as opposed to how a female may manipulate and intimidate the female she's bullying. Are boys more likely to use physical violence and girls more likely to resort to verbal? Distinctions among genders aren't definitive, of course – Cohen's novel is worth considering in light of Robert Cormier's classic *The Chocolate War*, as well, which showcases how males can be manipulative and intimidating without resorting to physical brutality. Are our ideas of gender and bullying socially constructed?

- Also worth discussing in this book is the absence (or presumed absence) of adult authority figures. Were there really no adults present for any of these incidents and/or were these adults choosing to ignore the situations going on? Why would an adult do that? Is this a perception by the teens in the story or was it a reality of the culture within the school and athletic department?

Harrington, Hannah. *Speechless*. Harlequin Teen, 2012. 288p. $9.99 Trade pb. 978-0-373-21052-7.

When Chelsea Knot walks in on two boys from school at a party being intimate with one another, she's shocked. And she opens her mouth. Because of her position as a popular girl at school, when she says something, the results mean certain punishment for the boys in question. It also turns her life upside down; no longer is she at the top of the social hierarchy. So she takes a vow of silence in order to protect not only herself but anyone else from what could result. Keeping silent doesn't solve her problems, though, as she finds herself the target of bullying, too.

- Harrington's novel offers an array of potential topics to discuss, the first being that of what is and is not within someone's rights to share of others. Did Chelsea have a right to share what she saw at a party? If so, who does she have the right to share it with? In knowing she had the potential to make what she shared widely known because of her popularity, could she have known the consequences for the boys or for herself? Were the consequences either faced justified?

- Another worthwhile angle of dialog is that of what is and isn't appropriate punishment for Chelsea. She's become a target of bullying herself, getting a miniscule taste of what other people experienced on a daily basis. But Chelsea also punishes herself by taking a vow of silence. In doing so, she learns to be a better observer and listener, opening herself up to more meaningful relationships with people at school.

- This brings up a whole host of other issues to think about, including the benefits and consequences of silence. Does Chelsea learn a real lesson in the end? What, if anything, does she walk away with following this series of events? Has she learned what real friends are? Did her conscious efforts to listen, rather than to talk, help her discover something about the people she once called friends?

- Because the rumor Chelsea spread was about two boys in a relationship, neither of whom had been openly gay, this novel also tackles what can happen to those who identify – or don't readily identify –

as LGBTQ. As recipients of bullying because of this, there are channels opened to discuss hate crimes and how they relate to and differ from bullying itself. It's also worth thinking about what Chelsea discovers regarding other people's choices. What, if any, right does she have to cast judgment upon other people? And what, if anything, led her to choose to "out" these two boys?

King, A. S. *Everybody Sees the Ants*. Little, Brown, 2011. 279p. $17.99. 978-0-316-12928-2.

Nader McMillan makes Lucky Linderman's life a living hell by bullying him relentlessly. But this isn't the only challenge in Lucky's life. His parents are not getting along too well and he can't cope with his father's inability to get over his own father never coming home from the war in Vietnam. When Lucky's taken by his mom for the summer to live with his Aunt Jodi, it's only a small escape – Lucky's being visited in his dreams by his missing grandfather. Or rather, Lucky himself visits his grandfather in Vietnam in these dreams. Lucky's also seeing the ants everywhere. They tell him how to act, how to think, how to behave.

- As much as the story sounds like it verges on fantastic, this book reads realistically if the ants and dreams with the grandfather are explored through the lens of coping. Lucky uses his time with his grandfather to learn about his own strengths and his own individuality, and he uses the ants as a means to seek revenge and solace in the face of bullying and hardship without having to raise a hand himself. When bad things happened to Lucky, he retreats to the dreams and the ants.

- What makes King's book worth opening a dialog about is precisely this aspect of being bullied: What are safe spaces? How does one escape the daily barrage of teasing and physical abuse and assault? If there aren't allies in one's life, how can someone get the help that he or she needs? Thinking about King's book in light of the other titles on this list, it's worth considering how Lucky develops his own coping skills that are unique and effective. But more than that, Lucky's sharing his coping mechanisms with the reader. While he may be withdrawing socially at times, he's doing so because he has a safe mental space to reside in. So even if he's exhibiting low social engagement, it's possible he's doing it because he needs to. It's how Lucky uses his coping skills in social settings that suggest he's not necessarily in a problematic place. He's not acting out some of the things he's thinking. He's allowing himself to think them, then packing those thoughts away in order to behave appropriately.

- As is the case in the bulk of the novels in this particular conversation starter, there is much to consider in terms of adult presence, adult attention to the affairs of the teens around them, as well as the perception of these absences as seen through the eyes of a teen character. King's book has ambiguity in meaning and in resolution, which only enhances the opportunities for discussing the heavy issue of bullying. Does bullying have an end point or do characters – and people – eventually find a way to live with what they're experiencing?

Stella, Leslie. *Permanent Record*. Amazon, 2013. 282p. $17.99. 978-1-4778-1639-4.

Badi, an Iranian-American boy, is starting at a private Catholic academy after a series of incidents at his old school. He was the target of terrible bullying, so this is his chance to start over again. He'll not only be starting over in a new school and meeting new people, he's now got a new name: Bud Hess. He's not thrilled about any of this, especially since it means giving up part of his own identity in order to fit in. When a series of anonymous letters start showing up in the school newspaper, pitting student organization against student organization, everyone suspects it's the new kid. He's there to stir things up. Since Bud refuses to take part in the annual chocolate bar sale that funds the student organizations, it seems like it could be no one else who wrote the letters. It's not long before Bud finds himself the victim of bullying again.

Stella's book isn't as cut-and-dry as it sounds like it might be. Bud isn't necessarily innocent himself. He was indeed the victim of bullying at his old school, but he sought retaliation, which is why he's being sent to a new school. Now, seeing himself again as a victim, he's hoping to seek revenge yet again.

- This book is packed with discussion fodder. First and foremost, like the other books here, what it means to be a bully and what it means to be bullied are front and center. But stepping even further back from that are the issues of identity and the issues of prejudice when it comes to race and ethnicity. At his new school, Badi takes on an entirely new identity and name at the request of his family in order to better fit in. One of the reasons Badi finds himself bullied at his new school has to do with his refusal to take part in school traditions (a la Robert Cormier's *The Chocolate War*), and there is much then to consider in terms of what it means to take a stand. In Badi's case, it results in being accused of misdeeds and having a vendetta against other students. But by bucking tradition, has he somehow opened himself up to this sort of backlash from his peers? Since he's the new guy, does he have the right to be different? Does Badi have the right to seek revenge for what he's endured from his peers? If he's Bud and not Badi, is there an additional layer of deceit and removal from self?

- Pushing Stella's novel even further are the issues surrounding why parents would encourage their son to abandon his racial and ethnic background in order to "fit in" at school. What happens if Badi isn't entirely on board with this plan? How does he remain loyal to his own heritage and also not disappoint his parents? Are there parallels between the abandonment of his identity and his refusal to take part in school traditions?

Summers, Courtney. *Some Girls Are*. St. Martin's Griffin, 2010. 256p. $9.99 Trade pb. 978-0-312-57380-5.

When Regina Afton is kicked out of the "Fearsome Fivesome" – one of the most popular cliques in her high school – for being accused of sleeping with the boyfriend of her best friend at a party, she finds herself the victim of their relentless payback tactics, ranging from name calling to back stabbing, to being frozen out, and having a hate website dedicated just to her. But things only get worse when her once-best-friends choose a method of revenge that puts her face-to-face with the person who started the hate spiral in the first place. No one believes that Regina was almost raped by her friend's boyfriend at the party. And when it seems like maybe Regina's found herself an ally, she has to come to terms with how she treated people when she was at the top of the social ladder. Seeking forgiveness is anything but easy. Not just that, though; seeking forgiveness is something Regina simply doesn't do.

• Summer's novel is relentless in its portrayal of girl-on-girl bullying, raising many discussion-worthy topics. Some of these include the thought processes behind psychological torment, the effects of the silent treatment, and impact that the use of degrading terms such as "whore" may have in demoralizing a female, particularly one trying to come to terms with the fact she was nearly raped at a party. Regina isn't an easy-to-like character in this story, either, raising questions about fault and about responsibility for one's actions. Did she deserve the treatment she got from her former friends because she, too, had perpetuated similar actions in the past? Does she deserve sympathy for losing her place among her friends and for her experiences at the party, despite the fact she's not a sympathetic or likeable person? Did she get what was coming to her? Moreover, did she have a right to redemption? And at what point, if any, should her own past behaviors influence the way people treat her now? Why does no one want to believe what happened to her at the party?

• There is much here to talk about in terms of social dynamics. What is it that makes a person a friend or an ally? Are there adults present at all in this story? Or is their absence something seen only through the eyes of the characters living in this world?

• Flipping the switch a bit, Summers raises a lot of discussion-worthy points more broadly about female relationships, about what lines can be drawn between support and encouragement, as well as disrespect and admonishment. Contrast the bullying in this book with Cohen's *Leverage*: What methods are employed when girls gang up on one another? How do they differ than when boys bully one another? Do these differences have anything to do with gender roles and subscriptions to them? Are they more biologically-ingrained or socially-learned? Does it matter at all or is this something that *we've* been socially ingrained to believe?

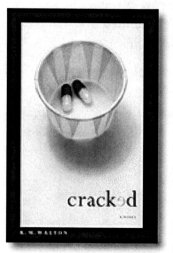

Walton, K. M. *Cracked*. Simon Pulse, 2012. 336p. $9.99 Trade pb. 978-1-4424-2917-8.

Bull never lets up on Victor, always making him the center of the bullying. It's been that way since elementary school and while Bull is definitely the aggressor, Victor doesn't make him stop and doesn't fight back. But what looks like a story of a bully and his target isn't that simple. Both boys have a lot going on in their lives. Bull comes from a poor family, one that's always scraping every penny together. He's told regularly that he was an unwanted child, too. Victor, on the other hand, comes from a home where there is plenty of money. The problem is that his parents are never around because they're always working in order to make more money. They never see Victor. He's their burden. The story comes to a head when both boys attempt suicide for and through different means and they end up in the same hospital room. Now they have to face their own healing as individuals and as a duo. Can the bully learn how to not bully and the bullied learn how to stand up for himself?

• Walton's book brings up a lot of insight into what elements may contribute to an aggressor's behavior, as well as what may make a victim not want to speak up. Are Bull and Victor playing these roles as bully and victim in order to garner attention for themselves? Is it because they aren't getting that attention from home? What is it that compelled Bull to choose Victor as his target?

- Both boys in this story have complicated histories apart from each other and with one another. Untangling them through therapy and through their forced time together allows for much discussion. Because this story is told through the eyes of both boys, readers can see what goes on inside the head of the bully and what goes on inside the head of the bullied. Is it possible the bully is himself bullied, too? How much can therapy and intervention help in changing the behaviors of both of these boys? What are the things they are missing in their lives that could help them choose to stop bullying and being bullied?

- Because of *how* Victor and Bull end up in this facility together, there is much fodder here for discussing suicide and the impact other people's behavior and decisions has on an individual. Their reasons for being here aren't the same, even if the perception is that both attempted suicide. Compare the outcomes of Walton's characters with the bullied character in Cohen's *Leverage* and the consequences therein.

- Another avenue of discussion in Walton's book is that of mental illness. While the overarching story is about bullying, what underlies the behavior for both Bull and Victor is what their mental states are during their encounters, as well as their mental states brought about in their home lives.

Chapter 17

Conversation Starter: Sex, Sexual Assault, and Rape

The Otis Library joined as a community partner for 'The Power of Purple - An End to Domestic Violence' event, a campaign to bring domestic violence out of the shadows and into the open. I asked to be part of this event. According to Love is Respect, 'One in three adolescents in the U.S. is a victim of physical, sexual, emotional, or verbal abuse from a dating partner.' Therefore, it's fundamentally important for teens to be aware of the signs of violent relationships, know how to get help, and to understand healthy relationships. As a YA Librarian, I know that reading about situations both similar and different from your own helps create awareness, understanding, and gives you strength.

For this event, the library created a display. I designed 'When Love Hurts,' a brochure for teens on dating violence. The brochure has four parts: dating violence book list, romance book list, a nonfiction list on sex/relationships, and empowering songs to listen to. To appeal to teens, I created the list to have serious merit, but also fun books to showcase both sides of relationships. At the event, I handed out the book list to adults and to teens. I hope that the list helps someone. I've included the list in a display at the library and will use it in the future, both in the library and in the community.

Additionally, in my teen room I have a wall display in the fiction stacks about unhealthy relationships, stemming from an article in Seventeen *magazine about Chris Brown and Rihanna. Their publicized incident created awareness that even famous people aren't exempt from violent relationships. Anytime I see something new on the topic, I post it there. Also displayed are book covers featuring books about dating violence. I often see teens reading the article and looking at the wall display. While I hope they never have to experience dating violence, I hope that they are armed with information on how to break the cycle if needed.*
– Jennifer Rummel, teen librarian

Sex is not new territory in YA, thanks in no small part to books like Judy Blume's *Forever*. Despite the fact sex in YA fiction exists, it's not without controversy. Adults sometimes worry that too much sex in the books teens read might lead them down a wrong road or give them ideas about engaging in sex themselves (and the truth is that sometimes teens are having sex and sometimes they aren't). There are the accusations, too, that YA books are too dark and that by tackling some of the more provocative aspects of sex, teen readers are going to find themselves learning about things they don't need to know about or "shouldn't" know about so young.

These books are essential and crucial to opening dialog. Teens who aren't ready to read about these things won't; they are amazing self-censors and know their comfort limits. But teens are also incredibly curious. It's through reading these honest and sometimes brutal stories where they can safely explore the things that they're interested in knowing more about. Yes, some of these books are detailed in their depictions of sex. Some may even be graphic.

Books that explore sex – including those that tackle sexual violence – should be made available and discussed. These books are safe spaces, and they're ripe with fodder about what healthy sex is, about what is appropriate when it comes to touch, and what it means to be a victim. These are heavy topics, but it's through reading and talking about books like these where we become more open about dialog on these topics. The more we talk about it, the less taboo the subject becomes and the more we're able to empower readers with tools for making choices in their own lives.

All of the books included here owe much to two of the classics on these themes: Laurie Halse Anderson's *Speak* and Chris Lynch's *Inexcusable*. Not only do both titles tackle these issues head on, but they did so through the perspectives of a female victim of assault and a male who raped a girl, respectively. These stories get inside the mindsets of the victim and of the criminal, and both force readers to consider what it means to be on either side of that divide. Readers are able to think about what it means to be good and what it means to do something out of character and irresponsible.

These topics are timely and they are timeless. Discussing healthy sex and the problematic aspects of sex is vital in helping teens not only feel comfortable and normal in their thinking about these things, but it helps them understand that these are issues they'll be confronting their entire lives.

Desir, Christa. *Fault Line*. Simon Pulse, 2013. 240p. $16.99. 978-1-4424-6072-0.

When Ani moves to town, Ben is immediately drawn to her because she's a challenge. She's hard headed, she's sarcastic, and she gets what she wants because she goes after it. When they start to date, the worst happens to Ani: She goes to a party, her drink is spiked, and she's coerced into a number of sexual situations she would never have initiated in any other state. It's never laid out exactly what happened, though it is clear that at some point, she was raped by at least one person at the party. Ben, who did not attend the event, blames himself for not being there to protect her. But the real discussion-worthy element of the book is what happens after: How can Ben be there for a girl who withdraws and feels as though she's lost any and all respect from her peers?

- Desir's title is blunt in its exploration of victimization, victim-blaming, and the sorts of responses aimed at a victim of assault and rape. It also explores the notion of what it means to be a support system and offer a safe space for that victim. How much is worth keeping quiet about and at what point do teens need to seek help and advice from those who are experts on handling these challenges? Ani wants no one to know what happened to her because she's received harsh response at school from those who were at the party. But the weight of what happened is heavy on her, and she can't go through it entirely alone. Even if Ben is there, he can only offer her support when she asks for it specifically – and Ani isn't the most open about what it is she needs. How far can or should he push her for information? Does she have a right to keep it all quiet?

- At what point does Ben, who has been there for Ani since the incident happened and promised not to tell her mother, have to break his oath in order to assure that Ani gets the kind of help she isn't getting from him or the counselor who helped her the morning after the incident?

- There is a lot more to talk about here, including ownership of one's body and sex life; what it means to have a healthy relationship that is both sexual and not; what it means to be a victim; what it means to be a victim's advocate; how people view victims of rape and assault; and at what point one's own behavior may or may not have contributed to other people's actions toward them, among other things. Desir's novel explores the phenomenon of victim-blaming, as well slut-shaming, and she does a great job of leaving more questions unanswered than answered.

Scheidt, Erica Lorraine. *Uses for Boys*. St. Martin's Griffin, 2013. 240p. $9.99 Trade pb. 978-1-250-00711-7.

Anna used to be the only thing in her mother's world, but when her mom started a cycle of dating new men, marrying them, moving her and Anna into a new home, then subsequently divorcing those men and beginning again, that relationship between daughter and mother waned. When she's thirteen, Anna has her first taste of what it is that makes her mother choose this life: The attention she received from boys. From then on, Anna lets boys touch her and she lets them have sex with her. Some of these experiences are healthy and good; some of them, though, lead to unhealthy consequences. Some of them make Anna question who she is at her own core – is she Anna or is she simply a tool for these boys to use and then leave hanging?

- Scheidt's book cuts no corners in sex and exploration of one's sexual desires. It's honest about the emotional and physical consequences that can emerge when a girl chooses to engage in sex from a young age. Anna has to make choices about her own body, despite the fact that, at times, it doesn't feel like her body belongs to her at all. That's not to say the sex in this story is all about the bad things that can happen. In fact, Scheidt does a good job of showcasing healthy sexual activity and healthy emotional relationships between Anna and a boy. Those are moments worth talking about and discussing with teens, as are the moments when sex has significant consequences, including pregnancy.

- There is much worth considering here when it comes to what craving physical attention from boys means in terms of Anna's reputation now and in the future. Are there words that adequately describe a girl who is curious about her body? Is it possible for someone to use her body and its physical responses to fill the gaps she has inside her emotionally and mentally? Is it problematic Anna chooses to put herself in these situations?

- This book raises many questions about parental and adult influence on the development of teens. Part of why Anna chooses to explore sex so much is because she's seen that this method is the one her mother chose to pursue. It brought her mother security and stability, even if it wasn't always long-lived. What roles do adults play in the lives of teens, especially when it comes to discussing relationships, both those which are sexual and those which aren't?

- Even though the topic of sex is at the heart of this discussion guide, it's also worth noting that this book is one of the few in contemporary YA titles featuring a high school dropout. That is itself a meaty discussion, both in light of and outside of the scope of Anna's use of physical intimacy for security, approval, and self-confidence.

- Ultimately, Scheidt's novel is about choices. Are there "right" choices? Are there "wrong" choices? What or who gets to decide what is and isn't appropriate for an individual's life?

Scott, Mindi. *Live through This*. Simon Pulse, 2012. 304p. $9.99 Trade pb. 978-1-4424-4060-9.

Coley's life is imperfect. It's not about the fact her mother is married to a man who brought new siblings into the family nor that Coley's not always getting along with other girls on her cheer squad. Nor is her imperfect life about the people who keep pressing her to make her relationship with Reece more serious because they'd be so great together. What weighs Coley down is the biggest secret she holds: she's a regular victim of sexual assault that comes not from a stranger, but at the hands of her own brother.

- Scott's story is a quiet one because Coley keeps what's happening to her as hidden as possible. She doesn't want to admit that it happens because she's embarrassed and ashamed by it. It's amplified because everyone likes her older brother. He's a likeable guy – it's just that his actions toward her are inappropriate. They leave Coley believing she's wrong for how *she* feels about it.

- Though this book explores sexual assault, the standout elements come through Coley's wrestling with her own conscious about the right course of actions for making the assault stop. She loves her brother, and she doesn't want him to get in trouble. But she also knows his actions aren't right and that she has the rights to her own body.

- This secret is one Coley feels like she can't hold on to anymore, but she knows that anything she says will have consequences. How can she stand up for herself and still maintain loyalty to her family? How does she come to admit to being a victim not just once, but repeatedly over a long period of time? Who are her advocates when she feels as though the biggest unit she has – her family – might not be there for her in the way she needs them to be? How does someone who feels she has no voice find that voice within her?

- Scott incorporates a number of other interesting and discussion-worthy elements in her story. Coley doesn't always get along with her fellow cheerleaders, but some of them may turn out to be her strongest advocates. How could she know where to seek help when it feels like everyone has turned against her? Her brother's popularity and likability complicate the situation further. What happens to Coley's long-time, supportive, and caring boyfriend when the truth comes out? Can they have a normal relationship ever again? Do either of them want to have a normal relationship?

Whitney, Daisy. *The Mockingbirds*. Little, Brown, 2012. 288p. $8.99 Trade pb. 978-0-316-09054-4.

Alex wakes up in a room she doesn't recognize, in a bed that isn't her own, and suddenly she realizes what happened the night before. She knows she should say something, but she's ashamed of what she let happen to her after the party. Themis Academy wouldn't care anyway. The administration believes none of their students would ever do anything bad. But it's with the encouragement of her roommates that Alex seeks justice through The Mockingbirds, a student-run vigilante group that tries student cases the administration would otherwise prefer to ignore. The more Alex thinks about the events that night, though, she wonders if she was really a rape victim or if she did something that implied consent.

When her case is heard by The Mockingbirds, Alex really begins to understand that she was indeed a victim and that she has the right to speak up and out about what happened. She feels determined and empowered enough to want to take a role within the justice group, in order to help other victims find their own voices.

- Whitney's book offers a lot in terms of talking about victimization, and it forces Alex and readers to pause and consider what the lines are between consensual intimacy and rape. At what point does a person give up his or her right to what happens to her or him: What if she drinks too much or is under the influence of drugs? Is there a line at all? Can a person be "asking for it?"

- Likewise, there's much to consider here in terms of vigilante justice and what it means to engage in hard but important conversations. What kinds of punishments encourage change, rather than simply ownership of blame? Is there a responsibility for people who are victims to then become advocates for change and justice? How much does an individual need to represent a class of victims? Do they have to do so at all?

- Maybe one of the most interesting discussion possibilities in this novel is the absence of – and ignorance of real issues by adults. Themis Academy administrators believed that their students would never do something bad and therefore, they didn't have a justice system in place for students who may need it. There aren't adults to protect or guide teens; instead, the adults in Whitney's book are there for themselves. Even if this pushes the boundaries of believability, it opens the case to how *teens* feel the adults in their lives perceive them and the real challenges going on in their lives. Are adults absent and unavailable because they don't care? Are they unaware of the huge challenges teens face? Or are they choosing to purposefully ignore these things in hopes they're just not happening?

Chapter 18

Conversation Starter: Teens and Technology

I think the biggest influences have been books with boy narrators. One of the first I read was Twisted *by Laurie Halse Anderson. It was such a pleasure being inside Tyler Miller's head. A teenage boy's mind is an undiscovered country for me.*

After that, I loved Eireann Corrigan's Ordinary Ghosts, *which also featured a boy narrator, but one that was extremely funny and wry alongside some very hard issues. The book's basically about grief and loss but I could read that book over and over.*

I also love what Andrew Smith does with line and language in Stick. *He's a very lyrical writer (though he'd probably kill me for saying so) and I love what he does with rhythm and repetition.*—Carrie Mesrobian, author of *Sex & Violence*

Teens use the Internet. Teens use cell phones. Teens have and check Facebook, Tumblr, Instagram, and many other social networks that adults do and don't know about. They're engaged with technology, and they're using it because it's part of their responsibility to their education, it's part of their responsibility to staying in touch with family and friends, and it's fun. Technology is a staple of today's world, regardless of how much screen time one devotes to it.

As technology continues to expand and reach new places and possibilities, so does the potential for how teens use it. But because teens are teens, the ways that using technology can impact them isn't always apparent to them. What seems like an innocent picture sent between a boyfriend and girlfriend can have immense consequences for both. What seems like a safe and caring person on one end of the screen may turn out to be anything but that in the flesh. What seems like a small joke put out on social networks may, in fact, backfire on teens who aren't careful.

How can teens use technology for their own benefit without falling victim to crime? How is it teens may use technology for bullying?

The following titles explore the impact of texting, cell phones, Internet predators, and more on teens. Although the stories and characters are fictionalized, the experiences shared in these books are ones that are a constant reality in today's world. These titles lead themselves to conversations about where and how technology can be used for good purposes and where and how it can be used for less praiseworthy purposes.

But more than the opportunities present to talk about technology use are the possible conversations about how what one does online now can and does impact them forever, since digital footprints don't erase easily.

Brown, Jennifer. *Thousand Words*. Little, Brown, 2013. 288p. $17.99. 978-0-316-20972-4.

In Brown's novel, Ashleigh must face the consequences of being caught sexting. It's not only about having to perform community service in order to be in compliance with the legal side of her actions. She must also learn how she can find a way back into her own social circles, including what to make of the boy to whom she sent the image.

• There's much to think about in terms of what the role of technology is in cementing and breaking friendships and other relationships. When can it be a tool to strengthen bonds and when does it ultimately become a problem? Another discussion-worthy element of this novel comes through Ashleigh's own thoughts and discoveries about what right and wrong actions and behaviors are. She's not only considering hers, but she's considering those of other teens who are completing community services projects like she is.

• Is it possible that Ashleigh brings her own prejudices to what it is that makes someone a good or bad person? If she herself has made a mistake and must face the consequences, does it make her a bad person? What about the boy she bonds with at community service? How does she make peace with the past in order to move on and have a fresh start? Is she even allowed to do that?

Lange, Erin Jade. *Butter*. Bloomsbury, 2012. 320p. $16.99. 978-1-59990-780-2.

At its heart, this book is about bullying and thus could fit in the bullying discussion guide. But the bulk of the story is about Internet bullying. Butter – not his real name – begins his relationship with popular girl Anna on the Internet. They chat all the time, though she has no idea the person she's talking to is actually Butter, the fat kid people make fun of at school. But when she learns the truth, the rest of the school learns too, and suddenly, Butter's life is unbearable. To get back at the bullies, Butter is going to commit suicide. And he's going to do it online, via live video, so every single one of those people can watch him as he dies eating.

- Lange offers a brutal depiction of cyber bullying, and the tension that surrounds Butter's announcement of his suicide plans is high. Will he do it or won't he do it? What does it mean to do this in front of an audience?

- Although this is a way of Butter enacting his revenge, it's also a sign of desperation and attention for him. He wants people to see that he really and truly is troubled by the way people treat him and torment him, both in person and online. By performing his "final act" in front of an audience, though, will he make the impact it is he wants to make?

- There is plenty of fodder here for talking about cyber bullying and also the ways in which we seek validation through the Internet and the legacies we may leave behind in our digital worlds. Likewise, as in the discussion guide on bullying, there's much to think and talk about when it comes to suicide as a means of removing oneself as the target of bullying.

- Of course, there is a notable absence of adult figures in the novel. Are they really absent or are they perceived as absent by the teens?

Littman, Sarah Darer. ***Want to Go Private?*** Scholastic, 2013. 336p. $9.99 Trade pb. 978-0-545-15147-4.

Starting high school is scary, but for Abby, it's made a little bit worse when she and her former best friend begin to drift apart. Faith wants to make new friends and Abby isn't yet comfortable enough to explore new relationships. Abby and Faith's friendship in recent months has been pretty much restricted to the time they get to talk on the social network ChezTeen because they've gotten so busy with school. Although most of the time Abby only chats with people she knows on the site, she begins to talk with a boy named Luke. He's been so nice to her and when they start talking more privately, he becomes the sympathetic and understanding ear she needs, especially when it comes to her needing to talk about what's going on between her and Faith. Before she knows it, Abby finds herself feeling like she loves Luke, even though she doesn't know him well. She does things for him she'd never think about doing for anyone else, including taking and sending nude photos. She's so comfortable with Luke that she thinks they should meet up in person. And they do – but it's not to a good end.

- Littman's book offers up a lot. What does it mean to establish trust in a relationship with someone who you don't know beyond their digital words? What happens when you choose to pursue meeting someone you have only talked with online?

- More than that, because this book is told through multiple perspectives, readers are privy to not only what Abby is thinking, but also to what her friends and family are thinking. How could Abby have opened up about her feelings regarding Faith better? As readers, we're able to see she had many avenues, but what was it that made her not see them or feel she could not turn to them? How could she have made better decisions regarding her relationship with Luke, if at all? How do we know who we can rely on and how do we know when we're being realistic about danger and when we're being paranoid?

- Maybe the biggest questions are those which come both through the use of technology and in everyday, real world engagement. What are our networks? How big are they? What value do they have in helping us through some of our toughest personal challenges? Do we have and use different venues for different purposes? How and why do we choose to share what we do?

Vaught, Susan. *Going Underground*. Bloomsbury, 2011. 352p. $16.99. 978-1-59990-640-9.

When Del makes a mistake of sending a sext message, he's prosecuted harshly. Unfairly, even. Del's no longer in school – he's been kicked out – and he works in a graveyard, since that is the only place he can get a job with the criminal record he now has. He resigns himself to this fate because he owns his actions, even if they were a complete mistake. But rather than feel depressed about the situation, Del takes it with a bit of optimism. He still maintains dreams and hopes, and he feels awful for what it was he did that got him into so much trouble.

- Vaught's book is a harsh look at the sometimes unfair consequences that befall teens who make a mistake and break the law by engaging in sexting. In Del's case, the incident isn't premeditated nor is it vicious. He has no ill will and he had no idea what the consequences of his actions could be. When they're this severe though, there's much to consider in terms of what legal mandates teens should be aware of that impact them directly. At what level do they need formal education on these issues? But more broadly, it's a question of the legal system: What is fair and just punishment for something like sexting, which may come from a place of innocence and fun, rather than a place of wanting to hurt or harm another person? What if it's between two consenting teenagers? What if it's between two teens who are ignorant of the law?

- Vaught's book deserves conversation with Brown's title, as the stories are told from slightly different time periods (and legal proceedings), even with just a short number of years separating their publication dates. Seeing similar stories through the perspective of a male and a female voice, how these individuals are perceived and judged by their peers and romantic interests, as well as how the legal consequences impacted each internally and externally are worth considering.

Chapter 19

Conversation Starter:
Unlikable Female Characters

I deeply believe that there is meaning in the everyday. That our lives are, after all, mostly an accumulation of the everyday. There are a lot of crusaders in the children's literature world. People have these personal crusades against bullying, or for self-esteem, or a calling to address eating disorders or abuse or whatever the issue is. I'm interested in these things, but if I'm a crusader for anything, I'm a crusader for the idea that everyday life holds extraordinary meaning. That the accumulation of all the little things that make up our common experience – the conversation with the barista, trying to love your family, eating a meal with a friend, how we deal with loss and what's going on in the world – matter. All of these things matter a great deal and are the very stuff our lives are made of. There's beauty there, as well as pain. It's all right here. – Sara Zarr, author of *How to Save a Life* and *The Lucy Variations*

Rather than tackle the topic of gender roles head on – though there are suggested titles for a discussion on that topic in the additional conversation starters section – this selection of books focuses on the "unlikable" female main character. For many readers, it's the unlikable female that's challenging to read because she bucks the socially-acceptable role of what it means to be a good girl. That's not to say these girls are bad or engage in risky behavior. Instead, the girls in these books aren't afraid to say what they're thinking, even if it isn't pretty. These girls make choices about how they behave and how they act and respond, and those choices don't always fall within what society accepts as pleasant to see or understand.

Readers may find themselves frustrated with the characters in these books but it's through the discussion of what makes these girls hard to like where insight into social politics, gender roles, and the greater idea of being a well-rounded, fully-realized, and authentic character can emerge. Maybe more interesting is how many of these "unlikable" females *aren't* seen by readers as unlikable at all.

These characters force readers to accept their less-than-pretty choices and also ask readers to take a mirror to themselves and question how it is they might react in similar situations. The truth is it isn't always without sharp edges, but it is about being true to self. What is it that pushes people out of the way they think they should act and into acting the way they really need to in order to feel right with themselves?

Jarzab, Anna. *The Opposite of Hallelujah*. Delacorte, 2012. 464p. $16.99. 978-0-385-73836-1.

What makes Caro an unlikable character in Jarzab's story is that rather than feeling content to see her sister Hannah return home after an eight-year hiatus at a contemplative order, Caro chooses to be angry and annoyed at her sister's return. She judges her sister as weird, casting Hannah's disordered eating, her social withdrawal, and her inability to connect with the rest of her family as signs of needing attention, rather than as a signs of her depleting mental health. Caro reacts selfishly to her sister, but it's not necessarily because she is selfish. It's because she's unable to cope with losing her status as an only child. That grief manifests in her ill-thinking and behavior toward Hannah. But when Caro takes a stronger interest in her sister and begins to understand why it is Hannah chose to attend the contemplative order, Caro starts to understand that not all choices are easy ones to make. For Hannah, coming home wasn't easy and she has many troubling things to work through herself.

- Jarzab opens up great opportunities to discuss topics such as mental illness and the way that those un-affected by it may react and respond. Caro doesn't understand that Hannah is pained by post-traumatic stress disorder and that she's suffering from an eating disorder because of it.

- There's also much to make here about resentment and grief and how those two emotions can interact and enhance one another. Not all is lost for Caro, though, just as it's never all lost for any unlikable character. It's through her toughness and her need to commit to her feelings that she's able to help and connect with her sister in a way she never expected.

- Another element contributing to Caro being a frustrating and potentially unlikable character is that her life has always been good. She comes from a bit of privilege, she's well-educated, and she's got a social life. But even having what seems to be everything isn't always enough. This is a theme that will emerge through many of the books on this particular list and may in fact be one of the reasons why many of these girls are deemed "unlikable."

Kelly, Tara. *Aplified*. Henry Holt, 2011. 304p. $16.99. 978-0-8050-9296-7.

Jasmine's life has always been nice and cushy. She's reminded constantly by her father that she's privileged to have what she has and she should take advantage of it by going to college, getting a job, and being "good." But she doesn't want that. What Jasmine wants is a career in music. Because she doesn't want to follow Dad's advice, she's kicked out of her house. Making it on her own in Santa Cruz doesn't worry Jasmine too much, and she knows she has the musical chops. It's just a matter of meeting the right people, finding a way to make some cash, and everything should be on the up and up from there. But when Jasmine finds a group she thinks she can jive with, things aren't easy. She's hard headed and stubborn, not to mention the fact she's not necessarily telling the whole truth when it comes to her background and experience in music. It may be the lies that break her.

- Kelly's book features a main character who is unafraid to go after what she wants, despite the fact it's not the thing anyone else wants her to do. She makes poor choices, including, but not limited to, lying to her future roommates and bandmates in order to get in. She also doesn't treat her father well in any respect. How much can and should Jasmine use other people for her own advancement, when it's other people who want to help her despite her unwillingness to listen to them? At what point does she need to strike out on her own completely and at what point does she need to understand that other people want to help her because they care about her? That they're not trying to drown out her dreams and goals?

- There are questions raised here about the value of being stubborn and about the point at which stubbornness becomes insensitivity. There are also many good questions here about the notion of gender norms more broadly, as Jasmine wants to be with the boys as much as possible, despite the fact that sometimes, the boys want nothing to do with a girl they think is playing them. Where does her own privilege and her ability to go back home further make her a problem to those around her who are truly independent from their families? Kelly forces the reader to also consider the value of lying if it's a means of getting what it is you want.

Rapp, Adam. *The Children and the Wolves*. Candlewick, 2012. 160p. $16.99. 978-0-7636-5337-8.

Bounce comes from the right side of the tracks. Her parents work for the local drug company, and they leave her unsupervised all the time. She lives in a nice house and has unrestricted access to Oxycontin. She's confident, even cocky. But when she's challenged in her English class by an adult, she suddenly begins losing her edge. She's knocked down. How dare anyone suggest she's not the queen of the world anymore? Now she's out to get revenge.

Two seventh grade boys, Wiggins and Orange, who have taken a shine to Bounce, become her toys. When Bounce decides to kidnap a four-year-old girl, she convinces Orange to keep the girl chained up in his basement. But as bad as that sounds, what it is that makes Bounce truly awful is when she decides she's going to employ Wiggins and Orange in a scheme, telling people they're raising money in order to fund a search effort for the missing girl they have chained up in the basement. That's the money Bounce plans on using to purchase a gun and seek her revenge on the poet who dared challenge her.

- Bounce is unlikable through and through, but what Rapp does in his book is force the reader to question what it is that made her tick. Is it the fact she was challenged by an adult? Or was it the fact that she has to be honest with herself and realize she is not the top of the food chain anymore?

- Even though she comes from the best possible background, she chooses to spend her time with two boys who aren't from the good side of town and who don't come from homes as well-nourished as her's. But is her life everything it seems? Her parents are absent and she may or may not have a prescription drug abuse problem. Do these things contribute to her choices and her inability to think logically about the potential consequences of her plans? Does she care?

- There is plenty of fodder here in terms of good and evil, as well as what it means to seek revenge and whether or not revenge means anything at all. Rapp offers us a bleak ending to this story, which furthers us to question whether any of this had to happen at all. And what of the four-year-old girl and her obsession with the video game she's allowed to play? In what ways does the idea of gaming play into the grander scheme of revenge and/or victory for these characters?

Saldin, Erin. *The Girls of No Return*. Arthur A. Levine, 2012. 352p. $16.99. 978-0-545-31026-0.

The Alice Marshall School, set in the sprawling and remote woods of Idaho, is where girls who have problems are left to work through them with intense counseling. It's a last chance resort, and supervision is high. When Lida arrives, she believes that her version of broken isn't as bad as other people's; her roommates are messed up beyond imagination and there is no way she'd ever trust them with her challenges. But it's when she chooses to befriend Gia, the new girl who has captured everyone's attention, that Lida believes she's finally found someone she can trust. It's too bad Gia isn't a good girl – the information Lida tells her will be used against her when Gia doesn't get what she wants.

- Even though it seems like Lida is the victim here, both girls are "unlikable" and, at times, even deplorable. They're both struggling with their mental health, but it's their external actions which make them ugly. They aren't the only players, either. Lida's roommate Boone is also a problem-riddled girl, and while Lida is initially frightened by her and the rumors she's heard about her, eventually, the two find they have some important common ground.

- Saldin also explores the ways that privilege can play against mental illness and contribute to character behavior. Privilege and wealth may buy things, but they don't necessarily help when it comes to social standing or internal struggles. At Alice Marshall, these are big things each of the girls must confront and understand.

- Another interesting point of discussion is adult supervision and guidance. Throughout the therapy sessions and the supposedly well-supervised free time, there are hardly any adults around. But is this purposeful? Are the girls truly without a lot of adults around or is this how they perceive their situation?

- There are also many questions about sexuality, and the power that sex can play in exerting power. Are Lida and Gia friends or are they something more romantic? Is it possible the girls are neither? How much of their relationship is based on them being unlikable and finding some sort of compatibility in those qualities? Saldin's exploration of power-wielding is fascinating and discussion-worthy.

Schmidt, Tiffany. *Send Me a Sign*. Walker, 2012. 384p. $16.99. 978-0-8027-2840-1.

Mia Moore, who is diagnosed with leukemia, doesn't immediately seem like she's an unlikable character, and many readers may argue that she's not unlikable at all. But Mia makes a choice. Prompted by her mother, Mia decides not to share her diagnoses with her best girl friends nor anyone at school. The only person who gets to know is Gyver, her long-time friend and neighbor. It's in making the decision to keep her illness a secret that her behavior toward her friends shifts. She chooses not to spend time with them, despite spending some with Gyver and with another boy who has shown interest in her. Mia lies to her friends about where she's spending her summer. She's not really spending time with her family, but is instead in the hospital getting chemotherapy.

- What Schmidt brings to her story of a girl struggling with leukemia is that question of whether or not Mia's choices are good or bad. Whether she's entitled to decide what information she shares with people and what information she decides to withhold. Even though it's her health and her future, what happens to her impacts those closest to her. Should she be telling them about her illness?

- Complicating this further is that Mia lies to her best friends. It's not just a conscious decision to withhold the truth. When she lets a close friend know what's going on, that friend suggests keeping it a secret – it's *her* means of holding power and withholding truth, even though it's a secret that's not hers to have. What are the implications of friendship and power when one friend knows and encourages the secrecy?

- In terms of high school friendship dynamics, Mia makes things worse when she *is* telling more than one boy what's going on. Does it make her unlikable that she picks a boy (or two) over her female friends? In making those choices, does she make a statement about what relationships matter most to her?

- What happens when Mia begins to flake out on her long-time friends enough that they decide they don't want to invest time in her anymore? Will sharing her secret with them change their mind or will it come off as a manipulative ploy?

- Maybe the biggest question undercutting the entire story is whether or not one's illness gives an individual an almost untouchable status: Is it okay to be angry with or frustrated by a character who might die from cancer? What is the meaning of cancer, if anything?

Summers, Courtney. *Cracked Up to Be*. St. Martin's Griffin, 2009. 214p. $9.99 Trade pb. 978-0-312-38369-5.

Something happened that turned the once-perfect Parker Fadley from the girl who had it all – friends, a hot-shot boyfriend, a spot on the cheerleading squad as captain, a bright future ahead of her – into the girl who is failing all of her classes and who wants to do little more than drink. But she's not opening her mouth about it. Parker wants to disappear and get through high school as fast as she can. Her parents and her counselor have her under close scrutiny. And now that there's another boy taking a shine to her, she can't get away. Parker might be responsible for something awful, and she can't talk about it at all.

- What Summers's book forces readers to do is endure a bitchy, rough, and hard-to-like girl on the outside who is very much guilt-ridden, anxious, and breaking down on the inside. There's a lot going on when it comes to what the outward manifestation of deep challenges on the inside look like. For Parker, it's being incredibly defensive and guarded as a means of working through the mental consequences she's punishing herself with. But is this how all people struggling with a terrible secret work through their problems? Or is Parker being unnecessarily unlikable and defensive? How does withdrawing help her or make her feel worse about what happened?

- This is a book where the unlikable girl has to endure her own unlikable nature and she *knows* it. She's almost as uncomfortable with herself as the reader is. And at the end of this book, perhaps what garners the most discussion is that Parker isn't a healed girl. Questions linger about whether or not she can ever be her true self again – and whether or not she wants to be. Is she being unfair to herself through her self-punishment? Does she deserve better? Could she have stopped what she saw happen? And if so, how? Would getting involved sooner have changed the course of her future?

Zarr, Sara. *How to Save a Life*. Little, Brown, 2012. 341p. $16.99. 978-0-316-03606-1.

Jill MacSweeney isn't pleased when she learns that her mother plans on adopting a new baby. After losing her father and keeping herself at a distance from her friends and her boyfriend in order to properly grieve, the last thing Jill wants to deal with is one of her mother's crazy schemes. Especially as it seems more like it's being done out of charity, rather than out of a desire for raising another child. Mandy, pregnant and left alone because of her own neglectful parent, wants nothing more than a good home for her baby. More than that, she wants a place where she, too, feels at home. Forced to deal with one another because of their common link in Mrs. MacSweeney, can Jill learn to let down her guard and find empathy for Mandy and her predicament?

- Zarr's novel is voiced by both girls, giving readers the chance to be inside the mind of one character who is desperate to shut everyone out, as well as a character who is desperate for a way in. The dual characterization may be part of why Jill comes off as abrasive as she does. Even though she's mourning her father, when compared to Mandy who seeks a good and solid life after making a number of mistakes that may be the result of her own poor upbringing, Jill looks even more "unlikable" and her behavior reads as more unbearable. Can the two girls come to find one another on solid ground? What is it that will ultimately make Jill understand that her behavior might not be tolerable to her family or to her friends? Does she have the right to her attitude and her actions if it's her way through the grief?

- Even if the girls are able to build a bridge between their lives, it's possible that Jill may never actually be the sort of person she was before losing her father. There is much to discuss her in terms of not just the likability and the different lives the two girls are living, but there's a lot to explore about what it means to *be* and to *have* a family. For Jill, it's something that she was born into, whereas for Mandy, it's something she has to seek out and create for herself. This divergence is illuminating when it comes to thinking about privilege and whether or not that's something Jill brings with her and her attitude. Though it's Mandy who makes a number of decisions in her life that are easy to judge – she is a pregnant teenager – it's Jill who commands reader attention for her attitude.

Chapter 20

Conversation Starter:
Young People and War

As a young reader I sought some version of myself in the pages of the books I read, some way to better understand my changing world, or some new lens through which to view my surroundings. This is what I try to provide as a writer of contemporary YA. It's what I know, what I love, and where I'm at home.
– Dana Reinhardt, author of *The Things a Brother Knows* and *How to Build a House*

War and combat have been a reality of this generation of teens since they were born. Many either know someone who served in the military – a father, an uncle, a brother or sister maybe – and many will have friends who choose to join the service. Some of them will enlist. Because war has been such a constant in their lives, it's not a surprise that more young adult books have taken on this topic. Today's YA fiction explores war from not only the perspective of those who know veterans and those who lost someone as a result of combat, but it also explores war from the eyes of the teen veterans themselves. This is the next generation of war fiction, complete with explorations of the social consequences and the political ramifications that accompany military action.

The books in this list cover an array of topics relating to war and teens. In some cases, the stories are steeped in heavily political issues that, as a result of time and of judicial processes, are not necessarily political issues any longer. For instance, two of the books below tackle issues of sexuality and military personnel. Thanks to the repeal of the controversial "Don't Ask, Don't Tell" policy, both Jackson and Kokie's books take on a different status. Though neither are historical fiction, their place on the shelf is now worth noting as indicative of the changing sociopolitical climate.

These stories engender the realities of both today's young adult readers, as well as those readers who will be coming into YA fiction in the future. For many years, war literature in young adult meant books set in far off places and battles fought by individuals unlike those who were reading their stories. However, today's war lit features the neighbors, the families, the friends, and individuals using our libraries, bookstores, and classrooms every day.

Someday these books will be historical fiction. But for now, they're as contemporary as it gets.

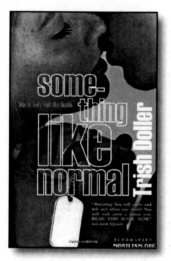

Doller, Trish. *Something like Normal*. Bloomsbury USA, 2012. 224p. $16.99. 978-1-59990-844-1.

When Travis comes home after taking a leave from his tour of duty, he's not welcomed back as a hero. He's an average nineteen-year-old boy who has to clean up the mess left behind by his girlfriend cheating on him with his brother, his parents who are on the brink of divorce, and not knowing if he has any friends left. Worse, he's torn apart by the loss of his best friend, Charlie, from combat. It's not just grief that tears at him, though. It's also the reality of post-traumatic stress disorder that keeps him awake at night with nightmares and the fear of what could happen. After apologizing to Harper, a girl he'd hurt in the past, Travis is able to make the kind of connection with another person he's longed to have since going off to war. And it's the kind of bond he needs in order to get through seeing Charlie's family at his memorial service.

- Doller's book brings up a wealth of important and interesting discussion topics, including what it means to be a member of the military. Travis isn't regarded as a hero. In fact, when he comes home and realizes he's hurt people in the past, he has to own up to not being a perfect person. Being in battle doesn't change that fact for him, and being a hero isn't automatic. Serving was a choice, and while he garners respect, that's different than garnering a status like "hero."

- But even bigger is what happens when Travis relives the events that caused Charlie's death. He's tormented by night terrors because of post-traumatic stress disorder. Even when he gets the chance for real closure with his friend's death, he's unable to shake his own mental illness. PTSD is a topic worth talking about and thinking about, particularly as it relates to today's youngest military members. Socially, it's becoming more and more well-known, but even as the conscious awareness of PTSD is heightened, it's not entirely understood by those who diagnose it or those who suffer.

- Readers will be interested in talking about the ways in which grief and death aren't made any less painful when it happens on the battlefield. There is a very human face to the consequences of war through Travis.

Jackson, Corinne. *If I Lie*. Simon Pulse, 2012. 288. $16.99. 978-1-4424-5413-2.

Quinn's boyfriend Carey is fighting overseas, but it's when a photo surfaces of Quinn and Blake in a compromising position that the true battle begins. In Quinn's small town of Sweethaven, North Carolina, everyone lets their feelings be known about what this photograph means. Sweethaven is a military town. Any and everyone who chooses to serve is a hero here. Now that Carey has gone missing in action, things only get worse. Quinn becomes subject to bullying, to torment, and to teasing at every moment and in every place in town. Her parents and Carey's parents can't even look at her because of what she did to him. And even though it is Blake in the picture, his face is obscured enough that the only person looking bad is Quinn. But the truth of the story is that Quinn was never cheating and that Carey was never really her boyfriend. He's gay, and Quinn has held his secret tight since she found out.

- Jackson's novel is explosive in its exploration of military mentality, in patriotism, and even more importantly, the challenges of being homosexual while serving. The risks associated with Carey's sexuality are huge. Quinn, knowing the devastating effects the truth could have on both him and his reputation in town, keeps it a secret.

- There is much to be discussed about the ways in which personal politics interact with social politics and politics more broadly. When should secrets be kept? When and why do things like sexuality need to be policed in any capacity? There are questions, too, about the ways in which Quinn is treated and mistreated. Despite the nastiness she endures, she remains loyal to Carey and her promise to keep his secret.

- One of the consequences that Quinn faces requires her to perform community service at the local veteran's hospital. Through the course of her work there, she befriends an older vet. Their connection and friendship is not only authentic and moving, but it opens up a channel for talking about the way war can impact people on different levels, especially as she comes to terms with what may or may not have happened to Carey. Additionally, the friendship that emerges between Quinn and the vet should prompt dialog about intergenerational friendships, as well as legacy and honor.

Kokie, E. M. *Personal Effects*. Candlewick, 2012. 352p. $16.99. 978-0-7636-5527-3.

When Matt's brother TJ dies in combat and he has time to move past the initial shock of loss, he finds himself devoted to seeking out more information about his brother's life. Matt and TJ were never close, but when two footlockers of TJ's personal effects arrive at home, Matt can't help himself. He needs to know more, even if it means going against his father's orders to forget about TJ altogether. Inside the footlockers, Matt discovers a pile of letters from someone named Celia who lives half a country away. Photos included with the letters feature her and her daughter, with whom TJ posed more than once. A million questions roll through Matt's mind and he knows the only thing he can do to get answers is drive to meet Celia and ask her himself.

- Like in Jackson's story, Kokie's novel is an exploration of secrets relating to being a member of the military and being homosexual. TJ was never married to Celia nor did he have a daughter, much as

Matt builds up this story in his head. Rather, TJ was gay, and this was a ruse in order for him to keep up his relationship with another male. Kokie's novel raises questions about the politics of sexuality and how they relate to an individual, as well as how they relate to serving in the military.

- There's much to discuss here in terms of family dynamics. Matt and TJ didn't live in the most supportive household, and the boys didn't have a strong relationship. TJ kept his sexuality a secret, and he kept his fake relationship with Celia a secret, as well. In what ways, if any, did TJ's decision to enlist have to do with wanting to get away from home? How much did keeping his sexuality a secret have to do with the fear of being found out at home? What impact did TJ's service have on the family? Did it make Matt and their father's relationship stronger or more strained?

- Another interesting avenue of discussion possible with Kokie's title, as in others on this list, is the notion of hero. TJ is one because he dies in combat, but is it a title he's earned or is it one he's given because of his choice to serve, rather than pursue another path? What, if any, impact does his sexuality have on his status? Because TJ wasn't open about being gay, does it change the impact of Matt's discovery? Does it change his legacy?

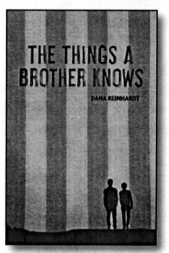

Reinhardt, Dana. *The Things a Brother Knows*. Ember, 2011. 256p. $8.99 Trade pb. 978-0-375-84456-0.

Boaz is coming home from a tour of duty, but his brother Levi is not really excited. Levi's in a weird place, both at home and at school, and he's not even sure where he and Boaz stand in their own relationship. When he gets home, things only get tougher. Boaz retreats into his room for weeks on end and he doesn't interact with his former friends nor anyone in his own family. Even though Levi wasn't originally invested in Boaz's return, now he's obsessed with finding out what happened to him. Why has he become so withdrawn and sullen? Levi wants to help Boaz however he can. What was it that made Boaz enlist in the first place? Does knowing that illuminate Boaz's current struggle?

- Levi has questions about what happened before, as well as what the fallout is now that his brother is back home and working through the horrific effects of war on his psyche. Reinhardt's novel asks questions about what it is that can drive someone who has what appears to be a promising college future ahead of him to choose to enlist instead. It's a non-traditional path, and it leads to questions about expectations from family, from school, from peers, and from society at a larger level. Levi wouldn't make that kind of choice. So why would Boaz? Is there lingering resentment on Levi's part for Boaz's choice?

- There is much to discuss in terms of what happens during and after war. Can a person return and be who they were before they served? One of the things Boaz does when he gets home is make a plan to walk from Massachusetts to Washington DC, and Levi plans on following. Will it unravel the clues to his brother? Will it help either of them make sense of war or of the PTSD Boaz may be suffering? Will it help them grow stronger as brothers in the way they never were before?

- This book is an excellent pairing with Kokie's above, as both explore what it means to be a brother. How important is family when it comes to breaking through mental illness? Does a brother know how to be the best help?

Chapter 21

More Conversation Starter Ideas

Realistic/contemporary fiction comprise approximately half of our campus YA book club selections over the past three years and just less than half of the club's summer round robin titles. My co-leader and I have found that contemporary/realistic books encourage discussion between our college students and the faculty and staff members as the members tend to dig deeper into discussions of theme, purpose, and character intent. For our group, fantasy and graphic titles lead to discussion of author's intent rather than character-driven discussion. – Becky Canovan, academic librarian

These topics are far from exhaustive, as are the books listed within them. But each of these themes have emerged over the last few years in contemporary YA, and each are worthy of discussion and consideration in their own rights. The suggestions below are meant to prompt creative thinking and dialog.

■ Body Politics

There are a number of books tackling issues related to weight and body image. They're worth discussing as a whole, whether the battle in the story is about an eating disorder or about finding a way to help a character with his or her obesity. The following explore both ends of the spectrum, with plenty of potential to talk about the political aspects of the body, about what the ideal body is, about body image, and much more.

Anderson, Laurie Halse. *Wintergirls*. Speak, 2010. 288p. $9.99 Trade pb. 978-0-14-241557-3.

Cooner, Donna. *Skinny*. Point, 2012. 272p. $17.99. 978-0-545-42763-0.

Price, Nora. *Zoe Letting Go*. Razorbill, 2012. 288p. $16.99. 978-1-59514-466-9.

Sanchez, Jenny Torres. *The Downside of Being Charlie*. Running Press, 2012. 272p. $9.99 Trade pb. 978-0-7624-4401-4.

Sheinmel, Alyssa B. *The Stone Girl*. Alfred A. Knopf, 2012. 224p. $17.99. 978-0-375-87080-4.

Trujillo, Ee Chalton. *Fat Angie*. Candlewick, 2013. 272p. $17.99. 978-0-7636-6119-9.

Walton, K. M. *Empty*. Simon Pulse, 2013. 256p. $16.99. 978-1-4424-5359-3.

Vaught, Susan. *My Big Fat Manifesto*. Bloomsbury, 2009. 336p. $8.99 Trade pb. 978-1-59990-362-0.

◼ Gender/Sexual Roles and Identity

What makes someone a male or female? Is it possible to not identify with a single gender or to identify with the gender that is opposite of your biological sex? These books explore gender and sexual identity, and they also take a look at what it means to be either a male or a female or either or both in the modern world. What are the expectations thrust upon each and can those expectations be bucked? Is there a reason for expectation at all?

Beam, Cris. *I Am J*. Little, Brown, 2012. 352p. $8.99 Trade pb. 978-0-316-05360-0.

Brezenoff, Steve. *Brooklyn, Burning*. Carolrhoda, 2011. 210p. $17.95. 978-0-7613-7526-5.

Cronn-Mills, Kirstin. *Beautiful Music for Ugly Children*. Flux, 2012. 262p. $9.99 Trade pb. 978-0-7387-3251-0.

Hassan, Michael. *Crash and Burn*. Balzar + Bray/Harper Teen, 2013. 544p. $18.99. 978-0-06-211290-3.

Vivian, Siobhan. *The List*. Push, 2012. 336p. $17.99. 978-0-545-16917-2.

◼ Rural Life

Has living in a rural area become a topic worth discussing? It seems like more and more, stories have been taking place in rural parts of North America. It's not just that the setting is worth discussing, though; it's how the setting is used in these stories and in the lives of these characters that make this topic interesting. Can a small town eat a character alive? Is it a place that someone outgrows? Or is rural life something that can positively impact an individual? What about the stories where a character doesn't want to "get out," but instead wants to continue living in a small, rural area?

Backes, Molly. *The Princesses of Iowa*. Candlewick, 2012. 464p. $17.99. 978-0-7636-5312-5.

Bick, Ilsa J. *The Sin Eater's Confession*. Carolrhoda, 2013. 320p. $17.95. 978-0-7613-5687-5.

Cronn-Mills, Kirstin. *The Sky Always Hears Me: And the Hills Don't Mind*. Flux, 2009. 288p. $9.99 Trade pb. 978-0-7387-1504-9.

Whaley, John Corey. *Where Things Come Back*. Atheneum, 2012. 256p. $9.99 Trade pb. 978-1-4424-1334-4.

Whitaker, Alecia. *The Queen of Kentucky*. Poppy, 2012. 375p. $17.99. 978-0-316-12506-2.

Woolston, Blythe. *Black Helicopters*. Candlewick, 2013. 176p. $15.99. 978-0-7636-6146-5.

■ What Comes Next: Life Beyond High School

These books talk about what options exist after high school that aren't limited to the somewhat traditional path of going to college, getting a job, finding a spouse, and having children. Of course, some of the teens in these stories choose to pursue these paths and to no ill effect. The following explore what other options are out there, as the teens themselves live through them. Included are books featuring high school dropouts, as well.

Forman, Gayle. *Just One Day.* Dutton, 2013. 320p. $17.99. 978-0-525-42591-5.

Griffin, Paul. *Stay with Me.* Speak, 2012. 192p. $8.99 Trade pb. 978-0-14-242172-7.

Hubbard, Kirsten. *Wanderlove.* Delacorte, 2012. 352p. $17.99. 978-0-385-73937-5.

LaCour, Nina. *The Disenchantments.* Speak, 2012. 336p. $17.99. 978-0-525-42219-8.

Scheidt, Erica Lorraine. *Uses for Boys.* St. Martin's Griffin, 2013. 240p. $9.99 Trade pb. 978-1-250-00711-7.

Violi, Jen. *Putting Makeup on Dead People.* Hyperion, 2012. 336p. $8.99 Trade pb. 978-1-4231-3485-5.

Chapter 22

Advocating for Contemporary YA Lit

My sophomores just finished an inquiry-based research project and many of them chose YA titles to read to help answer their big questions. One of my students learned more about what it means to be a hero when she read The Mocking-birds *by Daisy Whitney. Another student learned how the war can affect families when he read* Personal Effects *by E.M Kokie.* Something Like Normal *by Trish Doller helped a student understand how grief and PTSD affects a person. Geoff Herbach's* Stupid Fast *series has turned multiple boys into enthusiastic readers; those boys have found pieces of themselves in Felton Reinstein. A student who lost a boyfriend to drugs/suicide and a brother to meth addiction found solace and understanding when reading* Crank *by Ellen Hopkins. I have a community of readers in my classroom, thanks to YA literature. Some of my students enjoy reading the classics and appreciate them, but they are connecting with Jordan from* Catching Jordan *and cheering for DJ from* Dairy Queen *more than any character they encounter in a classic piece of literature.– Sarah Andersen, high school literature teacher*

Now that you have the tools, the titles, and an idea of how to use the two together to build meaningful conversation, how can you advocate for contemporary YA lit with readers and with other professionals?

Contemporary YA doesn't have the marketing and publicity behind it that other titles do. While there are well-known contemporary authors who see advertising behind them, the bulk of contemporary fiction falls to the middle of a publisher's list. It doesn't mean that these books are bad or that they do not have merit or value. It simply means that there are other titles that have stronger, more compelling hooks that are, in many ways, simply *easier* to sell.

Consider the pitch for Suzanne Collins's *The Hunger Games* over a title like Swati Avasthi's *Split*. Collins's book is heavy on action, adventure, and the stakes are high from the onset and remain high throughout. While Avasthi's book contains high stakes, the pacing is slower, the development more internally focused, and the adventure isn't based on page-turning action. Collins's title appeals to a larger demographic of readers, whereas Avasthi's appeals to a smaller readership. One is not better or more important than the other. Each is meant for different markets, which means they receive different plans in terms of push behind them from the publisher (and often, librarians and teachers).

Readers Who Want These Books Matter

The reason these books are published is because there *is* a market and an interest in these titles. It's a matter of making the connections between the book and the reader. It is through youth advocates – those working on the ground with young adult readers – where these books can be put into those right hands.

Part one of this book talked in depth about reader's advisory and how to line up appeal with reader interests. Part two talked about the vast array of titles out there, as well as appeal factors.

Advocacy Takes It to the Next Level

How can one advocate for contemporary YA fiction? Start by reading it. Read wide and read deep. Find those authors whose work speaks to you and find the books that speak to you. Then pass them on to other readers who want those stories. Know the appeal factors and know your readers; match reader to book, book to reader.

Be an advocate for those books by taking the time to talk about them with other professionals who may not be reading them. Speak about them during book talks. Speak about them at conferences when you're asked what you've been reading and what it is you like to read.

It is important – it is part of the job of any youth advocate, in fact – to know those best sellers that your readers want. Know why your readers are asking for them. Did they hear about it in a magazine? In a movie preview? An author was talking about it? It is as important, if not more important, to know about the other books, too. This is an opportunity to book talk, to make comparisons among other authors and titles, and to highlight the appeal factors of the books that aren't getting a lot of press or that may be back list titles which have fallen out of the sphere of memory in the light of those high-profile titles. These are the books that aren't going to be easily discovered by chance because they're titles lying beyond the bookstore end caps or displays, the books that don't end up with full-page advertisements in trade journals, and books that don't get reviewed in big-name publications like *The New York Times*. Advocate for contemporary YA and readers by taking the time to browse the shelves to discover new and different titles and styles.

Readers who become the best reader's advisors and the strongest advocates for reading and books are those who *seek out* the books which aren't the easy reaches. When you take the time to share a contemporary title that's not getting all of the glory of other titles or when you spend the money to purchase one of those "smaller" books for your library or classroom, you're advocating for the book and the readers who would be served by that book. You're putting an author and a book out there, and you're helping expose new voices. Readers are devoted and devour the things that matter to them. Often they will buy the book and spread the word about it.

The more books you know as a gatekeeper, the more you can talk about books, the more knowledge you can spread to your readers, and the more you're supporting both the titles and the authors. You're playing a part in the system on the ground level.

Stay Ahead of the Game

Know what books are coming out, know what authors are writing about the contemporary issues that you know matter to your readers, and read the books. Browse blogs aimed to inform you as a gatekeeper and aimed to reach young adult readers. Share these resources with your readers.

Take Time for Your Passion

If you don't make time for your passion, reassess your priorities. As gatekeepers, our passion should be meeting the needs of our readers. It can be daunting keeping tabs on and fiercely advocating for contemporary YA, but it will make you an authority and a partner in the growth and development of your readers.

Connect your readers with the authors. Many young adult authors have strong social media presences, and many are willing to chat with classrooms or library groups via SKYPE or other means.

Take the time to nominate strong contemporary titles you read or that your readers recommend to the award and selection lists that ask for field nominations. All of YALSA's award and selection lists allow for field nominations, and the annual CYBILS awards pull their lists only from those titles nominated by readers. Nominate titles for state or provincial award lists. Do your part to spread the word about the lesser-buzzed titles by reading them and by speaking up about the qualities that make them great books. Just because they receive less push behind them doesn't mean they aren't strong, compelling stories that can – and do – have the power to change the right reader's life.

The tools are all here. So are the books. It's our job to put them to work together.

Appendix

Resources for Contemporary YA Lit

There are a number of great books and blogs worth knowing about that feature contemporary YA fiction, as well as feature further information about topics covered in this book, including book talking, appeal factor analysis, critical reading, and more.

■ Books

Cart, Michael. *Young Adult Literature: From Romance to Realism*. American Library Association, 2010. 256p. $58. 978-0-8389-1045-0.

Cart's book is the gold standard for a historical overview of young adult fiction. This is a must-read for anyone interested in the growth and development of YA, as well as those interested in genre distinctions within YA.

Horning, Kathleen T. *From Cover to Cover: Evaluating and Reviewing Children's Books (Revised Edition)*. Collins, 2010. 240p. $14.99. Trade pb. 978-0-06-077757-9.

Everything you could want to know about how to critically read and assess children's books can be found in Horning's guide.

Wadham, Rachel. *This Is My Life: A Guide to Realistic Fiction for Teens*. Libraries Unlimited, 2010. 431p. $58. 978-1-59158-942-6.

Readers who want to know more realistic YA fiction titles – those published prior to 2009 – will do well reading Wadham's genre guide. Included with each annotation is a short list of appeal factors for titles. Those may be helpful in making read alike suggestions between the titles in this book and older books.

■ Blogs

The Contemps – *http://thecontemps.blogspot.com*

A group of YA contemporary authors build this blog around advocating for and celebrating contemporary YA in 2009. Although it hasn't been updated regularly, the resources available on this site about contemporary fiction are well worth bookmarking and knowing about.

For the Love of Contemporary – *http://fortheloveofcontemporary.blogspot.com/*

Although this blog ended in 2012, it is still available as a resource for readers who want to explore contemporary YA. There are reading lists and suggestions for how to get started in the genre.

Real Life YA Fiction – *http://reallifeyafiction.wikispaces.com/*

This well-designed and easy to navigate wiki offers an historical overview of contemporary YA fiction, defining authors and titles, and more.

STACKED Books Blog – *http://www.stackedbooks.org*

One of the goals in my own blogging has been to highlight contemporary YA fiction because it's a genre I love. Aside from reviewing titles, I've developed more than one week-long series devoted to contemporary YA fiction. I've solicited strong guest posts from contemporary authors ranging from Geoff Herbach to Patricia McCormick, and I've developed book lists, reading guides, and more.

Author Index

Title Index

Topical Index

About the Author

Kelly Jensen has worked as a teen and youth librarian in Illinois and Wisconsin since 2009, which is when she began blogging about books and reading at *stackedbooks.org*. She also writes at Book Riot (*www.bookriot.com*), and she's had her writing featured in *VOYA Magazine*, *The Horn Book Magazine*, *School Library Journal*, BlogHer, as well as The Huffington Post. She has a degree in English, writing, and psychology from Cornell College in Mount Vernon, Iowa, and she earned her masters in information studies at the University of Texas in Austin.

After serving on the Children's and Young Adult Bloggers' Literary Awards (CYBILS) for three years, she discovered her love for contemporary YA fiction and learned how wide-ranging the idea of reader appeal really is. When not reading or writing about reading, she's enjoying black licorice, cooking, glitter, robots, and traveling.